"So, What Are The Boys Saving?"

"So, What Are The Boys Saying?"

An Inside Look at Brian Mulroney in Power

16270 26 30

Michel Gratton

McGraw-Hill Ryerson Limited
Toronto   Montreal   New York

Design by Dan Kewley

Printed and bound in Canada

ISBN 0-07-549562-7

1 2 3 4 5 6 7 8 9 0 W 6 5 4 3 2 1 0 9 8 7

Canadian Cataloguing in Publication Data

Gratton, Michel
"So, what are the boys saying?": an inside look
at Brian Mulroney in power

Includes index.
ISBN 0-07-549562-7

1. Mulroney, Brian, 1939–   . 2. Canada – Politics
and government – 1984–   .* I. Title.

FC630.G73 1987   971.064'7   C87-094951-9
F1034.2.G73 1987

For Valérie, Marie-France and Brigitte;
and for their mother, who brought them up
without me.

Acknowledgements

My thanks and undying friendship to Hubert Bauch, one of the finest writers I know, who understood me and my writing, and to Jill for making him work. Thank you to Mike Duffy, my dear friend and colleague, without whom I never would have written this book; to Nancy Colbert and Denise Schon, the wonderful women who believed in it and, for no good reason, in me; to Charles Lynch for his kind advice; to my mother and father, for teaching me to stand up for what I believe in — I just wish she was alive today; to my friend "Flocon" (she knows who she is) for standing by me when very few would; to Maurice Godin and John Udvarhelyi, my best partners in crime who kept my morale up; to Ginette and Darryl, for keeping me company in the long and lonely times; to Suzanne, for saving me from myself; to Fox, Bonnie, Ann, Stu, Charley, Bernard and all the others who took part in the adventure . . . I hope they understand.

Contents

The Man and the Media

"So, what are the Boys saying?"

It was the Prime Minister's ritual way of saying hello, in person or on the phone, in English or in French; over the space of almost three years, I must have heard that phrase a million times. The Boys in question were the representatives of the nation's media, and, more specifically and most of the time, the learned correspondents of the Parliamentary Press Gallery. Some of the Boys, of course, were girls; all were embraced by that oft-repeated, all-purpose question.

Sometimes it was heard just after the Prime Minister had finished a speech, a press conference or an interview; sometimes he would have just emerged from a stormy Question Period; sometimes, there was no triggering event — he just felt like chatting. He didn't want to know anything in particular, it was more like a kind of reflex that kicked in whenever he saw my face. It reminded him of what at once frustrated and intrigued him most: reporters.

So, our conversations inevitably started the same way, with the same question. Bill Fox, my predecessor as Press Secretary, had had to get used to the repeated ritual, as did all those who worked in the Prime Minister's Office and were liable to be dispatched on special missions to Medialand when the need arose in the Prime Minister's mind. In time, I came to await these moments with apprehension; maybe because, too often, I didn't have a clue as to what the Boys were saying right then; maybe because the Boys didn't have much of anything to say; or maybe because what they did have to say wouldn't be the kind of thing that would help the Prime Minister of Canada sleep soundly that night.

Perhaps it would have been easier if "The Boss" had only asked the question once during the course of a single conversation. But most of the time, he wasn't altogether satisfied by the first answer. He'd sit there and think about it for a while, his eyes turned elsewhere, then break the silence with the same question, "So, what are they saying?" The first few times he did this, I thought there was something wrong with me. I was sure I'd just told him what the Boys were saying. With practice, and since my profession of the moment quite often required me to juggle words, if not facts, I'd try to embellish my tale by retelling it in other phrases. I also learned to limit my responses and to hoard my information, like a general holding troops back for the final push. After a while, I'd always keep a few Boys in reserve for the second go-around.

At times like this, particularly when I had favourable commentary to impart, the Prime Minister would remind me of an adolescent schoolboy with a crush on a new girl, hounding her sister to find out what the new flame was saying about him. "Yes, but what's she saying?" The question would roll out, over and over. What could you reply except, "She's saying what I just told you"?

The ritual was particularly demanding on trips, when we were often together at the hotel, in the car or on the government Challenger jet. There's really nowhere to hide on a Challenger. I'd try to scrunch down in my seat and look small, but inevitably the Gaze would seek me out and land on me, and the reflex would kick in. When I heard that basso-profundo voice intone "Michel . . ." I knew I was in for a session in the principal's office.

All of this is to say that from the very outset, and for the duration of my sojourn in the Prime Minister's press office, the media held a disproportionate importance and fascination for Brian Mulroney. What hurt most is that the media knew it. After the ego-bruising they suffered at the hands of Pierre Trudeau, who regarded them all as some sort of lower life form, they were served up a media junkie on a silver platter. And they proceeded to devour him with relish.

What was it that fascinated him so about the media? No doubt in part it was the years of dreaming about politics and imagining himself as Prime Minister. But it was also, in part, the media mystique. The camaraderie, the nonchalance, the kind of cynical *joie de vivre* affected by journalists whose power to pontificate about anything that moves — without suffering any noticeable consequences for their errors and omissions — have outgrown rational bounds. But the Prime Minister, who knew this, never really understood it. Who lives by the headline, dies by the headline. Heroes are created one day and reduced to ashes the next, particularly in politics, and particularly in the politics of this country, where people tend to resent those who stand out and those who speak out.

With Brian Mulroney, it was only a matter of time. The target was just too easy. And when they started sticking the knives into him, they did so in a merciless frenzy. Since he attached so much importance to the media, the wounds went all the deeper, and left him with a deep resentment at having been betrayed by people in whom he had invested a portion of his soul. He started to hold them responsible for all his problems, rather than seeking out the truly guilty parties within his own administration. I can't remember how often he railed against the media, calling the reporters ignorant fools who didn't understand anything. Often he was right, and never did it change anything.

And in the Prime Minister's Office, with perhaps the exception of the former ignorant fools now on staff — Bill Fox and myself — everyone else joined heartily in the media-bashing sessions. Even Bernard Roy, the Prime Minister's Principal Secretary, a man with a heart of gold, and unquestioned integrity, a man who had himself been stung — usually unfairly — would refer to journalists as "whores" in front me. My reflex was to remark that this came a little hard from a criminal lawyer, considering that there are many more lawyers behind bars in this country than journalists. (This was a line I had stolen from Allan Fotheringham, one of the Boys who mattered most.) Bernard chuckled, and admitted that it was so.

I myself didn't have a terribly high opinion of certain individuals in the exalted Parliamentary Press Gallery — but I knew better than to lump them all together. Having grown up in the news business, I knew that, as in every other profession, there are people less competent and less honest than others who nevertheless manage to float to the top — not the cream, exactly, more like the oil. The trouble is that it takes only one of these to launch a false rumour and throw the juggernaut that is the 300-member Press Gallery into overdrive. The scribes are like wolves; they hunt in a pack.

In the beginning, they were friendly, even fangless, wolves. We had just won the greatest majority in Canadian history in the 1984 election. Brian Mulroney, a consummate backroom boy, but neophyte politician, had humiliated John Turner, the blue-eyed, silver-haired Liberal slicker, who had returned to the party from the purgatory of Bay Street, and would lead it back to the Promised Land. Or, at worst, the land of Promises. Mulroney had sent him scuttling into opposition. The Mulroney party bestrode the country; Quebec was ours, as much as Alberta. Brian and his wife, Mila, were bright, beautiful, bilingual, model parents; in short, perfect. He, the boy from Baie Comeau, a true-blue Quebecois, even if his origin was anglophone. She, the daughter of immigrants from Eastern Europe, now a staunch Canadian as well as a fine lady, a woman of dignity, but ever-disarming, with her little-girl smile. They radiated charm; and we, the insiders, like the rest of the country, let ourselves be wafted off by the dream of a new era. Central Casting had done its part; now we would create Camelot on the Rideau.

Alas, it wasn't long before power, and its attendant pitfalls, brought everyone back to earth. From very high up, we fell very far, very fast. Especially He and She, even though their entourage spared no effort to create and maintain an unreal world around them. We forgot that Camelot existed only in the imagination.

Was the Prime Minister ill-advised? Most probably. I personally plead quilty to having held back things that might have hurt, but which might ultimately have been more helpful than the kindly platitudes and circumventions that were served instead. I know I wasn't the only one to do this, telling him — like the mirror in *Snow White* — what he wanted to hear rather than what he needed to hear. Access to the man wasn't a problem, making the most of that access was. It was easy for us see him or talk to him on the phone; it was harder to lay unpalatable truths before him; he had a way of suddenly becoming impatient and cutting short the conversation whenever it took a turn he didn't like.

However, this was not the only force behind the dismal descent. It might, perhaps, have been useful if we had had an idea ahead of time of where we were going. In nearly three years by his side, and in the close company of his principal advisers, I always had the impression that only one person knew all the details of the overall plan — if indeed there was an overall plan — and that person was Brian Mulroney. We would get glimpses of the way ahead in bits and pieces, just before arriving at a new bridge that had to be crossed. Sometimes, we crossed bridges without really knowing why. For some people, it seemed a good way to govern, but it was frustrating for many of those who had to carry out orders blindly. Bill Fox, whose commitment to Mulroney was total, tried to soothe us by quoting the Prime Minister: "Don't worry . . . You, you know a few pieces of the puzzle. I'm the only one who sees the big picture." This left unexplained whether the big picture was a landscape, an abstract, or a self-portrait.

To be fair, it has to be said that the Prime Minister had some reason to keep his own counsel, to be wary of his own personnel. His office was a veritable sieve. His closest advisers would regularly leak inside information to the media. Sometimes, we knew who the culprits were, sometimes we only guessed, but we had only to read the newspapers to know there were culprits. But, for one reason or another, they were kept on once the anger of the moment had passed. Every time he was betrayed, the Prime Minister would be bowled over by the idea that he couldn't count on even his closest associates. And so, he kept his grand plan to himself, despite the difficulties that that entailed. Gradually, the pressure of events forced him to open up somewhat, and to commission the preparation of an overall strategic plan. Still, I can't say that the Mulroney "vision" was ever clear to me or to anyone else. Everyone would chant the four points of the vision like a personal mantra: national reconciliation, economic renewal, social justice, and a constructive role on the international scene. These were the goals, but how were we to get there? We never knew. Instead of realizing a vision, we were playing a game — Follow the Leader.

And then, when, predictably, things turned wretched, the Prime Minister, egged on by his caucus and cabinet, put the blame on "the lack of a first class communications strategy." In other words, Bill Fox, who had risen from Press Secretary to Communications Director, and I were held most responsible for the mess the government was in. But we were not the authors of the tainted tuna affair, Suzanne Blais-Grenier's pricey peregrinations, the first Wilson budget, the Sinclair Stevens mess, the Michel Gravel scandal, and the Oerlikon affair. As scapegoats, on the other hand, we were made to measure. In my case, the true Conservatives were deeply unappreciative of my way of dressing (often rumpled, sometimes in jeans and leather vest), or the length of my hair. In the eyes of certain hard-core elements of the party — who for me were symbolic of the Conservatives Canada had rejected for most of the twentieth century — I was, not to put too fine a point on it, a hooligan. No one ever said it to my face, mind you, but I heard it often enough behind my back. I didn't cling to my untidy ways out of arrogance, but because I thought the worst thing I could do would be to change my character now that we were in power. In the eyes of my former media colleagues, with whom I had to deal on a daily basis, the conclusion would have been that the job had gone to my head. And my shirt.

The Prime Minister, tolerant by nature, never reproached me directly. Indeed, he was visibly displeased by an outburst from Clément Côté, the MP from Lac St. Jean who, during a national caucus meeting behind closed doors, came down hard on my appearance. Still, Mulroney would make the point indirectly. Sometimes he'd find himself combing his hair in front of a mirror when I was around, and say, in mournful tones, that he needed a haircut, when it was obvious to all that my locks began where his left off. Once, when we were in the washroom just off the lobby of the House of Commons, he said in a loud voice, "I need a haircut; I'm starting to look like a Beatle." Seeing me smiling in a corner of the mirror, he added, "I'm starting to look like Gratton." And everybody laughed. I did, too.

But there weren't too many occasions for hilarity. The Tories are serious people. They are nothing if not serious. Unfortunately — and this accounts for many of their problems — they take themselves very seriously indeed. Life on that level isn't often a fun proposition, and someone like me, a francophone from the Ottawa suburb of Vanier, who hesitated to set foot in Ottawa West when he was a young lad, feels like a fish on terra firma in the company of such solemn and high-falutin company. During the last two years of my adventure at the heart of the power structure, there were far more occasions to cry than to laugh. There were days when I desperately didn't want to get out of bed in the morning. I was Press Secretary, but I was terrified to open a newspaper or turn on the radio. I'd jump when the phone rang, wondering what piece of the sky was about to fall on me this time. Every task turned into monumental drudgery, particularly the trips out of the country. I wasn't blasé, I was burned out.

What I came to dread most were the words that should have been the most comforting: "The government appears to have taken control of the agenda." Inevitably, those words, intoned by the CBC's Chief Parliamentary Correspondent, David Halton, or one of the other Grand Viziers of the Press Gallery, turned out to be the precursor to yet another disaster. The last time I heard the incantation was just before the Oerlikon affair exploded, and the Prime Minister had to fire André Bissonette, the junior transport minister. The agenda the government had taken over, apparently, was the one that knocked the bottom out of the Conservative Party's popularity across the country.

On March 9, 1987, two years and eight months to the day after I joined Brian Mulroney's staff, I was hastily summoned back to Ottawa from Montreal. The previous Friday, I'd asked Bernard Roy if I could go to Montreal on Monday and to Quebec City the next day. He could see no problem with this, even though we both knew that the Prime Minister had told me he would reflect over that weekend on the letter of resignation I'd submitted three weeks earlier.

On the Friday, Mulroney had phoned to tell me, "Michel, I got your letter of resignation. I have to say I haven't reflected on it up to now. I'll think about it this weekend. And no matter what happens, you'll be there . . ." I never really understood what he meant by that last little bit.

So I went to Montreal, thinking that I'd be left dangling for a while yet. But then on Monday, my secretary called to report that Bill Fox was desperately trying to reach me. After a few tries, I got through to Fox. "I think you should come in this afternoon," he said.

"What's happening?" I asked him, already knowing the answer.

"The Boss wants to see you."

I arrived back in Ottawa late Monday afternoon. Fox himself came to get me at my office in the Langevin Building, the limestone block across Wellington Street from Parliament Hill that houses much of the Prime Minister's staff. He walked with me to the Prime Minister's Office in the Centre Block of the House of Commons. We didn't say a lot to each other on the way; we'd been through too much together, and travelled too many miles over the past three years. We both knew there was nothing left to say.

The Prime Minister didn't keep me waiting long.

When I entered his office, he had his feet up on an open drawer of his desk. His jacket was off, and the sleeves of his always immaculate white shirt were rolled up. I think he asked me what the Boys were saying, but I'm not positive — maybe for once he said it in a slightly different way. Then, all of a sudden, he straightened up in his chair, crossed his hands in front of him and, in a voice almost devoid of emotion, with the air of a coach cutting a player who doesn't fit in with the team's plans, he explained that he was accepting my resignation. I replied in the same manner, without flinching. A bystander would have thought we were conducting a real estate transaction.

That concluded, he laid aside his formal tones and became animated, talking about the media, and what they had done to me a few months earlier, when two female members of the Press Gallery charged me with unbecoming conduct. Now it was clear to me — as I suspected would be the case when the story first broke — that these allegations were my undoing. It was also clear that Mulroney hadn't changed very much. The media were still calling the shots.

It was a short conversation. When it was over, he got up, shook my hand and said, almost awkwardly, "In any case, I just want to say thank you. My wife and I are thinking about you and your three daughters."

It was over at last, and my overwhelming reaction was one of relief. I was out of it, sadder but wiser. The rest of them, the Prime Minister, the Progressive Conservative party, the government itself, were still thrashing around in the ruins of blasted hopes. What went wrong? Was it our arrogance, our inexperience, our incompetence, or simply misfortune? I don't know for sure, although I have some ideas, which will be explored in the pages to come. Perhaps the Prime Minister had it right when he remarked, after the dreadful autumn of 1985 when the slide began in earnest, "Nobody ever wrote a manual about how to be prime minister."

What follows is not a manual on how to be prime minister; it is, instead, one insider's report of what happened to one prime minister, and the people around him, during the fastest and most furious fall from grace any government in this country has ever known.

This is not a judgement, but an account of what transpired behind the locked doors and drawn blinds of an administration under siege.

PART ONE

A (Nearly) Perfect Campaign

"Politics are a jealous mistress. If you aren't careful, they will take more of your time than you bargained for."

Ralph Campney, 1958

CHAPTER ONE

Through a Glass, Darkly

For me, the adventure that would change my life began the way many of life's adventures begin — during the course of a bar-crawl. Bill Fox was a friend of mine. He was also the Press Secretary to the leader of Her Majesty's Loyal Opposition. At the time this story begins, I was writing a political column for *Le Droit*, Ottawa's only French language daily. After five years on Parliament Hill, I liked to think I had built up a certain following, particularly among our younger readers, who were used to the slightly gonzo, no-holds-barred style that I'd made my trademark. As one of my esteemed colleagues told me one day, I'd become a wizard at writing columns that took up to two hours of my time every day. Maybe so, but that was just the time it took to write them; the real trick was to find an idea every twenty-four hours, and to that end, my days were spent joyfully poking around here and there and everywhere along the corridors of power on Parliament Hill.

An essential, though unofficial, adjunct to the House of Commons is the bar of the National Press Club across the way in the National Press Building at 150 Wellington Street. The Press Club can be depressing at the best of times. Its most conspicuous sight is the crowd of aging regulars, past their prime, rehashing past glories that exist largely in their imaginations, and suffering the sneers of a new generation. Spilled beer and spoiled dreams are their staples. Beside them crouch the media bigshots, the current favourites, heavyweight political scribes for whom the club is a handy watering hole, only a few steps from their offices. It is a place for soothing old hangovers and starting

3

new ones, for drowning anxieties and floating rumours, and a convenient clearing house for all the dirty linen in Ottawa. Along with the working press, the Press Club is a haven for assorted ex-journalists who have gone on to more dubious — and, mostly, more lucrative — pursuits in government offices or lobbying concerns. These are the "flacks," as opposed to the "hacks," the press secretaries, communications advisers, lobbyists and consultants of all stripes, whose subsistence depends upon an ill-defined, incestuous relationship that links the press, the power structure, the bureaucracy and the business community.

Actually, it is the last group that keeps the Press Club afloat. Business flacks are limited by the club rules to two-thirds of the membership, or there would be more of them. As it is, they keep the bar registers ringing with their generous expense accounts, which subsequently get written off as "promotion," and transferred to the taxpayer's account. We will hear more of this later.

After having been one of the best informed and most respected members of the Parliamentary Press Gallery, Bill Fox had been dispatched to Washington by the wealthy, prestigious, and Liberal-leaning *Toronto Star*, but he was lured back to Ottawa by Brian Mulroney, to take on the key role of Press Secretary to the opposition leader. He was still in that role on Wednesday night, June 27, 1984. Another cocktail hour at the Press Club at the end of another inconsequential day in Ottawa. He was at one end of the bar. I was at the other, along with my habitual accomplices from the Press Gallery's francophone gallery — we liked to call ourselves *la presse Québecoise à Ottawa* — confidently solving the problems of the world, even the universe, as we generally did on these occasions when we had nothing better to do.

The hangers-on in the national capital were, at this point, in an advanced state of excitement. The Liberals had come through their leadership convention two weeks before and John Turner appeared to be bringing off the miracle that had seemed impossible mere months ago. The public opinion polls were now suggesting that the Liberals, Canada's natural governing party of the twentieth century, looked as if they were about to make all the pundits who foretold their defeat look like false prophets by winning yet another federal election.

I didn't believe it. I didn't want to believe it. I had taken a dislike to Turner the day he gave his press conference at the Château Laurier to announce his candidacy. He nobly deigned to offer the services of his distinguished person to rescue the Liberal party, which was then mourning the departure of the godling, Trudeau, and dreading the possibility of losing the power that the party bosses regarded as theirs by divine right. In this setting, when he was asked about the right of franco-Manitobans to linguistic equality with anglophones in the province, Turner gave them the back of his hand. This was a matter of provincial jurisdiction, he said, not something for his lordly self. Not only did this make my franco-Ontarian blood boil, it hit me that here, in the space of a few seconds, Turner had disavowed all that the Liberal party had laboured to accomplish on the language issue over the past two decades. And on top of that, he equivocated. I have trouble putting any confidence in people who equivocate on such basic issues. Perhaps that explains the state of mind that made me jump the fence, and trade the implements of a journalist for those of a press officer. I joined the enemy.

The fact is that I was also more than a little bored and antsy for some strong sensations. That night in the Press Club, in a fog that thickened with each pint consumed, I made up my mind, and, in the end, wandered down to the other end of the bar where Bill Fox sat hunched over his glass. I tapped him on the shoulder, and motioned him to step away from the bar for a minute.

"Bill," I told him, "if you need someone for the next election, I'm available."

Fox seemed surprised, but nodded his head, and said simply that he'd get back to me tomorrow. The conversation didn't last long, and I still ask myself to this day whether I would have taken that stroll to the other end of the bar that fateful night if I hadn't consumed so much of the poor man's champagne.

The next day, I had a vague recollection of what I'd done. My first reaction, primed by morning-after guilts, was to wonder how I could have been so dumb. Here I was, a national political columnist, and, on top of that, President of the Press Gallery, openly offering my services to a party leader who was more than likely to be in an election campaign within the next few weeks. I was placing my fate in the hands of Brian Mulroney, a man who was not much more to me than a face on a TV screen, a figure under siege in Parliament Hill scrums.

With the help of some hair of the dog — it was quite a hairy dog — I was able to convince myself that last night's escapade meant nothing. I would forget this ludicrous notion of jumping into politics when I could spend the rest of my days churning out sage advice for the nation's leaders without ever having to submit myself to the judgement of the electorate. I've often thought that journalists, especially columnists like myself, are in fact politicians too fearful to practice what they preach. Or maybe too happy. I really didn't think the next day that the next tumultuous months would confirm the accuracy of my reservations about getting into politics and abandoning what I'd always thought was the best job in the world.

As the day wore on, calm returned; the events of the previous evening receded — along with the headache — into the distance and disappeared. That's how I found myself on Thursday evening, nonchalantly strolling down Parliament Hill thinking about whether I should go straight home, or perhaps make a detour across Wellington Street to the Press Club, when I heard a voice behind me calling, "Michel!"

Turning around, I immediately recognized the massive form and shambling gait of Bill Fox, the human grizzly bear. "Tomorrow, at eleven o'clock in my office," he said in his typically abrupt manner. "I think we have something for you."

"Right," I said, and that was it.

The next day, Friday, I was in Fox's office at the appointed hour. His assistant, Lisa Van Dusen, a woman blessed with an exceptionally fine mind — barely twenty-one, she had already worked as a Parliament Hill reporter — was sitting in a miniscule office, piled high with newpapers and folders. As the daughter of Thom Van Dusen, a long-time aide to John Diefenbaker, she had been brought up in politics and the media.

"Hi!" she said enthusiastically. "I hear you're joining us. I hope you accept."

"This is your office?" I asked, trying to sound sympathetic.

"Actually," she replied, "this is Fox's office."

I couldn't believe my ears. The Press Secretary couldn't get a better office than this broom closet!

"And where's your office?" I asked.

"Well, it's my office, too."

"And where's my office going to be?"

"I don't know," she laughed. "Here, too, probably."

At this moment, Fox burst into the chaos of his cubbyhole office like a man rushing to report a fire down the street. During the course of the coming months, I'd get used to his habit of blowing through doors like a misplaced typhoon. Lisa slid out from behind the desk and disappeared diplomatically down a corridor.

"We've created the post of Deputy Press Secretary," said Fox. "Obviously, we expect you to deal mostly with the French press, but all the others, too . . ."

The French press. Fox was one of the most francophile of the English-language journalists to have passed through the Parliamentary Press Gallery. He had lived in Quebec and in Paris, he had married an Ontario francophone, and he spoke excellent French. Some of his friends in the francophone ghetto liked to refer to him as "our favourite Rhodesian," an allusion to the Quebec nationalist tag "Westmount Rhodesians," used as a catch-all designation for Quebec anglos. Fox appreciated the easy camaraderie he enjoyed with the Quebec reporters; he knew he was one of the few anglo journalists admitted to a circle where most of his kind were viewed with distrust. As for myself, I'd grown up speaking French in an anglophone milieu, so it was easy for me to cross the bridge back and forth between the two.

That bridge had suddenly sprouted something of a barricade for Fox a few weeks earlier. During a trip to Washington with his leader, Brian Mulroney, there had been a run-in with the Quebec journalists, none of whom had been invited to a diplomatic reception in Mulroney's honour. They cried discrimination, and blamed Fox, and, as is the case in most of these stories, the truth got lost somewhere in the fog of internal quarrels that get inflated into national news.

Those of us who knew Bill Fox didn't believe the discrimination bit, but the charge bothered him, and he was marked by the incident. My entry into the political game couldn't have come at a more fortunate time.

I was offered $47,000 — about $5,000 more than I was making as a journalist at the time. It wasn't a whole lot more, considering that my new career could end abruptly if we bombed in the impending election. Fox was brimming with confidence, however. "Wait until we're on the other side," he said. By the other side, he meant the Langevin Block, home away from home for the majority of the Prime Minister's staff. Things would be better over there. So they were; I received a lordly $65,000 after the election.

In fact, I accepted this first salary arrangement without much comment. Fox didn't have to do a selling job on me, by then, I'd already sold myself. I felt like a second-string player who has spent the game warming the bench, and then gets the call with the clock ticking down towards zero, and the cause apparently lost. It sounds a little silly now, but what can I say? If you've got a romantic streak, you sometimes find yourself doing foolish things.

"Am I going to get an office?" I asked Fox.

He seemed surprised by the question, and slightly baffled.

"Well, um," he said, "we'll find you something by the bye."

He was more patient about that than he was about the week's notice I wanted to give *Le Droit*. Fox wanted me to jump on the ice right away. But in the end, we agreed to wait a week. The conversation in which I was hired didn't take more than ten minutes. Then he took me in to see The Boss.

This was the first of hundreds of encounters with the man who was to become Prime Minister of Canada. Brian Mulroney was slouched nonchalantly in an armchair, one leg flung over the side, his jacket off, his shirt-sleeves rolled up to the elbow, and his tie undone. Still, and as always, he looked like the best-dressed guy in the room.

"Salut, mon Michel," he said, in his most serious voice.

What followed was not a particularly memorable conversation, but I do remember him telling me that the current polls meant nothing, that the party had its own polls which told another story, and that he knew the temper of the electorate better than anyone because he'd been stumping in the regions for the past two months. He was trying to reassure me.

"I'm not worried," I said.

"No matter what happens, Michel," he said, "the party is a big organization." I took it that he was telling me that they'd find something for me if the Conservatives lost the election.

"I don't want anything," I said. And this wasn't just bravado. I wasn't altogether blind to realities. Up to now, I'd never had anything to do with this party; indeed, in Ottawa–Vanier, the riding where I was born and raised, we were issued with our Liberal membership cards before baptism. I didn't owe the Tories, and they didn't owe me. In the event of another loss to the infernal Liberals, the party sharks would be looking for victims to devour and one of them was likely to be labelled "M. Gratton." That was a simple fact of life. That night, I went home thinking that I'd just taken the most important decision of my life without knowing why. None the less, I felt good about it; I felt ready for a fight. At last, I was no longer a mere observer; this time, I was going to take on the establishment as a front-line participant. I was about to test the limits of my endurance.

During the week that followed the announcement that I had jumped aboard the good ship Tory, I was naturally warmed by words of wisdom by my colleagues in the Press Gallery, one of whom confided dolefully that she knew for a fact that Bill Fox was already regretting his move to Mulroney's staff. I was not alarmed by such dire tidings; more than a few of the gloom-spreaders, I knew, would have liked to be in my place. Nor did I feel guilty about crossing the line from the professional virginity of journalism to the flagrant whoredom of flackery. There are, after all, more things to life than those encompassed by journalism.

Ian Anderson, then Communications Director for the opposition leader's office and a former journalist himself, called to offer encouragement.

"Get all the sleep you can this week," he advised, "because in politics, you never sleep."

I took his advice and slept in until noon the next day, thereby missing my first appointment with Brian Mulroney's chief of staff, Fred Doucet, whom I'd met only briefly once before. But then, I'd already been told by some of the loose tongues in the opposition leader's office not to bother too much with Fred, even though he was chief of staff. I didn't know it at the time, but I was already being exposed to the congenital infighting in the upper reaches of power that would prove so debilitating in the months and years to come.

Doucet, a sweet person by nature, didn't seem put out when I phoned to apologize for sleeping in. We arranged another rendezvous for Saturday, July 7, at Yesterday's restaurant, just down the street from Parliament Hill, and it was there that I received my first bombshell.

"It's not altogether decided," Doucet told me, "but I'm sure the leader is going to run in Quebec. In Manicouagan."

I almost choked on my coffee. My first instinct was to run to the phone to call my news editor and tell him that I had the latest exclusive on the election campaign. I couldn't believe my ears. Mulroney had actually decided to abandon the iron-clad-safe seat of Central Nova in Nova Scotia — the seat bequeathed by Elmer McKay when Mulroney won the leadership — to throw himself into the jaws of the Liberal monster in Quebec. Up until then, Manicouagan had been one of the most solidly Liberal constituencies in an all-but-solidly Liberal province. This was a hell of a story, and it was mine.

But then I realized I wasn't a reporter any more. I couldn't tell anyone. I wasn't going to have my scoop. However, there was one consolation: I knew we were going to have some excitement.

CHAPTER TWO

The Fur, Among Other Things, Begins to Fly

"The Boss told me, 'Give this one to Michel Gratton . . . Let a pro handle it.' "

The tone was unmistakable; something was afoot. Hubert Pichet, executive assistant to the leader, had interrupted my rueful contemplation of the dimensions of my new office — a closet at one end of the conference room — to bring me my first assignment from The Boss. I had the impression he was handing me the keys to some powerful machine and telling me, "Drive!" Trying to look like the consummate pro The Boss apparently believed me to be, I glanced at the newspaper clipping Pichet slipped under my nose.

This was the morning of July 9, 1984, my first full day in the service of Martin Brian Mulroney. It was, as it happened, the very day that John Turner, recently ordained as Liberal leader and subsequently installed as Prime Minister, had chosen to hold the press conference that the entire country was awaiting with bated breath. Well, maybe not the entire country. But at least those who take themselves for the country, the Parliament Hill hangers-on, of whom I was one.

However, the air of excitement that radiated from Hubert

Pichet like some powerful new cologne, had nothing to do with the possibility that a general election might be called this day. Actually, it didn't take me long to learn that Pichet always seemed excited. He had only one speed — fast forward. Five foot five, 120 pounds soaking wet, Pichet, a genial young lawyer from Quebec City, was forever talking as fast as he walked, that is to say, like a character in an old movie with the film speeded up. Moreover, another little lesson was being imparted to me: whatever The Boss wants, he wants it now, not the next day. Nothing was too trivial for prompt action.

The cause of Pichet's alarm this morning was a convoluted article in a Montreal paper about a stolen car, in the trunk of which there were two fur coats. Because the car had been rented by the local Conservative party executives for the use of the Mulroneys, it was assumed in the press that the couple, who were about to embark on an election campaign, might be forced to alter their election schedule to appear in court in Montreal to testify. But, as Pichet explained, neither the car nor the coats belonged to them. Apparently, according to the story I was told at the time, they (the fur coats) were to be tried on by Mila Mulroney's mother.

That was it. Pichet wanted me to issue a press release immediately, denying the whole sordid affair. I tried to grasp the extreme gravity of the situation, but somehow it eluded me. Still, I solemnly promised to get to the bottom of this, and suggested, to Pichet's great astonishment, that I didn't really see the need for a press release right away. He suggested that I call "Maître" Bernard Roy, our Quebec campaign director, and an intimate friend of Mulroney's. I wondered why he used the formal reference to Roy, perhaps to remind me that he, too, was a lawyer, and thus entitled to be called "Maitre."

After a few calls, including one to Roy in his Montreal office, I was satisfied that there was no cause for undue alarm. Bill Fox couldn't understand the fuss, either, any more than I; it appeared that the crisis existed mostly in Pichet's imagination.

Fox, in any case, had larger matters on his mind, to wit, the press conference Turner had already scheduled for that day. Fox had sacrificed a brilliant journalistic career to clamber aboard Brian Mulroney's uncertain ship, and now he might be about to go down with it, in the all-or-nothing gamble of an election campaign.

"Don't harbour any illusions," he told me. "If we lose this election, your head and mine are going to be the first to roll down Parliament Hill." Then he asked, "What if he decides not to go?"

11

The question took me aback. What was Fox talking about?

"Turner's not necessarily going to call the election," he said. "What do we do if he doesn't?"

I couldn't believe my ears. Turner had jetted over to England to see the Queen, to postpone a Royal Visit that would have con flicted with a summer campaign. Everybody from Her Majesty on down was convinced that the Prime Minister would announce the kickoff at any moment, and here were the Conservatives worrying about what to do if he didn't. Would Brian Mulroney give a press conference anyway? What would he say if he did? "Say, boys, about that election we aren't having . . ."

But after my initial astonishment, I was impressed. They thought of everything, these guys. Another lesson in the perfect little press attaché's primer — always envisage the worst-case scenario. God knows, in the times ahead we often didn't have to use our imaginations, because the worst thing that could happen so often did.

Fox and I agreed to meet later in the opposition leader's office across Wellington Street from the West Block of the House of Commons. It's called "the South Block," but is, in fact, the former headquarters of the Metropolitan Life Insurance Company — fit milieu for the heart of the Conservative operation. Researchers, translators, communications specialists and consultants, all the key personnel in the leader's support system were lodged here. Today, Mulroney would be on hand, sequestered with a handful of key advisers, in his own office, a few feet from the conference room where most of us would gather.

I arrived at the South Block just before Turner's press conference. Fox was already there, along with a few of the senior strategists, including Harry Neare, one of the mighty cogs of Ontario's "Big Blue Machine." They were talking about things of which I knew little and understood less, so I tried to look intelligent by keeping my mouth shut. One of the topics was the estimated cost of proposed Conservative election campaign promises. The deep thinkers were aware that the media, spurred on by the Liberals, would seize at once on what promised to be the Achilles' heel of our carefully crafted campaign. It was all well and good to promise the earth and the sky, but what was it going to cost? How were we going to cut the deficit and, at the same time, pry open the public coffers to finance new programs? It turned out that the decision had already been made not to issue cost figures with every promise — no sense in supplying our adversaries with ammunition. Instead, we'd promise to produce a price-tag at some unspecified future date. As I listened to this, I was impressed; these guys had matters well in hand.

These ruminations were interrupted by the bustle around the television sets that presaged the press conference. The sets were turned on, and everyone stopped working. We were hoping that Turner would not only announce the election, but make some sort of blunder at the same time. Maybe it was too much to hope for, but at this point, with an eleven-point deficit in the public opinion polls, we needed every little edge we could get.

Prime Minister Turner didn't upset any odds that afternoon — the election would be held on September 4, the day after Labour Day. His answers to the reporters' questions were evasive, but in no way maladroit. Since his triumph at the Liberal convention, he sounded more sure of himself. He looked like a prime minister. It hit me that this was an image we would have to chip away at in the campaign; but how could we, in the space of a few weeks, shred the myths that had been building up around Turner for more than a decade? How to beat him on the issue that the experts said was crucial — competence? All the polls had him far ahead of Mulroney in that category.

A few days later, The Boss, letting on as usual that nothing bothered him, told me, "It's normal that Turner should be ahead when it comes to competence. He's been prime minister. I've never been prime minister." What he didn't say was that he had been a Member of Parliament for less than a year and leader of the party for barely more than a year. Beyond that, he had never been a candidate for any elected office except for his costly and disastrous run for the Conservative leadership in 1976. Still, his Irish blood percolated with the confidence bordering on arrogance that Mulroney affects when confronted with a challenge. "Don't worry," he'd say, "let your pony go and watch him run." In this case, the pony was himself.

Mulroney said such things to inspire confidence, but on this July day I didn't need to be pumped up. The die was cast, the Rubicon crossed; it was too late for second thoughts.

Watching Turner perform, I concluded that he wasn't going to be an easy mark. Oh, it is true enough that, beside me in the conference room, Bill Pristanski, Mulroney's other executive assistant and the anglo equivalent of Hubert Pichet, was saying, "I can't wait to get that guy in a debate. He'll get eaten alive." But I wasn't so sure; those glacial blue eyes were getting to me.

And then, at the end of the press conference, he gave us what we had hardly dared to hope for — an election issue on a silver platter. The patronage issue. In one fell swoop, Turner named seventeen Liberals to posts in the federal bureaucracy or the Senate. The appointments, it seemed, were part of a deal he had worked out with his predecessor, Pierre Trudeau. Turner said he had legal advice that he was obliged to make appointments of sitting MPs to other posts after the House rose, in order to preserve the Liberal majority until Parliament was dissolved for an election. This was an outrageous misrepresentation. But what made the arrangement most appalling was the fact that, down the list of grateful appointees was a name that leapt off the page like a squirt of grapefruit juice in the eyeball. Bryce Mackasey, one of the most pathetic of the old Liberal warhorses still nudging around for a place at the trough, had been named ambassador to Portugal.

Incredible as it was, here, already, was a decisive turning point in the campaign. The importance of the patronage blunder on Turner's part cannot be over-estimated. Nothing that happened subsequently during the campaign was more important to the fortunes of the principals.

Then Turner's press conference was over, and it was our turn at bat. I went to join Fox, who told me that the two of us would flank the leader on the stroll from the South Block to the National Press Building, right next door. This was the first time that the Boys were to see me in my new official function. I was anxious to get on with it, and I'd dressed for the occasion as best I could. I was wearing a sports jacket, tie, slacks . . . and cowboy boots. I mean, I didn't want to eclipse The Boss.

We left the conference room and stepped into the elevator. The doors closed and there we were: Mulroney, Fox and I. It was my first elevator ride in the company of the leader of all the nation's Conservatives. It would not be my last, but I made the most of it. Rapid-fire, I offered two bits of advice. Mulroney was referring to "Her Majesty the Queen" when speaking in French. "The Queen" would do just fine for most Quebeckers. Then, I told him that if we had to pick out just one target in the Liberal cabinet, it should be the porcine André Ouellet, a long-time cabinet minister, and chief fixer and apple-polisher of the Liberal organization in Quebec. At all costs, we should avoid attacking Jean Chrétien, who had made a lot of friends among the electorate for his gutsy run against Turner for the Liberal leadership. I don't recall if Mulroney followed the first bit of advice, but I know he seized on the second with a vengeance. For the entire campaign, André Ouellet — who, as a good student of Machiavelli, must have looked on with a certain amusement — was thoroughly raked over the coals at every opportunity.

The elevator doors opened.

Once out on Wellington Street, we were surrounded by the hedge of cameras and microphones that would mark my horizon for the next three years. The Boss, in full stride, kept smiling every foot of the way. I smiled, too; I liked being there, at the centre of the action.

Once we were at the National Press Theatre, on the ground floor of the Press Building, where the conference was to take place, I found myself at a bit of a loss. No one had told me what to do now. The leader, as usual, took his place at the centre of the table onstage, to the right of the new President of the Press Gallery, Judy Morrison, a CBC radio correspondent. Bill Fox went to sit down on his right, but what was I supposed to do? I hesitated a moment, then slipped into the empty chair beside Fox, much to the delight of the media mob in the cheap seats. "Will you name Gratton to the Senate?" cried one. "Will you give him a clothing allowance?" yelled another. I thought it was funny, and The Boss was laughing, but he must have been asking himself what the hell was going on.

The Boss looked good that afternoon. He was able to skate around the Conservative election promises and zero-in on Turner's new weak spot by saying that the seventeen fresh appointments looked like a gang dividing the loot after a heist. And even as he spoke, the formidable electoral machine that the Tories had been polishing for months, like teenagers with their first set of wheels, was already, inexorably, in operation. Norm Atkins and his supposed pros from the Big Blue were thrown together — somewhat to their consternation — with the amateurs from the Quebec organization, later to be baptized, "Blue Thunder." The Big Blue Boys had already begun their favourite game, which is to rake in all the credit when you win, and avoid all the blame when you lose.

"The boys from the Big Blue," Mulroney would snort a few months later, while reading the account of one Ontario strategist congratulating himself on his role in the Conservative win, "they're all geniuses when they win. How many seats did they win in Quebec?" He added, poking his finger into his own chest, "The Big Blue is right here."

15

The next day, my second on the job, I went to Montreal to meet the famous Bernard Roy. "Now, there's a guy with class," enthused Bill Fox, who was generally sparing with his compliments. He implied, at the same time, that the rest of the gang in Montreal, with a few exceptions, weren't much.

When I got to Montreal — and I shared Jean Marchand's famous view that the best thing about Ottawa is the train to that city — I found Roy still preoccupied with finding a full slate of candidates for the province, and without much time for making conversation. He invited me to a strategy session on campaign advertising, about which my clearest memory is that I was drinking beer while the dozen or so others at the meeting were sipping soda — another reminder that I was no longer in the Press Gallery.

A group of us returned to Ottawa in a rented limousine, which impressed me a lot until I found out that, with five passengers, the limo cost not much more than five fares on the bus.

When we got to Ottawa, the driver headed straight for Rockcliffe, the dormitory of the capital elite, and pulled up outside Stornoway, official residence of the Leader of Her Majesty's Loyal Opposition. I tried to look cool, but inside, I was as edgy as an underage kid in a waterfront bar. We were about to drop in on the man my travelling companions referred to breezily as "Brian," but, not only had I never been invited, I had no idea what we were doing here.

The Boss, who knows all and misses nothing, noticed me at the outset, greeting me with a warm but somewhat perplexed, "Salut, Michel." I really knew I was not expected when he asked Hubert Pichet to go and eat at the coffee table, because I was there. The invitation was also for dinner.

"Would you like a little wine with dinner?" asked The Boss, who never drinks himself any more. Hey, I thought to myself, I was expecting club soda. This guy knows how to live. He may practice abstinence, but he doesn't impose it on others.

But what the devil were we doing here?

It didn't take long for The Boss to make that clear. In his most solemn manner, like a paterfamilias bestowing benediction on New Year's morning, he said, "I will be a candidate in Manicouagan."

I felt like blurting, "I know, Fred told me last week," but I restrained myself. It was Mulroney's moment, and not to be spoiled. I had seen earlier in the day how important this decision was, in conversations with my new-found allies from Quebec.

16

Of course, they all wanted him to run in his native province, but many of them would have preferred a safe riding, like Brome-Missisquoi in the Eastern Townships, which had a solid Tory tradition. For these people, Manicouagan was sheer madness. That very evening, the new candidate in the riding admitted that recent polls put him at least ten points behind the Liberal incumbent, André Maltais. What a way to come out of the gate — eleven points behind nationally, and ten points in the hole in the leader's riding! Up until then, Mulroney had suggested his intention to take this gamble to some of his closest advisers. But it was that night at Stornoway, that he settled it once and for all in front of his long-time friends Bernard Roy, chief organizer in Quebec; Montreal lawyer Jean Bazin, co-director of the national campaign; veteran organizer and adviser Rodrigue Pageau; and communications guru, Roger Nantel. Among those people, I felt like the mistake in "what's wrong with this picture"; but I was happy to be in on it.

However, pleasure is always short-lived in politics; on Wednesday morning, life in the opposition leader's office was back to normal — Bill Fox was fit to be tied.

"How could John Crosbie have done something like that?" asked Lisa Van Dusen, in wonderment.

"Because he's a congenital idiot!" shouted Fox.

John Crosbie, the flamboyant Newfoundlander, who was called many things, but rarely an idiot, even by Fox, had committed an extraordinary gaffe the day before. During a careless moment he had allowed a reporter to get a look at a document he carried on top of the pile of papers under his arm — and the document just happened to be a cost accounting of the Conservative campaign promises, which came in at a total of $20 billion. Whether the document was authentic or not, and whether the reporter had read it correctly or not, were issues of minor importance now. The media pack was already baying, and in fine voice. Even if the $20 billion figure were wrong, they could exploit it as evidence of discord between Mulroney and Crosbie, who had lost to The Boss in the Conservative leadership race a year earlier.

That same day, Mulroney was scheduled to make a public appearance at the official opening of the PC Campaign Headquarters. Going through with the ceremony at this point smacked of masochism; we knew we were walking into a minefield, but we went anyway. Brilliant strategy!

Predictably, The Boss did not fare too well that day. Things got off to a fine start when the reporters, spotting him, trapped him in a scrum. The term is borrowed from the bare-knuckle sport of rugby, and describes what happens when dozens of cameramen, sound technicians, radio reporters and print types waving their mini-recorders all try to interview some poor soul at once, with a barrage of shouted questions under the glare of floodlights. Mulroney declined to divulge the cost of his promises, or to confirm the validity of the $20 billion figure. But this was the kind of issue that could haunt us for the rest of the campaign.

Amid the shouting and the jostling, the genius of the Conservative organization, which had put together this state-of-the-art election Campaign Headquarters, somehow went unnoticed and unappreciated. It wasn't only the $20 billion figure that stung, it was the whole question of credibility. Could people believe what Brian Mulroney promised them?

The campaign marathon began in earnest the next day. In keeping with our reputation as one of the finest electoral machines ever put together in Canadian politics, we confidently boarded our leased Boeing 727 at Uplands Airport, while the disconcerted media pack following John Turner had to scramble for seats on commercial aircraft. The Liberal jet was not ready yet, and that confirmed what we had suspected for some time — that the party was lacking in both funds and organization. We had money to burn and organization coming out of our ears, and we knew that, in politics as in baseball, a good organization won't necessarily make you win, but a bad one can consign you to the cellar.

The first 727 we used wasn't the one that would later be baptized "Manicouagan I"; that one, which would become our home for most of the summer of 1984, was still being outfitted to campaign specifications. This one wasn't quite as nice, but it wasn't shabby, either. And the drill on board varied little, whichever airplane was used. The leader and his wife would sit at the front in a private compartment set apart by a portable screen. Most of the time, they would be joined by their policy adviser Charles McMillan, tour director Pat Kinsella, and aides Peter Harder and Patrick MacAdam. McMillan and MacAdam were Mulroney's personal friends, while the other two were emissaries from the Big Blue Machine in Toronto. The executive

18

assistants, Bill Pristanski and Hubert Pichet, were often up front, as well, to make sure The Boss lacked for nothing and to run errands to the back of the plane when Fox and I, for instance, were being summoned to the Confessional.

Fox, Lisa Van Dusen and I had seats immediately behind the leader's partition, and Bonnie Brownlee, Mila Mulroney's executive assistant, who was then embarking on a personal relationship with Fox, was also with us most of the time. It was more crowded up front, and besides, she found our company more amusing. In addition, there were three secretaries, a clerk, and a half dozen technicians, whose crucial task it was to hastily set up the sound system and stage backdrop for the candidate's public appearances. In terms of Tory strategy, they were as essential to the operation as policy advisers; without them, The Boss would look lousy on television, that most unforgiving of all the media, which has made perception more important in our age than reality. Later, we added a platoon of singers and musicians, but they didn't last long; by popular demand, they were kicked off the plane a few weeks after they signed on.

The technicians and, while they lasted, the band, formed a kind of buffer between us and the reporters who took up the rest of the plane. There was an unwritten rule aboard that no journalist would cross the imaginary line roughly across the middle of the 727, without being invited to do so by someone in front. Finally, to cater to every (well, almost) whim of the forty to fifty media personnel regularly assigned to our tour — and who would become difficult if we didn't have enough beer on board — we had the wagonmaster. Next to the leader, there is, in fact, no more important person on a campaign tour than the wagonmaster, that modern descendant of the heroes who piloted hapless pioneers through hostile territory. The political wagonmaster makes sure the media are briefed on the minutest details of the leader's itinerary. He shepherds them on and off planes and buses, tells them exactly what door to enter for which event, where to plug in their equipment and where to find the telephones. And the johns. He wakes them every morning, and sometimes in the middle of the day. He makes sure that all their needs are met, hunts for their lost objects, and even helps the air hostesses serve them drinks. He is part mother hen, part father confessor, part drill sergeant — and all-important.

For this campaign, the Conservatives were fortunate to have Ross Reid as wagonmaster. They could have done no better. Always calm, unfailingly pleasant, Reid had been borrowed from

Public Affairs International, a top-ranked consulting firm. A Newfoundlander, he had previously been one of John Crosbie's top aides, both when he was Finance Minister during the short-lived Clark government, and during the Conservative leadership campaign. He was supported by two assistants: Camille Guilbault, whose charm soon won the hearts of all the Boys away from home, and the indefatigable Perry Miele, another Big Blue product. They were usually the one who had the thankless task of rousing reporters each morning from the comatose state in which most of them reposed.

Fox assigned me to the task of media surveillance. It was my job to join the journalist's conversations, to make note of what they were saying, and to detect signs of impending trouble. According to the plan, I'd spend most of the campaign with the reporters, while Fox stayed close to the leader. A few months later, someone I was about to hire as my secretary asked one of the old hands what I did during the campaign, and she replied, "He waters the reporters." Obviously, she had understood perfectly.

Our destination this Thursday, July 12, was Toronto, where, under a leaden sky, Brian Mulroney, flanked by his Yugoslavian-born wife, addressed a crowd of 10,000 at Esto'84, an Estonian festival held in Nathan Phillips Square. The speech was anti-Soviet and pro-American; we would come to hear a lot about "our American friends" as the weeks wound by. After the speech, we went to the Westin hotel, and I was in the midst of dinner when Hubert Pichet came bustling across the dining-room.

"He wants to see you," he said.

"Why?"

Hubert shrugged his shoulders. What on earth could I have done? Brian Mulroney was waiting for me in his suite. He was comfortably installed on a sofa, wearing a robe and slippers. Somehow, that reassured me; he didn't look like the kind of guy who put on airs.

"So, what are the Boys saying?"

I took him to mean the reporters. I didn't have much to relate, and I tried to steer the conversation elsewhere, but talk was made difficult by the sound of a piercing signal, like the wail of a phone left too long off the hook. It was so loud that it brought Mila Mulroney in from the next room; she was most displeased, and demanded to know what was making the noise.

"I don't know," I answered, "but it's all over the hotel."

I'd been hearing the damned racket for fifteen minutes now, and I was eager to get out of the room and give my ears a rest. Mrs. Mulroney called in hotel staff, who checked the smoke alarm, the phones, anything that could emit a noise, without result.

I went downstairs to the press room — I wasn't going to be caught twice not knowing what the Boys were saying. As I walked into the room, one of the TV technicians looked up and asked, "What's that noise?"

"I don't know," I repeated, "but it's everywhere in the hotel."

"No, it's not. It started when you walked in."

"That's right," said someone else, "it's coming from you."

"Come on, how can it be coming from me?"

"It is. It's coming from your pocket."

Incredulously, I put my hand in my jacket pocket and touched an object. What infernal thing was I carrying around? Gingerly, I pulled it out, and discovered the little tape recorder Fox had given me to record the leader's comments during scrums. I had forgotten to turn it off, and the cassette, having run to the end, was causing the recorder to give off the nagging sound. I didn't know whether to laugh or cry. Later, I explained the mystery noise to The Boss, who looked at me as though asking himself what manner of turkey he had here. To this day, I wonder if he thought I was secretly trying to tape him.

The next day, Friday, we flew to Central Nova, the Nova Scotia riding where Mulroney had been returned to the House of Commons in a by-election the previous August. He came to tell the poor constituents that not only wouldn't they have him as their MP much longer, they wouldn't have a prime minister as local representative, either, because his roots were tugging him home to Quebec's South Shore. It was an emotional moment, maybe too emotional. His voice cracked as he broke the news, and by his side Mila looked as grave as a widow. Evidently, she had received her instructions, but she didn't really need to be told what to do. She knew her role.

"Good theatre," remarked one of the media pack, as we stood in the audience.

The next morning, our little drama concluded in Central Nova, we flew to Manicouagan. Our first stop would be Sept-Iles, whose population of 25,000 made it the largest community in the far-flung riding. It was also the most hostile, as opposed to Mulroney's home town of Baie Comeau, at the other end of the riding, whose 9,000 people he had in his pocket.

In Sept-Iles, Fox assigned me to preside over my first press conference. Leaving nothing to chance, as usual, we traced the route Mulroney would take from his hotel room to the room where the press conference would take place. On the way down, we passed a men's room.

"He'll want to stop here," said Fox, sounding very sure of himself.

"How can you be sure?"

"Because he always wants to stop here."

A few minutes later, trying not to look as nervous as I was, I went back down with the leader. As we passed the washroom, he stopped and went in. Timidly, I followed. It was another ritual to which I eventually became accustomed — chatting beside the urinals with the future prime minister.

I didn't disgrace myself at my first press conference, and after an uneventful stop-over in Baie Comeau, we went on to Montreal, where Bernard Roy was to unveil his slate of Quebec Conservative candidates. During the flight, The Boss left his compartment for a stroll to the back of the plane, to exchange pleasantries with the reporters. It seemed like good PR, and Fox and I didn't pay much attention. It would make the Boys happy to be able to talk informally with The Boss, and there was an unwritten campaign convention that these conversations were off the record. We thought.

In Montreal, it became evident that internal tensions within the organization were bubbling to the surface. The Ottawa strategists and Mulroney's Montreal brains trust could barely tolerate each other. The press release that was to have been distributed had not been translated into English, and it contained serious errors of fact. Pat Kinsella, a unilingual anglophone, tried to sort out the mess with Roger Nantel; Fox got involved and the squabble began to get noisy, right there in the hotel lobby. It would get worse before it got better. Throughout the campaign the Big Blue Boys treated the Quebec organizers with thinly-veiled contempt. Kinsella eventually despaired of being able to reform them into his own neat image. Jean Bazin, the Quebec campaign co-chairman, was forever being called in to make peace between the Quebec organizers and the leader's travelling entourage, particularly Bill Fox and Ross Reid. I was caught between the two: my natural sympathy was with the Quebeckers, but I owed my loyalty to Fox. In time, I came to understand that these internal quarrels were part of the political process, and that people regularly detested other members of the same party.

I went to join the reporters in the press room at the Queen Elizabeth hotel, and guess what they wanted to know about? The possibility that the Mulroneys might be called to testify in the case of the stolen car with the fur coats in the trunk. I felt like a perfect idiot; I didn't know what to say; I thought this little business was behind us. The journalists were aggressive and demanding answers, so much so that I told Fox later that I was lucky that I'd just left the Press Gallery ranks. If I'd been just another press attaché, they'd have chewed me up and spit out the pieces. I promised to make inquiries.

It was with a sinking feeling in my gut that I made my way to the leader's suite and shuffled around the open door. Bonnie Brownlee spotted me first.

"Do you want to talk to him?" she asked gently. "Come on in."

If Bonnie said so, it must be all right. I edged inside. The Boss and Madame were seated on separate sofas. Both looked preoccupied, and, in time, I would come to recognize these moments when it was unwise to disturb them. Still, Mulroney gave no sign that he was put out.

"So, Michel," he said.

I started to tell him that we might have a bit of a problem over the stolen car caper, and as soon as he got the gist, he cut me off in mid-sentence. The voice went up.

"What are you telling me? I thought this thing was settled." And he let loose a bellow: "Hubert!"

I was lifted about two feet straight up in the air from my arm-chair. Poor Pichet, in the next room, must have hit the ceiling. In a flash, he was at The Boss's side, white as a sheet, and stammering apologies. I'd heard about Mulroney's towering rages, but never expected to be on the receiving end of one. And so soon. Pichet began to stammer an explanation.

"Well, uh, Maître Roy told me it was all looked after . . ."

"If it's all looked after, what's Michel doing here talking about it?"

Pichet shot me a look at once pleading and accusing. Anxious to defuse this bomb that I had just dropped in the leader's lap, I got up, explaining that I'd see to it immediately. I probably hadn't got it right. Everything would be looked after. Hubert Pichet and I left the suite together, but not happily. He, needless to say, was supremely honked off at me. I apologized and promised to be more careful. Once our heartbeats returned to normal, I saw Bernard Roy, who assured me that this business would go no further; the Mulroneys would not be testifying in the case. So that's what I told the reporters.

I'd put out my first fire. But I felt somewhat singed myself.

On Sunday night, we flew back to Ottawa, wrapping up our first week on the campaign trail. The routine would be much the same for the weeks to come. Weekends disappeared, because the strategists discovered that it was easier to get air time on Saturdays and Sundays than on weekdays, when there's other competing news. Our off days would be Mondays, and, sometimes, Tuesdays. This was going to do wonders for my social life.

Never mind, one week was over, we thought. And not a bad week at that. We little dreamed of the drama already hatching aboard the plane, or what hell on earth the next few days were going to be.

CHAPTER THREE

Of Whores, Old, and Bums, Patted

I ought to have known from the start. I should have begun worrying from the moment I saw the lanky frame of Neil Macdonald of the *Ottawa Citizen* in the group of reporters decanting from our campaign plane at Uplands Airport at the end of our first week of campaigning. I knew him well. I knew of his penchant for "original" stories, that others didn't or wouldn't write. I knew he wouldn't let anything get in the way of a good story. As well, he wasn't a member of the Parliamentary Press Gallery, so he was less inclined to run with the Hill pack. Most of the regulars who would dutifully trot forth the official line of the day didn't appreciate Macdonald and his deviationist tendencies. As I say, I should have known that his presence meant trouble, but I didn't, and, that Sunday night, I slept the sleep of the blameless, little realizing that Macdonald had already fired the torpedo that was about to punch a gaping hole in the hull of the good ship Tory.

I was still slow on the uptake the next morning. Bill Fox had called Lisa Van Dusen and me in for a working breakfast at the Four Seasons hotel in downtown Ottawa, and he asked, in a worried tone, what I thought of Macdonald's piece on page one of that day's *Citizen*. I'd seen it already but right then I didn't think a whole lot. The article related a conversation that Mulroney had had with some reporters during the Saturday evening flight from Baie Comeau to Montreal. According to Macdonald's account, Mulroney was bantering about Turner's patronage appointments earlier that week and speaking of Bryce Mackasey, he said:

"There's no whore like an old whore. If I'd been in Bryce's place, I would have been the first with my nose in the trough, just like all the rest of them."

Mulroney often privately used coarse language, despite his image of a leader forever careful about what he said. Aside from that, the comment didn't seem to me to be any big thing. Rightly or not, I was convinced that, deep down, a majority of Canadians agreed with his view of the *fin-de-regime* awards. But, on reflection, that was not the real sting of the piece. It suggested that Brian Mulroney was denouncing patronage in public and condoning it in private; he had one line for the nation at large and another for the Conservative faithful. The issue was no longer merely patronage. That one had been joined by another — hypocrisy.

The worst of it was that neither Fox nor I had heard the conversation in its entirety. I'd heard bits and pieces of it, but not enough to be able to confirm or deny the *Citizen* version. Macdonald had written that other reporters sitting close to him had been witness to the incident. We didn't even know if he himself had heard everything he had reported, or was simply writing what others told him. (He says today categorically that he was in on the conversation.) Nobody, it seemed, had recorded the conversation. It didn't help that both Fox and I had heard Mulroney use the same "old whore" reference privately, so it was probably true. Fox was called away to the restaurant phone during breakfast, and when he returned, he said, "Guess who that was?"

Indeed, it was The Boss, deeply troubled by the possible ramifications of the *Citizen* story. Still, our reaction remained low key; there were too many unanswered questions for us to get excited, yet. Was the article going to be taken seriously? If other reporters had heard Mulroney saying the same thing, why weren't they writing it? We hoped this would be a one-day wonder, soon buried amid the avalanche of other campaign news. We decided to play it cool and hope for the best.

The party bigwigs, on the other hand, with Norm Atkins of the Big Blue Machine at the forefront, saw it in an entirely different light. They wanted the leader to issue a denial, a clarification, excuses, anything to defuse this time bomb. What worried them most was that Mulroney might just have blown the juiciest campaign issue the Tories had — patronage.

I went home that night thinking that the brains trust was overrating the story's importance and that the whole thing would soon be forgotten. Fox agreed. He succeeded, or at least he thought he had succeeded, in convincing the organization to leave things as they were for the time being, to wait and see what happened. That evening, he went out for a quiet dinner — a rare luxury for him in recent months.

It was about nine-thirty that night when the phone rang at my place. I was sound asleep; I'd gone to bed early because the pace had worn me out, and when I picked up the telephone, my head was still fuzzy. On the line was Ian Anderson, the party's communications director. His voice carried an unmistakable undercurrent of anxiety, not to say panic.

"Michel," he said, "you have to do something. You have to talk to The Boss. They're going to put out a press release on this *Citizen* story that makes no sense."

"You want me to call The Boss?" I asked, incredulously. I might have been asleep, but I wasn't off my rocker.

"You or Fox. He wants to talk to one of you."

"Okay."

After I hung up, I wondered how I had let myself get talked into calling The Boss so easily. I didn't even know what Anderson was talking about. What press release? Besides, it sounded serious, and I wasn't sure that I was the man of the hour.

"What is it?" my girlfriend asked, sleepily.

"I have to call Mr. Mulroney," I said.

In a few minutes, with the aid of the operator in the opposition leader's office, I had The Boss on the line.

"Michel," he said, obviously straining to remain calm, "I've got a draft of a press release here." And he began to read what he and his immediate advisers thought would put an end to this whore story, or maybe this whore of a story, once and for all. The proposed text had one fundamental flaw. His entire defence rested on the contention that his remarks had been off the record, and should therefore not have been brought to the public's attention. Even in my half-conscious state, I could see that this would be a big mistake — it was admitting the most damaging implication of the *Citizen* story, that he had one line for public consumption, and said something else in private. He didn't take this line of reasoning too well.

"Where's Fox, anyway?" he grumbled, and hung up after saying that he'd get back to me.

By this time, I was wide awake. Anderson had been right; the situation was serious. What fool could have written something like that? It was barely an hour, but it felt like eternity before The Boss called back.

"Michel," he said, "we've decided to take your advice for tonight."

I wanted to say, "Hold on a minute, I was just joking. Deep down, I don't know what I'm talking about." I didn't want to be the one making these crucial decisions. But then, I'd just found out why I was being paid a wage by the Conservative party. It wasn't the most restful night of my life.

The next day, Fox was in a supremely foul mood, which didn't improve when I told him that I'd taken the call from The Boss in his stead, and that They had been looking for him.

"Looking for me, were they?" he snorted. "I know they were looking for me. What did they expect me to do? When I left, everything was fine. We were going to wait, and then, all of a sudden . . ."

Fox was mad at himself for not having been there when needed, but what really steamed him was the scheming to make the leader issue a press release when he had been advised that there should be none for the moment. The internal battle raged all day, and Mulroney became convinced that he had to do something. He was bowled over by the fact that the hue and cry over the story, instead of abating, seemed to gather force with every newscast.

Mila Mulroney came by the office; she had to get out of the house, where her husband was prowling around like a caged bear.

"How is he?" I asked.

"Right now, he's not too bad. But he feels betrayed."

Betrayed? What was beginning to look like a dangerous lurch off the rails of a careful campaign had been the result of a stupid mistake by Brian Mulroney. And Brian Mulroney knew it. The blame belonged to no one else. How could he have thought the reporters were his allies, his confidants?

Lisa Van Dusen was particularly demoralized. I didn't know why then but, as she often did, she would confide in me the next day.

She had actually known of Macdonald's intentions since the previous Saturday night. After having a few drinks with me on the town, she had returned to her Ritz-Carlton room to find a note pinned on her door. It was from Macdonald, who also happened to be a good friend of hers. He wanted to talk to her about something. She went to his room. Sitting on his bed smoking a cigarette, the *Citizen* reporter told her that Mulroney had said these things on the plane and that he intended to write them. She argued with him, saying among other things that nobody on that plane would ever talk to him again — including reporters — if he did that. She left his room thinking she had succeeded in convincing him.

Obviously not. She was livid the morning the story appeared and her mood deteriorated further after that. Two days later, as we were about to leave for our next campaign swing with Macdonald on board, she went straight to him and said sarcastically, "Well there's the Carl Bernstein of Canadian journalism," referring to the famous American investigative reporter who had broken the Watergate story while at the *Washington Post*. Macdonald, more out of anger than anything else, said that it was her who had dared him to write it when they had their conversation at the Ritz. And poor Lisa, at that point, was starting to feel guilty about it. As Macdonald himself put it to me later, he would have written it anyway. But on that day, Lisa Van Dusen had the weight of the world on her shoulders.

Another day went by during which we did nothing, except that already an apology was being drafted. Eventually, we produced a masterpiece of semantic contortions that allowed Mulroney to save face, at least for the short run. I say we produced it because, once the din died down, a number of people emerged to claim credit for the text of Mulroney's statement. In fact, it was hammered out by Bill Fox, sitting at the typewriter, with Dalton Camp the bald guru, advertising genius and party stalwart dictating.

Now we had a statement. All we had to do was to get the leader to recite it to the voracious media, who were out there baying for blood. We decided to do the deed at a press conference at our first campaign stop on Wednesday July 18, at Sault Ste Marie, Ontario. The conference would be held at noon, to avoid a morning mob scene in Ottawa.

There were few jokes among the entourage on the flight to the Soo that morning, and tension built as word spread through the media contingent that something was afoot.

"Is he going to apologize?" everyone wanted to know. The francophone reporters, who hadn't taken the story as seriously as their anglo counterparts, were perplexed by all the fuss.

A few minutes before this fateful press conference was due, I was sitting with the media in the hotel press room, when a Quebec reporter came up with what was, for him, a very serious question. He wanted more details from The Boss on a speech in which he referred to the possible abolition of import quotas on shoes. I thought I must be dreaming. We were about to throw ourselves off a cliff with our fingers crossed, and here this guy wanted to talk to me about shoes!

"I'll ask him about it," I said, trying not to snarl. I left the press room and went to the leader's floor, to the room of Charley McMillan, the man in charge of policy and speeches. I mentioned something about shoe quotas; were we about to abolish them? "The Quebec guys want to ask some questions," I added.

Charley, the perfect image of the brilliant-but-absent-minded professor who puts on different coloured socks in the morning, and is the only one who can understand himself when he talks, was looking particularly haggard this morning, and my news didn't cheer him up any. Somebody in the room said, "If what they say is true, then ten seats just went down the toilet in Quebec." The shoe business accounts for a lot of jobs in Quebec, and dropping import quotas would threaten those jobs, which would not make the voters jump for joy.

Charley busied himself checking with the party research office in Ottawa, to find out exactly what our footwear policy was, and so, the press conference over which the entire brains trust had been biting its nails was delayed fortunately some twenty minutes during which time we got our line straight on shoes. The question was asked, and the leader had the answer — the shoes he was referring to were not in competition with the Quebec industry.

The Great Shoe Crisis was almost a refreshing break in the action for Mulroney. For a man with his kind of pride it couldn't have been easy to plant himself before the cameras and say, as he did say, "I don't deny having made these comments, but I simply say they were not said with any serious intent, since they do not reflect my attitude nor my position with respect to this important matter of public interest."

"It was wrong of me to bring up so important a question in a manner that might be misinterpreted, and I regret having done so."

The media reaction: "Why did he wait so long to apologize?"

No matter. It was done; the breach had been plugged. We could get back to serious business. No one really knew how important that convoluted statement would be to the outcome of the campaign, and, given what followed, there is no way of telling whether Mulroney would have become prime minister without having made it. In the meantime, there were new hurdles to face. The next day he was scheduled to campaign in Winnipeg, and as he himself said, "The last time I set foot there, they threw bottles of beer at me."

This was a reference to a courageous speech he had delivered in Winnipeg the previous March, in which he stuck up for the linguistic rights of franco-Manitobans before a hostile Conservative audience. People who were with him at the time say he was so nervous before going onstage that he grabbed a pitcher of water and downed half of it without using a glass. But he stuck to his principles and came away with his stature enhanced. After that, he rarely passed up an opportunity to remind people that he had stood four-square behind the franco-Manitobans, implying, correctly, that John Turner had declined to do the same.

Now he was going back to Winnipeg to deliver a speech in the riding where Tory Bud Sherman was running (in vain, as it turned out) against Liberal heavyweight Lloyd Axworthy. Sherman, a member of the provincial legislature, had been one of the most virulent opponents of the French rights package proposed by Howard Pawley's New Democratic government and supported by Mulroney.

"We're insane to go to Winnipeg," I said. But the senior strategists didn't agree. We'd have to go at some point; better to get it out of the way early in the campaign. They were right.

One thing about this visit was certain, as far as I was concerned. Mulroney always spoke some French in every speech, if only for symbolic purposes. He had to do so here, or the Quebec media would crucify him. He did — not much, but enough to make the point — and the Quebec guys, knowing full well what was going on, were unable to complain.

Later on, Mulroney told me how hard he found his trips to Manitoba.

"They don't like me there," he said, "I can feel that they don't like me."

However, the Winnipeg visit was, if not a success, at least not a failure, and we winged west to the delights of Vancouver. *Toronto Star* veteran Val Sears, who has the demeanor of a British peer and the humour of a hangman, told me, "Wait until you see those mountains, my boy. Compared to them, Mount Royal looks like a little pile of shit."

The joshing was a relief; if the guys were in a mood to kid around, then maybe we had some breathing space.

And, in the meantime, John Turner was having problems of his own at the other end of the country. A CTV cameraman had compiled evidence of Turner patting Liberal Party President Iona Campagnolo's behind during a campaign appearance. The bum-patting began in Edmonton when the Prime Minister, as part of his introduction, gave Iona a tap on the butt right there in front of *le tout Edmonton.* And the whole country, in fact, once CTV screwed up the courage to run the tape. Iona, to her credit, whacked his bum right back.

It was a ridiculous episode. It was not a thing for the Prime Minister to be doing, and especially not in front of television cameras. It smacked of another era, of locker rooms and ignorant jockdom. We knew that CTV had the tape, because Montreal's *La Presse* had published a notebook item on the episode, but, for reasons we couldn't fathom, the network was holding back. They weren't altogether ready to air a tape of the Prime Minister manhandling his party president's buttocks. This struck us as double-standard journalism. The press was ready to have Mulroney saying "there's no whore like an old whore" but not to expose the Liberal leader's bum-patting proclivities. However, CTV finally aired the clip and Turner, amazingly, tried to make light of the incident in Montreal five days later, this time to the posterior of Lise Saint-Martin Tremblay, a Liberal vice-president. Suddenly old whores were old hat. Bum-patting was now the media rage.

I still don't believe these incidents, important as they were to the campaign, reflected the respect John Turner holds for women. But this image of him patting ladies on the backside raised questions about what kind of person he really was. Here was the Prime Minister behaving like a buffoon in public. Moderates, machos and militant feminists for once shared a single reaction — the white knight's armour had been tarnished, if not pierced.

On board our aircraft on the flight back to Ottawa, the leader wasn't saying much. When I brought up Turner's travails, he just looked at me with a little smile tugging the corners of his mouth, as if to say, "Didn't I tell you?" Mila Mulroney was more forthcoming; she'd met Turner socially, and judging from his behaviour then, she wasn't surprised.

There wasn't much for the press corps to do on this flight but to get drunk. Since it was my duty, I forced myself to join in the revelry. But I couldn't help thinking that it was a little early for celebrating, even though the booze was free, and we were ahead on the week.

Next week would be the big one.

CHAPTER FOUR
The Debates

The subject came up two years later aboard Brian Mulroney's government-issued Challenger jet, and he could barely contain his anger.

"Do you know what Marcel Masse said the other day? He gave a speech in Cabinet about why we won the election. He said that people in Quebec decided to vote for us when the polls showed that we could win the country. He didn't say a word about the TV debates. Not a word! That's where I won the campaign."

During the summer of 1984 Mulroney wasn't the only one in the Conservative organization who regarded the scheduled face-to-face confrontations with John Turner, and with NDP leader Ed Broadbent, as crucial; but he was probably the only one who was absolutely convinced, even before the fact, that the whole campaign would turn on these encounters. And that he would emerge the big winner.

Some of the Tory brains trust were unhappy with the format. They had hoped for a series of debates across the country, but there would be only one debate in each official language plus one debate on women's issues. They would also have liked to see the debates later in the campaign; but the Liberals, as incumbents, held the whip hand, and they got the fixtures scheduled early, reasoning that few people watched TV in the summer, and those who did had short attention spans. And so it was arranged that the French debate would take place on July 24 and the English version the next day. At least we had ensured that there would be separate French and English debates.

This was perhaps the most important point for Mulroney. As he had done a year before when he won the party leadership, he was counting heavily on the Quebec card. Without Quebec, he always argued, the Conservative party would remain in opposition forever; it was his theme song.

The strategy was as lovely as it was simple. We knew that Turner's French was rusty — we'd heard him stumble along at press conferences — but most Quebeckers didn't know this, just as most weren't aware that Mulroney's French was their own colloquial speech. Putting the two men together, face-to-face for two hours, would drive the point home. He would be the Quebecker, the native son. In his home province, Tory advertising exhorted the populace to vote for Brian Mulroney; in the rest of the country it was "Vote for the Conservative Party." In Quebec's eyes, Mulroney had to be seen as the logical successor to Pierre Trudeau, and the French debate was the window of opportunity to make him so.

It also helped that Mulroney had a sound grasp of the issues that concerned French Canadians everywhere, as he had shown when he staked his credibility on support for the franco-Manitobans, while Turner had retreated into the thickets of semantics. The Boss was supremely comfortable in the language, and understood the French-Canadian mentality, but that was more than could be said for his generals from the Big Blue Machine. They were mostly unilingual anglophones who had come to regard Quebec as the land of lost seats and cruel disappointments, and some of their antics drove Mulroney almost to despair. On the very day of the French debate, a video crew dispatched by the generals showed up on his doorstep to record election advertisements.

"Don't they realize that I'm going to win the election tonight?" Mulroney bellowed, and ordered the crew tossed out in the street forthwith. Ever after, he would tell that story on the geniuses from the Big Blue Machine.

To prepare the leader for the debates, we hired a veteran journalist, Tom Gould, who quickly fastened on a couple of his quirks. What counted above all was the image we created of Mulroney, a man, after all, who wasn't well known to the Canadian public. We had unlimited confidence in his handling of the issues, and no one questioned his capacities as a verbal brawler — he'd been honing his style since high school. But he had a tendency towards a half-smile half-grimace that would distort his features when he was thrown off by a tough question. In time, he conquered it, but, going into the debate, it was a small worry.

The bigger worry was harder to define. For myself, I was never worried about the quality of his French; my concern was that he might try to overreach himself, to use sophisticated expressions that he ill understood to impress the Quebec intelligentsia. This is what the Press Gallery cynics would jump on. For most of the anglos, the French debate was little more than a warm-up for the big showdown the next day, but for Brian Mulroney, this was the big one. He was betting not only the election but his Quebecois soul on this encounter, and one was as important as the other to him.

The two debates were taped in the studios of CJOH, in Ottawa's west end. The reporters who showed up at the station could either watch it on TV monitors elsewhere, or live, in the studio, from little bleachers that looked as if they'd been whipped from a high-school gym. Now why, you might ask, would reporters trundle out to a TV studio in the suburbs to watch something on TV that they could see just as easily at home? In case of some unforeseen catastrophe — which would make them quite happy — or in case one of the party leaders had something exceptionally brilliant or, better yet, stupid, to say on the way out. When they talk about "coverage" for an event like this, they're not kidding; it's like being draped with a giant horse blanket. The idea, for the recipients, is to avoid suffocation.

That night, when Mulroney arrived at the studio, there was a furious scrum during which one of the security guards bowled over the CBC's superstar Mike Duffy like a linebacker flattening a wide receiver. The Boss solicitously asked after Duffy's health afterwards — body fine, dignity not so hot. Then there was that unavoidable ritual, the pre-event photo opportunity, in which platoons of photographers elbow and claw for that "exclusive" shot that no one else has. Turner decided to take over the photo op. When the cameramen and photographers came in, he put one arm around Ed Broadbent's shoulder, and held out the other arm for Mulroney. He wanted to appear in the newspapers the next day with one adversary under each wing, but Mulroney refused to, as he put it, "get caught into that one," so the next day the pictures showed Turner embracing Broadbent, and The Boss keeping a wary distance.

The debate went by the book. Only one of the three participants spoke really good French, and Quebeckers were shocked to hear John Turner stumble and fumble. Their memory of him stemmed from the mid-seventies, when he was regarded as one of the more bilingual members of the Trudeau cabinet, but Bay

Street had seized up his tongue. As for Broadbent, most people were surprised at how much his French had improved since the last election. His vocabulary was still barely beyond the Dick and Jane stage, and he was the first person they had ever heard speak French with what sounded like a Texas accent, but he was game, and, a lot of the time, you could even understand what he was trying to say.

As usual, I was with the journalists during the debate, to get reactions for the inevitable moment when The Boss would pop the question, "So, what are the Boys saying?" Turner's media people were there, too, and they were nervous. They were as aware as we were of their leader's language difficulties. The reporters picked up quickly on this, to the point where they spent as much time on linguistic inflections as they did on the content of the debate. The Quebec reporters took some delight in mimicking Mulroney's tendency to confuse the acute "e" with its grave counterpart. It wasn't terribly serious, but I worried that it might take their minds off the hash Turner was making of the language.

I was the first to greet the leader when he emerged from the studio.

"So . . ." was all he said, the anxiety evident in his voice.

"All right," I said. I was sure he'd come out the winner, although I had nothing solid yet to go on. Later, the Boys from Quebec assured me that Mulroney had carried the day.

Now there remained the English debate. For this, John Turner's problem was the opposite of ours. While he could count on the secular Liberal tradition in Quebec, he had to convince English Canada's electorate to extend the Liberal reign by posing as the agent of change. We wanted to drape ourselves in Trudeau's mantle — at least in Quebec — he wanted to shuck it off. And, while he could use his rusty French as an excuse for his mediocre showing in the French debate, this time there would be no excuses. He had to carry the day, and to do so decisively.

No one expected a knockout. Debates don't usually change much unless someone makes an astounding blunder, and the format was such that the three leaders never actually engaged each other all at the same time. After the opening statements, there were separate one-on-ones: Mulroney against Broadbent, then Turner–Broadbent, then Mulroney–Turner. Until that final segment, the debate had been largely desultory, with no one staking out a clear advantage; Broadbent got in some good shots, but that was about it.

I was sitting in the bleachers among the reporters, wondering why on earth anyone would sit in front of his TV set on a lovely night like this to hear such an exchange of platitudes, when suddenly the roof caved in on Turner. Mulroney pulverized him, like a crafty fighter waiting for the right moment, late in the fight, to deliver the knock-out punch. The fateful flurry began with Turner leaving himself open by raising the patronage question, hoping to score points by evoking the "old whore" episode. It wasn't the first time that he'd done so during the debate, but Mulroney had let him get away with it. This time he seized the moment and moved in for the kill.

MULRONEY: The appointments which we discussed earlier, I think, confirm the fact that it's the "old Boy" network back in town, that the boys are back and the Liberal Party doesn't want to change.

TURNER: I would say, Mr. Mulroney, that on the basis of what you have talked about — putting your nose in the public trough — that you wouldn't offer Canadians any newness in the style of government. The style that you have been preaching to your own party reminds me of the old Union Nationale. It reminds me of patronage at its best. Frankly, on the basis of your performance, I cannot see freshness coming out of your choice.

MULRONEY: Mr. Turner, the only person who has ever been appointed around here for the last twenty-odd years has been by your party, and ninety-nine per cent of them have been Liberals, and you ought not to be proud of that, nor should you repeat something that I think you know to be inaccurate.

You know full well that was a figure of speech that was used, and I do not deny it. In fact, I have gone so far, because I believe what you did was so bad, I have gone so far, sir, as to apologize for even kidding about it. I have apologized to the Canadian people for kidding about it. The least you should do is apologize for having made these horrible appointments. I have had the decency, I think, to acknowledge that I was wrong in even kidding about it. I shouldn't have done that, and I said so. You, sir, at least owe the Canadian people a profound apology for doing it . . .

May I say respectfully that, if I felt I owed the Canadian people — and I did — an apology for bantering about the subject, you, sir, owe the Canadian people a deep apology for having indulged in that kind of practice with those kinds of appointments.

It was brutal. Mulroney, now totally sure of himself, drove home his advantage, pointing an accusing finger at Turner. Turner looked like a trapped animal, cringing as Mulroney punished him mercilessly. Mulroney told me afterward, "I could see him start to shake . . ."
Turner's stammering reply was almost pathetic.

TURNER: Well, I have told you and told the Canadian people, Mr. Mulroney, that I had no option.

MULRONEY: You had an option, sir. You could have said, "I am not going to do it. This is wrong for Canada, and I am not going to ask Canadians to pay the price." You had an option, sir, to say no, and you chose to say yes to the old attitudes and the old stories of the Liberal Party. That, sir, if I may say respectfully, that is not good enough for Canadians.

TURNER: I had no option. I was . . .

MULRONEY: That is an avowal of failure. That is a confession of non-leadership and this country needs leadership. You had an option, sir. You could have done better.

Turner had gone rigid by this time, so much so that the moderator felt compelled to intervene, thereby compounding Turner's embarrassment.

MODERATOR: Mr. Turner, your response, please.

TURNER: I just said, Mr. Moderator, taking the Canadian people through the circumstances, Mr. Trudeau had every right to make those appointments before he resigned. In order to do so, yes, I had to make a commitment to him. Otherwise I was advised that, with serious consequences to the Canadian people, I could not have been granted the opportunity of forming a government.

In the room reserved for the reporters, all conversation had ceased during the exchange. Everyone was aware that something extraordinary was taking place. Slumped in their seats, Turner's press people knew it too. I could barely contain my joy. This was it, the turning point.

Again I was the first to greet the leader as he emerged from the studio. And as he had done the day before, he said to me: "So . . ."

"We've just won the election," I told him.

The congratulatory phone calls that started coming in almost immediately confirmed this view. Mulroney, curiously enough, was unusually subdued. He told me later that he was worried that he might have gone too far. "At a given point, I thought I had to stop," he said. Just as well. Otherwise, Turner might have run out of the studio in mid-debate.

We were all smiles as we climbed aboard the 727 next morning. This was the first time we would fly aboard the aircraft that would be ours for the rest of the campaign. "Manicouagan I" had been stencilled onto the fuselage, and the interior had been modified to our needs. A beaming Mulroney posed at the controls of the plane, with the name of his riding on the side, and we knew the shot would appear on the front page of most newspapers. That morning, he didn't have to force himself to smile.

We took off from Ottawa and headed for Sherbrooke. After Sherbrooke we took a swing through southern Ontario, where The Boss sang the praises of Niagara wines. Easy to do for someone who had taken up teetotalling. From there, we headed back to Ottawa to catch our breath and to savour the spectacle of John Turner flailing desperately as his campaign platform dissolved into quicksand beneath his feet.

He had to backtrack twice in the same week. The first time came when he accused Mulroney of wanting to fire 600,000 federal civil servants — more than there were — when he meant to say 60,000. Then, he had to apologize to Manitoba Premier Howard Pawley because, during the TV debate, when Ed Broadbent had pointed to falling unemployment in Manitoba, Turner had riposted that this was due to a declining provincial population. Now the facts were in, and he was proved wrong, so he had to eat crow. It was becoming a staple diet.

However, you can't win them all, and as July closed with a visit to Moncton, New Brunswick, our side was treated to the vision of one of our brilliant local candidates attacking the metric system in a speech about "millimetres and centipedes" to the delight of the assembled journalists and the discomfiture of the rest of us.

But it was here in Moncton that I really smelled victory. I sensed it in the reaction of the crowd of 4,000, which wasn't merely friendly, it was almost frenzied. It took forever for Brian and Mila Mulroney to make their way out of the hall, through the crush of people who wanted to get in a word of encouragement, or just to touch him as they went by. The debates had generated the momentum that would carry us to the finish line. The Liberal strategy had boomeranged; having the debates early on didn't seem like such a good idea any more. There was time for word of the debacle to spread, and by now, even people who had missed the live broadcast and all the replays were aware that Turner had blundered. Our strategy henceforth was to avoid mistakes. We were ahead; all we had to do was stay ahead.

The Boss was flying high. In seventh heaven, in fact. Maybe even, as events would soon show, a little too far up.

CHAPTER FIVE

Brian Brings It Off

Augusts began with what came to be known as "the Chatham Massacre," or "the martyrdom of Charley McMillan." Everything was coming up roses for the Conservatives, both inside the organization and in the eyes of the electorate. The pratfalls of the early days had been forgotten. The debates had enhanced the leader's image and credibility, and our daily public opinion samplings showed our popularity on a steady, inexorable rise. We had one more month on the campaign trail, and then we would savour the spoils that awaited us back in Ottawa.

Ah, but a month in politics, as anyone who has ever so much as licked an envelope in a committee room will tell you, can be an eternity; our troubles weren't over yet. We were lucky that Mulroney's consistently strong performance obscured some of the clangers along the way. Suddenly, he was emerging as the media darling, and it was John Turner's lot to play the part of campaign stumblebum, providing comic relief on the national newscasts. Every gesture, every speech, every manoeuvre by the Liberal organization pointed to the same conclusion: the wheels were falling off their wagon.

We on the Big Blue Bus, meanwhile, had developed what high-rollers call "the built-in edge," a saving grace that wafts you past a few awkward moments. There were few moments more awkward than those in Chatham, New Brunswick in early August.

Mulroney was still doing his Santa Claus impersonation across the country, descending from the skies to dispense promises out of what seemed like a bottomless sack of goodies. There were promises every day, great rafts of promises, and there always had to be more, in keeping with our strategy to make a pledge of local import in every region we visited. We had yet to come up with a cost figure for all of this, and while the campaign reporters had eased up on the topic somewhat, they would come back to it inevitably, once they got bored with The Boss' new-found allure. The Big Blue Machine was humming along nicely, but there were still a few bugs in the motor. We discovered one of them in Chatham, a quiet town in northern New Brunswick.

The promise-of-the-day there had to do with the small armed forces base outside the town. The Liberals intended to close it, although it contributed substantially to the local economy; Mulroney promised to keep the base operating at current strength. It was a lovely speech, and it went well. The problem was that neither the leader nor the brains trust had any idea what it really meant.

We might have slipped past this unscathed had it not been for the fact that our media entourage that week included Jim Munson, of CTV. Munson, who has gone on to become the network's London correspondent, is not only a feisty and competent reporter, but a native of this area. He was considerably more interested in what Mulroney said than the other journalists, and there was no way we were going to sneak anything by him. What's more, we weren't dealing with a local boy from some fifteen candlepower station; Munson would appear on TV screens across the country.

After the speech, we went back to the motel to give the reporters time to file, and The Boss time to catch his breath. When I strolled into the press room, I expected to find the usual cynical back-and-forth about the day's deliverance, instead of which I found an uproar, and, at the centre of it, Jim Munson, the hometown boy. He was in his scrapper mode, which did not bode well. Despite a diminutive stature, he was known for his aggressiveness and once, during a particularly arduous Parliamentary scrum, actually got into a shoving match with Pierre Trudeau and gave as good as he got.

So I was a trifle nervous when I saw him brandishing The Speech and demanding, "What's this supposed to mean?" Damned if I knew.

"There's nothing in here," he declared. "Let's have Mulroney out to answer a few questions. How many jobs will be saved? How many people are working at the base now? How much money will this cost?" These were all good, sensible questions

43

and it would have pleased me more than anything to give them good, sensible answers. Mumbling something that was supposed to sound convincing, I retreated to warn Bill Fox.

"We have a problem," I told him. His first impulse was to charge in and straighten the whole thing out by himself, but I convinced him that if he tried that, he'd find himself in a starring role on network news that night. Wouldn't The Boss love that! Instead, we decided to send in Charley McMillan, the rumpled professor. He was, after all, the senior policy adviser on the tour, and if anyone knew what Mulroney's promise meant, it had to be Charley.

Well, no. Charley didn't know anything about this particular situation, so he got on the phone to Ottawa while I went down to the press room to try to soothe the raging beast. I didn't do too well, but then, I didn't have a lot to go with. Every five minutes or so, I'd dash back to Charley's room, but he was still on the phone, taking forever. Finally, Fox and I pried him loose long enough to deliver an ultimatum: time was up; we had to face the horde. Charley didn't seem too worried, so off we went. He should have worried.

The meeting in the press room opened with a brief row between Fox and Munson. Munson wanted a warm body to go before his camera, but Fox explained that McMillan could only be identified as a spokesman for the leader. The reporters could use the information he provided, but he could not be quoted directly, and he would not appear on camera. Munson didn't like it, but these were the rules he worked under every day in Ottawa, and after some more grumbling, the briefing went ahead. Of all the moves Fox made during the campaign, this was perhaps the sneakiest. It didn't save poor Charley from being savaged by the assembled journalists, but his humiliation was witnessed only by those in the room, not a TV audience. Even after his chat with Ottawa, he knew diddly-squat about the cost of that day's promise, and when the reporters discovered that they dissected him, without benefit of anesthetic. It was not a pretty sight, and, after a while, Fox and I turned our backs and took an unusual interest in the sandwich plate across the room while Charley paraded his cheerful ignorance before the press. In the end, an exasperated Munson abandoned the chase; it was like beating on a turtle that has retreated into its shell.

When the carnage was over, I accompanied McMillan back to his room. "Thanks a lot, Charley," I said, radiating comfort and sincerity. At that moment, I truly loved the man for his guts and

44

good humour under pressure. He had been worked over like a street drunk outside a dive, but he was still laughing.

That night, huddled around the TV set in the leader's room, we expected the worst. To our delight, there was nothing in Munson's item about the afternoon *brouhaha*, We had lucked out. Fox snapped off the set with a triumphal cry: "I love you, Jimmy!"

However, Munson, that sly fox, had another one for us in his bag of tricks. The next day, we were in Halifax, where the leader was to give a press conference, something he enjoyed less and less the more he was exposed to the experience. The day started well with Robert Stanfield, now sainted in Tory circles, delivering a stirring endorsement of Mulroney, although he had preferred Joe Clark at the leadership convention. Stanfield was particularly pleased with Mulroney's stand on the language issue.

Mulroney's press conference was to follow and Munson, with an angelic look on his face, approached me to ask if I could make sure he got a question in. Preferably, the first. I suspected some kind of trap, but Munson's request was within the rules of the game, so I had little choice. Besides, I liked him. So, he got his question, and set off his firecracker: was Mulroney in favour of making French an official language in Ontario?

The question caught The Boss flat-footed. We were ready for everything but this. His response was tortuous. At all costs, he wanted to avoid using the term "French as an official language," because he knew he'd be opening a can of worms not only in Ontario, but everywhere, particularly in Quebec, where language questions always get a lot of play. Still, he had his reputation as the champion of minority language rights, so he couldn't vacillate. Damn Munson!

Mulroney found it in himself to say that he thought it "abnormal" that thousands of franco-Ontarians did not get the benefit of services offered to their English-speaking fellow citizens. However, his answer was laborious and convoluted, and, as usual, it fell to the press secretaries to handle the hot potato once The Boss had heaved it. The reporters wanted elaboration, but we didn't know much more about what he was trying to say than they did and we did know that Mulroney hated to be second-guessed by his subalterns. One of the delights of the media pack is to catch an aide making a statement that contradicts the leader. The best way to deal with such situations is to shrug the shoulders and say that The Boss said what he said, so we did that.

The business about official languages was particularly worrisome because we were just about to embark on a swing through the heartland of southern Ontario. Accompanying us would be Premier Bill Davis, who had graciously offered to front for Mulroney, a favour he had not extended to Joe Clark during the previous federal election. Davis, in fact, was our card in the hole in Ontario, and while he had made great strides in providing French services in the province, he had remained firm in his refusal to declare French an official language. We knew that within minutes of Mulroney's statement, every news editor was going to be issuing orders to get a reaction from Bill Davis. So we got to the premier first, briefed him on what had been said and reassured him that we were in no way trying to rock his orange-cart.

Once the reports got out, a few of our candidates, notably Flora MacDonald, MP for Kingston and the Islands, voiced alarm at the effect Mulroney's stance might have on voters, no matter how softly it was couched. Davis, who was making a campaign appearance in Timmins, graciously let us off the hook by saying that he understood how Mulroney, as a federal party leader, might see things differently; as for himself, he was sticking to his guns. I still don't understand how this fundamental disagreement didn't create more fuss than it did. The gods must have been smiling on us.

This wasn't the only bit of trouble that emerged from this August 2nd press conference. In response to a question about when exactly he planned to produce the promised price-tag for his election goodies, Mulroney was more evasive than ever. In fact, he left the distinct impression that he had changed his mind about telling Canadians about the cost of Conservative proposals. Perplexed, I went to Fox, who seemed equally disturbed.

"I hope he doesn't plan to back off on giving the costs," I said. Fox shrugged; he feared precisely that. By now, the problem wasn't the size of the bill so much as the impact of a refusal on Mulroney's part to honour his commitment. I was sincerely alarmed, and a conversation with The Boss did little to reassure me.

"Do you know what the polls are saying about how important the cost of our programs is to the average voter?" he asked me. I knew I wasn't expected to reply, and, sure enough, with a sneer on his face, he held up his thumb and finger to form a zero. History will record that he finally respected his promise and delivered a cost accounting during a Toronto appearance on August 28th — six days before the vote, when it obviously didn't matter much. But I'm convinced he came that close to backing out entirely.

Despite the scary moments, the Big Blue bulldozer was rolling along, right over the opposition. Our next destination was the picturesque Saguenay–Lac St. Jean area, where Mulroney blew it. We were in Roberval, the riding of future cabinet minister Benoît Bouchard. The local community hall was tarted up with streamers and bunting in a style that hadn't been seen much since the days of the Créditistes, who, like the Parti Québécois, were once very strong in the area. Now, it's important to remember that Roberval is situated in the Lac St. Jean part of the region, and, as might be expected, people in Saguenay don't look kindly on those who confuse Saguenay with Lac St. Jean, and vice versa. Earlier that day we had arrived in Chicoutimi, the area's largest city, which is in Saguenay, and proceeded by bus to Roberval, which is in Lac St. Jean. Got that? Apparently Brian Mulroney didn't.

After the grand entrance with the theme from "Rocky" blaring from the speakers, The Boss spoke, as he liked to at every opportunity, of his small-town roots on the North Shore, which happened to be the region next door to Saguenay–Lac St. Jean. In what was meant to be a resounding oratorical finish, Mulroney declared:

"And I don't need a roadmap to know where the region of . . ." and then he stopped abruptly in mid-phrase. He had forgotten where he was. Then, awkwardly, as they rolled out of their chairs at the press table, he finished, "the region . . . where we find ourselves today."

I didn't mention this gaffe to The Boss afterwards. I didn't need a roadmap to know that he preferred to extricate his foot from his mouth all by himself.

However, the day was saved. Jim Munson, Lord love him, our black sheep all week, gave us reason to rejoice by announcing that night that a CTV poll had the Conservatives nine points out in front. It was with happy hearts that we settled down in Baie Comeau, the Boss's hometown. Finally, we got a good night's sleep, and for once we slept longer than the reporters.

I was staying with the leader's entourage at the Manoir Comeau; the reporters were lodged across town at the Motel Le Comte.

47

The agenda for the next day had our first event scheduled for 9:00 a.m., a crazy water-ski race across the St. Lawrence River between Baie Comeau and Rimouski. The competitors would roar out of the harbour, then come roaring back a few hours later; in between, the crowd would mill around the dock drinking beer.

That morning, Camille Guilbault, who was in charge of rousing the reporters in time, asked the motel desk clerk to wake her up at 6:00 a.m. A couple of hours later, she started to make her calls to the media troops, only to find that she needn't have bothered. The hotel management, a tad overzealous, had taken her instructions to mean that the whole group, scribes and all, should be rousted at 6:00 a.m.

When I got on the bus I was greeted by a collection of long faces, grey with fatigue, and a furious barrage of complaints.

"Why the hell did they wake us up at six o'clock?" cried Gilbert Bringué of Radio-Canada. "We've been sitting around doing nothing for two hours!" After all they'd put us through, the journalists deserved a little shot of discomfort, but I thought it better not to point that out. Instead, I got on the second media bus determined to jolly them out of their foul mood.

"Good morning, Fred," I said cheerily to Fred Ennis, the normally good-humoured Newsradio correspondent, "it seems you got an early start this morning."

"Michel, I have just one thing to tell you," he said, his voice hoarse. "There was a young man from the motel who phoned me this morning, and I knew I wasn't the first one he called, because he asked me in French, 'What does it mean when someone tells you, fuck off?' "

That was the beginning of a memorable weekend in the leader's riding.

We had set aside three days in Manicouagan, starting with a trip along the lovely North Shore, from Baie Comeau to Sept-Iles, stopping off at all the little villages in between. Mulroney had chosen Sept-Iles for his "national reconciliation" speech. This was written by Lucien Bouchard, who was later to be appointed ambassador to France. Another of Mulroney's cronies from Laval University, Bouchard possessed a writing style combining a touch of poetry with a precise grasp of language and the nuances of political rhetoric; he was The Boss's favourite speech-writer. The text of the Sept-Iles address, in which Mulroney outlined his plan to bring Quebec into the Canadian constitutional fold "with honour and enthusiasm" would be oft-quoted, and would be reflected in reality with the Meech Lake accord in 1987.

It was one of the key speeches of the campaign, and somehow I managed to miss it. I got to the hall late and stayed outside — I hadn't even asked what the speech was to be about. The Quebec reporters who came to see me afterwards were full of praise; The Boss was going to win a lot of points in the province. For once, I knew what the Boys were saying, but I didn't know what they were talking about.

Even the triumph in Sept-Iles didn't cushion the rude shock I got when the next week opened with a fresh contingent of scribes, just off the Turner campaign, scrambling aboard "Manicouagan I." It is general policy for the media to rotate reporters on the campaigns on the assumption that a journalist left too long with one candidate will become either too enamoured or thoroughly hostile. The new group, which included some of the most high-spirited souls in the Press Gallery, brought along their satirical songs and their horror stories about the man they called "Chick" — Turner's nickname from college days at the University of British Columbia. The song they sang on the Turner plane, while the leader cringed in his seat at the front, was to the tune of John Lennon's "Give Peace a Chance," and began:

"All we are saying,
"Is give Chick a chance,
"All we are saying,
"Is give Chick his pants."

The reference was to the moment on the campaign trail when someone spilled coffee in Turner's lap, and Geills, his wife, took his pants into the ladies' room to try to repair the damage while the Prime Minister fidgetted bare-legged next door in the gents, with André Ouellet (who always seemed to be there when things went wrong) guarding the door.

It was refreshing, but dangerous, to have the new Boys on board. On one hand, they hadn't yet had time to memorize The Speech, whose familiar clichés and jokes their predecessors had learned by rote, and could deliver, word for word, with the candidate. The old gang had also come to appreciate the thespian talents of Mila Mulroney, who would sit through The Speech night after night and laugh on cue at the same jokes as if they were brand new. On the other hand, the new arrivals had just spent several weeks making life tough for John Turner, so they were full of spunk and determined to show that they could give Mulroney just as rough a ride.

They made up a new song for Mulroney. Reaching back to the "old whore" incident and the tune of "There's No Business Like Show Business" they would bellow:

"There's no whore,

"Like an old whore . . ."

We had to get used to a new set of personalities, and we were far from out of the woods.

This second week of August would turn out to be, at least for me, the longest and hardest of the campaign. We criss-crossed southern Ontario by bus, which meant spending a lot of time in cramped quarters, and by the end of the week the bus resembled a dump that smelled partly like a locker room, partly like a tavern, and partly like an abandoned fruit stand with decomposing wares. In five days we made our way from Windsor, in the deep south-west, to Kingston at the eastern tip of Lake Ontario, zig-zagging from one small town to another in between. There were places like Blenheim, Glencoe, and Talbotville, and many more whose names I don't remember, and which I'd just as soon forget.

The francophone reporters began showing signs of rebellion on the first day out. In Windsor, Mulroney delivered a sharp rejoinder to Turner's charge that there were separatists among his Quebec candidates — but the rejoinder was delivered in English. This was not much use to the French broadcasters, and in addition, Gilles Paquin of *La Presse* wanted to ask The Boss a few pointed questions about the front-line role he claimed for himself in the Quebec referendum battle of 1976. The Boys began agitating for a scrum.

The notion spread like a cancer. We got through Tuesday, but there were rumblings from the back of the bus all day Wednesday, and by Thursday morning, they were ready to mount an assault. They tried to trap Mulroney after a routine event in St. Thomas, but he managed to slip into his bus without saying a word. I begged Fox to convince him to do something, but in vain. Then at the next stop, Simcoe, the reporters, with Gilles Paquin as the main instigator, refused to board their buses after the speech.

"We've got a mutiny on our hands," I told Fox.

"Oh, yeah?" he replied, "I'd like to hear what their editors have to say when they find out they didn't get on the bus . . ."

I didn't think this was the best attitude, but maybe I was still too close to reporters. I bravely announced to the mob that there would be no scrum. They ignored me and massed around the door of the leader's bus. Finally, Fox appeared and announced that there would be a mini press conference at the next stop, Woodstock. Still grumbling, they headed back to their own buses.

As I began to follow them, an elderly lady who was having trouble backing up her car in the hotel's crowded lot asked me to help her, and, since all of us who go into politics are naturally good Samaritans, I climbed behind the wheel and backed the thing out myself. I was still basking in the glow of the lady's praise when I realized that there were no more Tory Blue Buses around. I was just beginning to panic at the thought of being stranded in Simcoe when I spotted a police cruiser. It was a local cop, wearing a big beer belly and aviation sunglasses. He could have stepped out of a B movie set in Georgia.

"You work for Mulroney?" he asked, when I accosted him.

"That's right."

"You're not with the press?" There was a note of suspicion, and derision, in his voice.

"Oh, no," I replied happily, convinced that if I had replied otherwise, he'd have shot me on the spot.

"Get in," he said. He revelled in the ride that followed; I thought I was going to die of fright. Lights flashing, siren wailing, he took off like A.J. Foyt. Masses of cars parted before us, like the Red Sea. When we caught up to the leader's bus, he tried to intercept it by pulling slightly ahead and fishtailing his back end.

"Not that one," I cried, "I'm on the one up ahead."

"I thought you told me you weren't with the press?" This time there was an undertone of menace.

"No, no, but I work with them . . . It's, uh, my job."

Looking mightily put out, the cop flagged down one of the press buses and let me off, giving me a long, hard look.

"You're sure you're not with the press?"

"Don't worry about it," I said, and fled onto the bus, where I was greeted, of course, with the royal raspberry.

At the next stop, The Boss gave his promised press conference. According to a strategy that allowed him to choose the moment to end the proceedings, Mulroney stationed himself just in front of the bus door, and when he had had enough the door popped open and swallowed him. After all the furor, the scrum provided nothing particularly newsworthy, but afterwards everyone was much more relaxed.

The next day, a poll commissioned by the Southam chain of newspapers had us almost twenty points ahead of the Liberals, and the journalists' resistance began to fade. Knocking Mulroney, one of them told me, was "like throwing rocks at an express train."

That Saturday night in Barrie, a town on Lake Simcoe, we stumbled on the best party of the whole campaign. It all started innocently when I got a call from Gilles Paquin of *La Presse*. I was staying at the Holiday Inn with the leader, and the media were up the street at another hotel. I was just having a little nap to prepare myself for the evening's exertions when the phone rang, about nine o'clock.

"Do you have two beds in your room?" asked Paquin.

"Two beds? Yeah, I've got two beds."

"Good," he said. "I'm sleeping in your room."

"What do you mean, you're sleeping in my room?"

"Damn right. I can't believe what kind of dump you've put us in. It smells bad, it's hot, and it's filthy. There's a huge garbage bin just outside my room, and I can't get the window closed. I'm coming over."

He already knew I had two beds, so I resigned myself to company and tried to catch a few more winks, but the phone rang again. This time it was Lisa Van Dusen, telling me that I'd better get over to the media hotel, because the scribes were about to build a bonfire in the parking lot. With the walls of the hotel!

I jumped into a cab and went straight over. The first thing I noticed was that Paquin hadn't been exaggerating. Maybe a little, but not much. The place was a dive. However, a bonfire didn't seem the best solution, and, after a few beers, we decided that the best way to survive the disaster was to stay up all night. Bob Parkins of the *Calgray Herald* offered his room for our bacchanal. He also had two beds in his room, so to make space we hoisted them on their sides and leaned them against the wall. Somehow, the room had more allure that way. And that's how we spent our night in Barrie.

The next morning on the bus, Glen Sommerville of Canadian Press, who had been one of the evening's leading lights, was talking to Camille Guilbault.

"Camille," he said, "did you see Bob Parkins' room?"

"No," she replied, "what was so special about it?"

"It was amazing. I haven't seen anything like it in years. They had Murphy beds!"

There was still the women's debate to be gotten through, a campaign novelty we could have done without. We knew we were starting at a disadvantage. For us, as for John Turner, appearing in a hall packed with militant feminists was a little like a staunch federalist going to argue his case at the St. Jean Baptiste Society. We were in a no-win situation.

On the whole, it was Ed Broadbent's evening. He and his party had vigorously catered to the feminist vote, and the room was brimming with his ardent supporters. I never doubted Mulroney's sincerity on women's issues, but he was weighed down by a party groaning with dinosaurs. Our only hope was that no one was really interested.

The televised debate took place at the Royal York hotel in Toronto. Almost all those in attendance were women, and they applauded and heckled the speakers in defiance of the ground rules. But in the end, the format worked for us. Since the debate was conducted in both languages, seventy-five per cent of the country heard only the dreary monotone of the translator whenever there was a question and answer in French. This was bound to bore all but the most committed, who probably wouldn't vote for us under pain of torture. It was one of the worst pieces of television ever, and just dandy for us.

Mulroney told me after the debate that he had met Premier Davis just before kickoff, and Davis told him to "act like a prime minister." So he did that, to his boring best, and, after the lights had been switched off and the cameras shut down, he smiled and said, "I survived."

And then, flashing his toothiest smile for me, "How did you like my courageous silence on abortion?"

Indeed. That had been another stroke of fortune. When the panel asking the questions got around to abortion, John Turner struggled mightily, while Mulroney said not a word. To my great astonishment, and his, nobody asked him for his view — opposed — before moving on to another topic.

There could be no doubt now that the momentum was behind us; it was just a question of how far it would take us. Our grass roots polls, particularly in Quebec, were showing a steady rise that even our organizers there found hard to credit. As one result, Mulroney was getting ever more sure of himself. At the outset of the campaign, he had been careful to lay off Jean Chrétien; now he was freely advising him not to stray too far from his riding. For Chrétien to lose his seat in Shawinigan we'd have to take 282 constituencies out of 282.

It was during this period in mid-August that I began to worry that The Boss was starting to believe his own myth. He'd always been obsessed by the Trudeau legend, and, though he respected Trudeau's intelligence, he thought him overrated. And he chafed at the knowledge that, in any comparison, he came off second best. He started asking us why the reporters were deliberately down-playing the size of the crowds at our rallies.

"He doesn't think we're pushing the crowd counts enough," Bill Fox told me.

I asked him, "What do you expect me to do? I'm the last person the reporters are going to consult for a crowd count. They're not crazy."

I tried to impress on The Boss later that times had changed since Trudeaumania sixteen years before, that the media hadn't been the same since TV took control of the reporting process, and since Watergate heightened everyone's suspicions. I could sympathize with him, but I found it unsettling that in the midst of a staggering electoral victory he was fretting because the papers weren't talking about "Mulromania." I was later told that part of the reason for his pique was the "Milamania" some papers had discovered, but I never believed that. It was simply an extension of his media complex; he thought they had been out to get him from the beginning, and even in his hour of glory the old insecurity was coming to the surface. The future was going to give his paranoia something to work on.

For the final weekend of the campaign, we headed home to Manicouagan. During a stop in the northern mining community of Wabush, Mulroney was confronted by an angry crowd of unemployed workers, who looked as if they could quickly turn into a mob. In a scene reminiscent of Trudeau's defiance of the St. Jean Baptiste Day rioters on the eve of the 1968 election, Mulroney grabbed the mike from his clearly petrified local representative and defied the demonstrators with the fervour of an Old Testament prophet having a few words with the lads from Soddom and Gomorrah. Mila Mulroney said later she was genuinely frightened — something that didn't happen often. The Boss, however, kept railing at the hostile crowd all the way to the bus, taking energy, it seemed, from their growing hostility.

He had fire in his eyes and a smile on his lips when he got back on the bus.

After the final emotional landing in Baie Comeau, the last stop on the two-month campaign haul, the election itself, on September 4th, was a bit of an anti-climax. We were confident that we had done our jobs, and that all we had to do was await the bestowal of power. Mulroney spent the day in a cottage attached to the Manoir Comeau, just down the street from where he was born and raised. That evening his closest advisers, most of whom were also personal friends, joined him. Once the polls in the Maritimes had closed, The Boss's great preoccupation was with how we had done in the five northern New Brunswick seats — heavily Acadian and traditionally Liberal. When our spotters confirmed that we were ahead in four of the five, he knew the dimensions of our triumph even before the CBC went on the air with the official results.

With 211 out of 282, we had won more seats in the House of Commons than any party in Canadian history. With a small joke that would ring prophetically across the months to come, Mulroney would say:

"Okay, we've won. What do we do now?"

PART TWO
Glory Days

"I sensed that power is a blind and omni-present force, that it is indiscriminate and immoral, and that men who wield it are also prisoners of it."

Dalton Camp, *Gentlemen, Players and Politicians*, 1970

CHAPTER SIX

Portrait of a Prime Minister

Before we plunge into the events that would first engage and then ensnarl the new government, we ought to pause to look for a moment at the man who, almost single-handedly, brought it into being. Canadians didn't know Brian Mulroney. We kept hearing it again and again; it haunted our dreams when the days turned darker following the sunshine victory of September 4th. No matter how many clever communications strategies we devised, no matter how many cute camera angles we worked out, no matter how honeyed were his words, and no matter how much we tried to adjust his comportment, Brian Mulroney remained a vague and elusive personality.

Not a mystery man, like Pierre Trudeau. Trudeau was a closed individual, who tended to keep the world at arm's length, but at least you had the impression that you knew where you stood with him. With Mulroney, the situation was reversed. No one could be more gracious, more charming, and more open, yet his personality somehow failed to impress. The smile hung in the air unsupported. The image was a little too perfect, the dialectic a trifle too sweet. The anglo reporters called him "slick," and the more cynical claimed, "Deep down, he's shallow."

It wasn't really fair, yet there was something undeniably troublesome in the public perception of the new prime minister. A major reason was the long legacy of Pierre Trudeau. Canadians, for better or worse, had got used to a prime minister in the Trudeau mould. His successors have had to deal, not only with the man, but with his out-sized shadow. Getting out from under it was not swiftly done — ask Joe Clark or John Turner.

Mulroney was obsessed with Trudeau and his enduring myth. Often, he would get on the subject during the long flights on foreign or domestic trips. He resented the myth the media had created of Trudeau's flair for international affairs, when many of the world leaders that Mulroney had met spoke of the man with contempt. During a meeting of Caribbean leaders in Kingston, Jamaica, in February, 1985, — our first major foreign trip — Mulroney told me that the other leaders complained about Trudeau treating them like schoolboys.

"He'd come here and give them philosophy lectures," The Boss snorted. He regarded himself as the better man; he didn't come to lecture on philosophy, but humbly to listen and work towards the calm resolution of problems. After meeting with British Prime Minister Margaret Thatcher, Mulroney reported with some glee that her description of Trudeau was unprintable. Thanks to the Watergate tapes, everybody knew what Richard Nixon thought of "that asshole Trudeau," and, from all accounts, Ronald Reagan felt much the same. But the media never seemed to get the message.

Mulroney regarded his policy of constructive international relations as the antithesis of Trudeau's confrontationalist approach — and it certainly seemed to work in hammering out a Commonwealth approach to South Africa. He was out to accomplish things; Trudeau, he believed was only out to spread his aura. But it wasn't only on the international excursions that the spectre of his predecessor would haunt the troubled soul of Brian Mulroney. The obsession was evident back home, as well.

On trips outside Ottawa, he and Mila would get out and mingle with ordinary Canadians, and inevitably a crowd would gather around them, perhaps to exchange a few words, or maybe touch one of them as they passed along, much as they would mob a rock star who strayed into town. The Boss loved these scenes; they were like a drug for him, and would lift his spirits for days. Inevitably, afterwards, he would ask me what the Boys were saying. I'd have to tell him that he'd performed well, but that the Boys wouldn't give him much credit for it this time, either. He'd shake his head.

"If it was Trudeau," he'd say, "they'd be talking about Trudeaumania."

He did have something of a point. It bothered Mila, too. One day, when we were flying back to Ottawa on the Challenger, she told him, "Why don't you stop talking about that? You know it's never going to change."

As he'd often do when reproached by his wife, Mulroney smiled softly at her and reached out to take her hand. They were still intensely in love. I've rarely seen two people who were so frankly smitten with each other. It struck me from the very start of the election campaign, but it was even more evident during some of the dark days to come.

He showed the same warmth to his children. I never heard him raise his voice to any of the four youngsters, who often came with us on trips. Mila sometimes bridled at this.

" 'Hello, nice baby. Hello, nice baby.' That's all you can say," she complained when he refused to take a tougher line with their youngest son, Nicolas. The Boss would talk to me about my own three daughters, and ask how they were doing. Whenever I said I was going to visit them, he'd say, "Ah, that's fun, that." Mulroney, with one daughter and three boys, said, "You're lucky, Michel; girls are a lot of fun."

I was always happy to see the kids along; it always put the Boss in a better mood. There were practical considerations, too. A picture of Nicolas or Mark had a far better chance of getting on the front pages than a hundred shots of Brian and Mila alone. Canadians, being vastly less cynical than reporters, were delighted to see the Mulroney family together, so it was heartening to hear The Boss chirrup to Nicolas, "Get ready, baby, we're going out on campaign!"

Although I never heard the Prime Minister shout at his children, I can't say the same thing for adults.

There has been much talk about Mulroney's towering rages, and I've been witness to a few. One came early in the new administration, when Finance Minister Michael Wilson, during an interview with Canadian Press, cast doubts on the continuation of universal social programs. Perhaps they should be provided free only to some Canadians, he suggested, although, during the election, Mulroney had spoken of universality as "a sacred trust." This plunged the government, and the Prime Minister in particular, into an embarrassing imbroglio of backtracking and explaining. When I first showed Mulroney the CP wire story, he went white as a sheet, then started shouting that it was "terrible," and "outrageous," along with some phrases that would make a stevedore blush. Turning to me, he said, "I want you to pick up the phone, talk to Wilson or his chief of staff, and tell them . . . "

Then, seeing my helpless expression — I was going to bawl out Wilson? — he stopped in mid-sentence, and decided to make the call himself. On the phone, he did no shouting, for one of the curious things about his rages was that he would rarely explode in front of the person he was angry with. Someone else would get it, by deflection. So, whenever he started screaming in my presence, I knew that I was safe, at least for the time being. On the other hand, I'd start worrying when he'd fold his hands on his desk, look at me over the tops of his glasses, and talk in his deepest tone. It would always start with, "You know, Michel . . . "

I knew then I was in for a sermon.

While Mulroney had an explosive temper, his humour and his desire to make people laugh were far more important to his makeup. On a trip to Zimbabwe, where the President — a strictly honorary title — rejoiced in the name, Banana, (actually, the Rev. Canaan Banana) we had a hard time restraining ourselves from making cracks, lest we wind up in somebody's column saying something that would breach protocol. The reporters, of course, were not so constrained. The Prime Minister finally had his meeting with President Banana, and, in the staff briefing that followed, dwelt primarily on the far more important meeting he had had with Prime Minister Mugabe. When I was able to slip in a question, I asked, "And how was your meeting with President Banana?"

"Very fruitful," he replied.

Alas, however, he found it hard to laugh at himself, an essential quality for any successful politician. He bombed lamentably in his first speech as Prime Minister at the annual Parliamentary Press Gallery dinner. This is a somewhat decadent rite where the party leaders deliver satiric speeches which must be funny — otherwise the journalists feel free to throw buns and sugar cubes at them. Mulroney tried to make fun of everyone but himself, and it went over like a 300 pound pole vaulter. He took it hard that he, the brilliant orator of the election campaign, had laid an egg before this crucial audience. But he learned from that disaster, and his Press Gallery speeches since then have been well received by the toughest crowd in the country.

That turnaround was the result of an incredible inner strength. It was an act of will, like the one that allowed him to stop drinking when it was obvious that alcohol threatened his aspirations.

Later, he gave up smoking, and, more recently, reading all the newspapers and watching almost every national news broadcast — no mean feat for a media junkie.

This was a man who read everything, and was always catching me out because I'd missed some item somewhere. Once, when were about to leave Ottawa for a goodwill trip, I made sure I'd read everything there was to read in Canada that might interest him. This time, I'd survive the quiz. No sooner were we strapped in the Challenger than he asked me, "Have you read this story in *Le Figaro*?" A French paper. I could have strangled him.

This was the man who was going to give up newspapers, and he told me of this last decision, in the winter of 1987, when things were at their bleakest in the midst of the Oerlikon scandal. I was stunned.

"What is there left to give up?" I asked.

It was bad news for a press secretary; now, I'd have to keep him abreast of all the news. His addiction became another of my burdens.

For it is a fact that rivalling his obsession with Trudeau was his obsession with the media. Every morning at dawn, the major dailies were delivered to the prime ministerial residence at 24 Sussex Drive, and he'd have read them all before his senior staffs' morning meeting. In the evenings, he was forever fiddling with a TV channel selector to make sure he didn't miss anything. When he wasn't there, he'd have someone record newscasts for him, and when we were overseas, he'd sometimes have the cassettes flown over. (Contrary to rumour, we never went as far as satellite feeds; the cost was simply prohibitive.)

I paid the price of The Boss's obsession one memorable night during the winter of 1986. We were staying at the Ritz Carlton hotel in Montreal, where, on Friday January 24, Mulroney gave an excellent interview to *Le Devoir*. The story appeared early Saturday, and Canadian Press put an item on the wire. That was fine; we had scored a small coup. All was peaceful as we settled down that night at the Ritz.

Normally, I would have left the hotel to savour the downtown joys of Montreal night-life, but a kindly fate kept me in my room like a good little Ontario boy. I was snuggled into bed at 12:30 a.m. when the phone rang. The Boss wanted to see me. At once. Good Lord, what could be coming down on our heads now?

When I got to his suite, he was sitting on the couch wearing a dressing-gown and a put-upon expression. Sitting in a nearby armchair in his pajamas was his principal secretary, Bernard

Roy, looking just antsy. Mulroney had been listening to the radio, as usual, and had picked up a report that was making him lose sleep. I no longer remember exactly why, but he was certain that the newsreader had dangerously misrepresented what he'd said to *Le Devoir*. I told him the announcer was probably reading from the CP story, and that he'd added a little something, as announcers often do.

"Get on the phone to Canadian Press," he ordered. "I never said that."

I turned to leave for my room, but he wanted me to make the call right there, in front of him. After speaking to the CP desk, I told him that, as far as I was concerned, the story that was read to me had been eminently correct.

"Then call the radio station."

There was, naturally, no one at the station but the wretched announcer, who played me a tape of his report. There wasn't anything terribly wrong with it, but, as I'd expected, he'd given the item a bit of topspin. I chewed him out, telling him that I'd been there for the interview, I knew what was in the CP story, and he had no right to put such distortions out on the air. When I hung up, the Prime Minister was looking at me anxiously.

"And . . . " he said.

"I think I scared him, but you never know."

Then he did something that will remain forever engraved in my memory. From the pocket of his dressing gown, he pulled out a small shortwave radio and began fiddling with the dial. I was so dumbfounded that I couldn't help blurting to Roy, "Isn't someone going to unplug him?"

Mulroney found that very funny, but he kept at the radio until he satisfied himself that the offending item had been dropped from the next newscast.

"Well," he said, "you must really have scared him." Then, almost shyly, he added, "I'm sorry I disturbed you."

Life was like that between the hammer and the anvil; between Mulroney and the media.

Yet, despite all the wounds he suffered at their hands, The Boss enjoyed the company of journalists. He didn't think much of their intellectual capacity, and lamented their feeble grasp on the nuances of power; he thought they were quick-hit artists, whose principal interests lay with the frivolous stuff that sells newspapers rather than the complex issues that drive countries — but he loved to shoot the breeze with them, and would have done more of it except for the still-tender memory of the "old whore" incident from the first week of the campaign. That soured his view forever. Above all, he couldn't tolerate personal attacks, especially stories that impugned Mila.

"This is disgusting!" he said of a piece by *Toronto Sun* columnist Claire Hoy. "Attacking my wife and children on Christmas Eve." Hoy loved to score cheap shots on the subject of the Prime Minister's wife and her role in the administration.

I had left the PMO when, in May, 1987, the *Globe and Mail* ran a series of stories on the extensive renovations to 24 Sussex, with descriptions of Mulroney's clothes-closets and Gucci loafers. These were harder on Brian and Mila than all the pratfalls and scandals since the election.

"For them, it was like being naked in public," one of their close confidants told me.

This brings me to the much discussed "Presidential" style which the media accused Mulroney of adopting. The reporters even took to bursting into "Hail to the Chief" to herald his arrival at press conferences. If there is a guilty party in all this, it isn't Brian Mulroney. The entire administration shares the blame, and I played my part. I'd always thought that the institution of Prime Minister wasn't accorded enough respect; I couldn't believe that the man who carried the responsibility of governing this very difficult country would have his integrity questioned over every little expense, every trip abroad, every effort that was made to make his burden more bearable.

My contribution to the presidential style came at the first meeting between Mulroney and the provincial premiers at Regina, in February, 1985. I plead guilty to having convinced Bill Fox to arrange for the Prime Minister to give his press conference from behind a podium adorned with the Canadian coat of arms, instead of seated behind a table. I even convinced him to announce, just as Mulroney entered, "Ladies and Gentlemen, the Prime Minister."

This announcement was greeted with much derision by the assembled scribes, and Fox never did it again, but the podium became a fixture for a time, although The Boss tired of it eventually. In fact, during the summer of 1986, when an aide set it up — just trying to please The Boss — Mulroney flew into one of his patented rages. Typically, this podium had been acquired, and often used, by Trudeau, but it was reported as if we'd borrowed it from Ronald Reagan.

The media also picked on the long corteges of cars for every official entourage, the overblown security, the travelling "butler and maid over in Asia," and the luxurious hotels where the Prime Minister stayed. However, the fact is that we had little control over the motorcades, laid on by our hosts, who were over-eager to impress The Boss. And the security measures were controlled by others, as well.

The Prime Minister could get criticized for travel extravagances that he didn't even know about, such as with the famous "backup" Challenger jet.

Contrary to what some believe, the Prime Minister doesn't have his own personal Challenger. He uses whichever plane from the government fleet that is most readily available. Some of the planes had eight places, some ten, and some had a dozen seats. I could never figure out how they decided how many seats to put into a given Challenger. It would often happen that we'd ask for a twelve-seater, mostly at times when the Mulroney children were travelling with the entourage, and we'd wind up with an eight-seater, much to everyone's embarrassment.

Who was responsible? The Armed Forces. Before we came to power, there were two fleets of government executive planes, one controlled by the transport department, the other by the military. To try to save a few pennies, and in a vain effort to put Challenger flights on a "national security" (thereby exempting them from access to information requirements) we centralized the operation at the Defence Department.

For reasons of security as well as efficiency, the Prime Minister used a Challenger wherever he went in the country, and sometimes on foreign trips. It wasn't easy, but we eventually convinced him to use the Challenger for his occasional Florida vacations because, despite the bureaucratic arithmetic involved, it was ultimately less trouble and less costly than putting the RCMP on alert every time the Prime Minister wanted to fly commercial, particularly if he was travelling outside the country.

As it was, our paranoia about the use of government planes had been induced during our days in opposition by a collection of Conservative dinosaurs from the back benches who made it their life's work to harrass the government over every flight logged on a government jet. And, naturally, when we got into power the Liberals, enthusiastically abetted by the media, made us pay the price for our previous displays of excessive piety, trailing out examples of Conservative ministers who appeared to be abusing their travel privileges. Mulroney tried to keep a tight rein on the use of the Challenger fleet, but there were still damaging incidents, such as the tale of Walter McLean's extensive travels in Africa, and the fact that a certain cabinet minister earned himself the nickname Marcel "Challenger" Masse.

However, the Tories had dug their own grave before they came into power. Brian Mulroney is paying today for the late Tom Cossitt's obsession with Pierre Trudeau's swimming pool at 24 Sussex Drive. That kind of attack is not something Mulroney would have indulged in so readily. In terms of travelling perks he was much better off as president of Iron Ore of Canada, and he'd often tell us that the company planes he used to fly on made the Challengers look shabby. It was the on-board phones in the Challenger that bothered him the most because most of the time they couldn't be made to work, particularly during the long distance flights. This meant that for extended periods the Prime Minister was practically cut off from the seat of government in Ottawa. It sounds difficult to believe, but it's true. I don't know how many times I watched one of the executive assistants pulling his hair out trying to get through to Ottawa from the Challenger. And once we did get through, the conversations were hardly confidential. Anyone tuned in to the right radio frequency could overhear everything.

Then there was the time in Baie Comeau when, at ten o'clock at night, the Prime Minister had gone all the way to the airport along with Bill Fox, only to be told that his Challenger was on the fritz.

"Okay, so we'll use a backup," he said, thinking there was a certain logic to this.

"There's no backup plane," was the response from the military commander of the fleet.

Here we were, in 1985, with the Prime Minister of a prosperous country of twenty-six million that is a member of the club of seven major western economic powers, a member of NATO and the British Commonwealth, a neighbour of the US as well as the USSR, stuck in a little town on the North Shore of the St. Lawrence because his army couldn't find him a plane. That night, Mulroney travelled back to Ottawa aboard a private plane belonging to a private company. I felt embarrassed for him. And needless to say, once we got back to Ottawa he unleashed his pit bull, Bill Fox, on the logistical geniuses at the Defence Department. But the incident didn't end there. After that the PMO issued an order that a backup plane always had to be available for the Prime Minister's use, should his own develop mechanical trouble. I don't know who was responsible for what happened next, but I'm sure Ollie North couldn't have done better.

On one of the subsequent flights, Fred Doucet happened to look out of the window of the Challenger carrying the Prime Minister and noticed another government plane about to take off. Curious, he asked whose plane it was. He almost choked at the answer. It was, he was told, our backup plane that was to follow us everywhere we went, in accordance with the PMO command. What had happened is that the military had apparently understood the order to mean that a spare Challenger was to travel along behind the PM's plane on every trip. Horrified, Doucet immediately put a stop to it, but at the office, we were all astounded that a simple order like that could have been interpreted so absurdly. And I wondered even more when the calls started coming in from the reporters, wanting to know if it was true that the Prime Minister now used not one, but two Challengers on every trip. Once again we'd been hosed.

In fact, the elaborate trappings of travel often irritated Mulroney, and once provoked him to outright rebellion. He hated the little flags that protocol types affix to the hoods of official cars, and when we emerged from a meeting in downtown Saskatoon in July, 1986 and he spotted an enormous white limousine at the curb, the size of the Queen Mary, he exploded, "I'm not getting into that thing!"

We walked back to his hotel, which was, fortunately, not far.

On the subject of hotels, I've never understood the media's fascination with the fact that the Prime Minister stays in the best available suite of any given establishment. To begin with, the hotel management usually insists on it. And, let's face it, the Prime Minister needs the room. Does anyone really expect him to receive guests perched on the edge of a bed? Finally, given the workload Mulroney imposed on himself while travelling, he deserved the greatest possible comfort, to allow him to represent the country's interests to the best of his ability. When he goes to New York, I'm sure most Canadians would rather have him staying in a suite at the Pierre than crashing at the Chelsea.

If Mulroney had trouble conveying his down-to-earth side to ordinary Canadians — as interpreted through the not-so-ordinary perspective of the media — it was not because of his presidential style. Rather, it had to do with three other crucial factors that tended to undermine his many positive qualities: his mania for perfection, the lawyer's syndrome, and his management — negotiator's reflex. These factors, I'm convinced, are what led to the widespread, and false, impression of Mulroney as a liar, or at least, someone who plays fast and loose with facts.

He was too perfect for most people. His tie was never askew in public, every hair was in place, and every movement appeared as calculated as the words he uttered. No normal human being can keep up such perfection under the relentless eye of the camera, and Mulroney's presentation of himself as the flawless man worked against him — people began to wonder if he could have the same human responses as they.

Consider the matter of his inner-ear problem, which affected his equilibrium whenever he was on any kind of platform for any length of time. It was particularly acute when he was tired or had a cold. The problem, I'm told, has since been medically corrected, but for a long time it meant enormous headaches for the staff, who had to organize around it.

It was hard, for instance, when he'd have to stand to attention on platforms for national anthems during foreign visits. I really felt for him in Beijing, during our visit to China, when he stood there for what seemed an eternity while the band played on. It was a difficulty, not a weakness that reflected in any way on his capacity as Prime Minister, but he went to endless trouble to cover it up. I suppose he was afraid people would laugh at him, the way they snickered when Joe Clark confessed that he couldn't swim because his head sank.

The truth finally came out in Washington, when the Prime Minister and President Reagan were supposed to stand on a small platform about four feet off the ground, not only for the national anthems, but also for the President's speech. We requested two chairs on the platform, and the Washington Press Corps immediately began asking why. The White House Press Office, although they had promised to say nothing about the chairs, reneged, as usual, because they wanted to avoid the inference that the President was feeling feeble; they leaked that the chairs were there at Canada's request. We had no choice but to come clean about the equilibrium problem, compounded that day by a severe case of flu. When Mulroney found out, he was almost relieved, and the media didn't make much of the incident. I'd thought all along that we were worrying over nothing, but that was part of Mulroney's insistence on being, or at least appearing, without blemish.

As for the lawyer's syndrome, it often got him into trouble because he would answer questions as if he were under cross-examination. One morning in London, Ontario, during June of 1986, the *Globe and Mail* made public a letter on the subject of free trade that The Boss had written to Reagan. The letter was authentic, and our office in Ottawa had already confirmed it as such.

I knew we were in for a scrum. Just before we faced the cameras, I told the Prime Minister that we had confirmed the letter's existence, and all he had to say was that he wasn't about to discuss his private correspondence with the President in public. Period. He seemed to agree. But when the scrum began, inevitably, with a question about the letter, he replied, "What letter?"

The reporter explained that it was the one that had appeared in the *Globe and Mail.*

"Ah, you've seen a letter," said Mulroney.

That evening, the exchange was played on national television and made him look like a man trying to hide the evidence. For a lawyer, such a delaying tactic might score points; for a politician, it was disastrous.

Mulroney's negotiator's reflex is the instinct that keeps a mistrustful card player with his hand glued to his vest, to prevent peeking. Okay in poker, not so good in dealing with his own aides. Often, we were sent out to sell the "line" on a speech of which we knew nothing. And, when we were bombarded with questions and demands for clarification, The Boss would refuse to let us interpret his words.

"Don't tell them anything!"

Again, in tense labour negotiations, it is customary to preserve your position; but we were on his side, and in refusing to open up to us, he left himself open to the wrath of a media mob that was far less sympathetic than we were.

Despite his faults, I still like and admire Mulroney tremendously. But as the legendary Liberal strategist, Keith Davey, has pointed out, in politics perception is everything, and the immovable perception The Boss created was one of an inward-looking, combative perfectionist. He is a glutton for work, a man of superior intelligence and keen political perception. He is, in the best sense of the term, a "good guy," and I never changed the view I had when I joined his staff that his heart was in the right place, and that he was a truly compassionate individual. But his obsession with the media, and with his predecessor, his constant striving for perfection, and his lawyer's tricks portray him instead as a mean-minded and dodgy operator, which he is not.

He has all the attributes to be a great prime minister. His greatest enemy is himself.

CHAPTER SEVEN

Riding High

I t was only when our campaign jet, "Manicouagan I," touched the runway on our return to Uplands Airport on the evening of September 5, 1984, that the full import of our election victory the day before hit me. The gamble I'd taken two months earlier, leaving a career in journalism that I truly loved, had paid off. Mine was not so much a feeling of joy or euphoria as a sensation of humility — not a journalistic staple. We were writing history, and it made me feel small. I had my first purely human thought, then, after two months on the campaign trail; I realized that it was autumn already, and that I had missed the sustaining joys of summer.

"What do we do now?" Many of us echoed the question. As a journalist, I had grown accustomed to almost instant gratification; you wrote one day and it was published the next. Some pieces were winners, some were not, but you could always redeem yourself next time at bat. This was not the same; waiting for us behind those mysterious doors of power was an eternal beginning. I was soon to realize that we were engaged in the labour of Sisyphus, that wretch of Greek mythology, condemned forever to push a rock up a hill, only to have it roll back to the bottom just before he made it to the top.

We had two weeks to clear out our old offices and move into the administration suites down the street. The party organization had taken care to set up a transition team, presided over by Bill Neville, the crafty and competent Ottawa pro who had served as Principal Secretary when Joe Clark was prime minister. However, nothing and no one could have prepared us for the wilderness that awaited in the Langevin Block. When I entered the press office evacuated by John Turner's media staff on September 17, the day we took power officially, I was alone with blank walls and empty desks. Not so much as a pencil or a notebook or a typewriter had been left behind; there was only a single monitor hooked up to a Canadian Press computer, and I couldn't seem to make it work. The phones were working, though, all ringing at once. Without a secretary or receptionist to help me, I tried to field a few calls myself, but it wasn't long before I unplugged the phones and beat a hasty retreat.

Thus, on the morning that the first Mulroney cabinet was formed, the Prime Minister's press office wasn't answering the phone. We could always blame technical difficulties.

I was in for a lot of shocks. I'd never really worked in an organized office before; I'd been raised in newsrooms, which operate more like a zoo. The Prime Minister called up one morning to see how we were settling in.

"So, how do you like it?"

"It's fine," I said. "I mean, I've never had an office of my own before."

"And now you've got a helluva nice one," he chortled.

It was his way of lending encouragement during those early days of power. He'd talk to us about facilities and about the trips we were going to make, as though we had all come into some deserved reward. None of us understood, then, that it was harder to stay on top than it was to get there. In fact, I had given some thought, over the two weeks between the election and our assumption of power, as to whether I wanted to be there. But in the end, the lure of power was irresistible — I couldn't turn my back on it before finding out what there was to it.

Between the endless briefings that accompany any transfer of power, the Prime Minister-elect spent the first two weeks of September pondering his cabinet-to-be. Some of the nominations were predictable; others, particularly from the astonishing fifty-eight member Quebec caucus that we reaped on September 4th — most of whom were unknowns outside their own block — were not so predictable.

Mulroney was consumed from the very start by the mania for secrecy that would quickly earn us a reputation for having a bunker mentality. I was therefore taken aback when he chose the Château Laurier hotel to hold his meetings with potential cabinet appointees. Why the Château? At this point the cabinet was the hottest story in town — why not the middle of Wellington Street? But The Boss was being crazy like a fox. Had he received the contenders at his official residence, the media horde would simply have camped on the front doorstep to determine who was in, and who was not. The Chateau, on the other hand, is practically an adjunct of Parliament Hill, a crossroads for politicians, bureaucrats and journalists, and the site of CBC radio's operations, which occupy the two top floors. The place teems with names in the news, and who was to know which of them were on hand to audition for the Prime Minister?

Once we knew this, we fell in with the plan, and carried on like schoolboys who had just put one over on the principal. As to the cabinet itself, my only advice to Mulroney was that there had never been, to this date, a unilingual anglophone communications minister and that was a tradition worth following. In the end, he named Marcel Masse to the post, although Masse was later replaced by Flora MacDonald, whose French was fairly shaky. The cabinet stars were familiar: Joe Clark, Erik Nielsen, Michael Wilson, Don Mazankowski, Flora MacDonald, Pat Carney, Roch LaSalle, Ray Hnatyshyn and John Crosbie. . . .

But, in looking over that list of the original Mulroney cabinet, not theirs but other names leap off the page, and for vastly different reasons: Sinclair Stevens, Robert Coates, John Fraser, Suzanne Blais-Grenier and André Bissonnette.

By and large, the new cabinet was well received by the Press Gallery, although there were a lot of questions about the new people from Quebec. The Quebec reporters were tickled that actress Andrée Champagne, one of the stars of a wildly popular TV series, "Les belles histoires des pays d'en haut," had been elevated to the cabinet. "Donalda" — her character in the series — had become a cabinet minister. She was not to survive the first major shuffle.

The day of the swearing-in, Fox and I were dispatched on a special mission by the Prime Minister. Our job was to tell the assembled ministers-to-be — and keep in mind that this group included several ex-ministers and a former prime minister — that they were not to say a word more than necessary to the media pack outside Rideau Hall, the Governor General's residence, after the swearing in. We passed the message to them, in both official languages, in the Opposition Lobby of the House of Commons, and got in return some looks meant to kill from the likes of Joe Clark, John Crosbie and particularly Ray Hnatyshyn, who ribbed Fox about it immediately after.

It got worse. Mulroney was determined that nothing was going to blemish the first day of his reign; there would be no more of the stupid mistakes we allowed ourselves in opposition. So lips were to be sealed. This did not take into account the panting horde of newsmen, and provoked the first public run-in between Fox and a member of the Press Gallery. Fox barked at Don Newman of the CBC who was attempting to scrum inside Rideau Hall, and Newman barked back. It went downhill from there, as thirty-nine ministers emerged from Rideau Hall and ran a gauntlet of reporters and cameramen, not the least restrained by the ropes we had carefully installed for their guidance. Fox and I were trying to hustle forty people to their cars as fast as possible, and the whole brilliant strategy collapsed the first time one of them — naturally — stopped to say a few words. Trying to separate newly minted cabinet ministers from microphones is like telling iron-filings not to respond to a magnet. The end result was a lot of yelling and shoving on the doorstep of Government House. Our media relations were getting off to a rocky start.

Still, as night fell we were able to reflect that no one had said anything compromising, which had been the main idea. The leader's plan to control the diffusion of information still looked flawless. It would be helped along by the appointment of the grim-faced Erik Nielsen as Deputy Prime Minister, responsible for government communications. He loathed reporters with an even deeper passion than Pierre Trudeau, and the reporters, in turn, dubbed him "Velcro-lips."

Nielsen became the enforcer who would play the heavy with civil servants and elected members who dared to violate the law of silence, although sometimes Mulroney took on this role himself. At one of his very first cabinet meetings, the Prime Minister raised the possibility of a plot against the Conservative Party involving certain mandarins and members of the media. To his great consternation, Joe Clark repeated this publicly in Edmonton, and Mulroney — who was not too keen on the man whose mandate he had usurped — called Clark in for a woodshedding. Still, Mulroney was generous with Clark, giving him his first choice, the prestigious External Affairs post. Many of his entourage would not have done that; for them, supporters of Joe Clark at the leadership convention — Clarkies — were as dangerous as the Liberal enemy.

Hubert Pichet asked me to help block the appointment of a certain individual in Marcel Masse's office, because he was "one of those Clarkies." Stephen Ash, Masse's chief of staff, reminded him that old quarrels should be buried. It was easy for me to say, too; I hadn't been through that war. But suspicions were contagious, and we were all anxious to protect The Boss.

Thus, the "nanny" incident.

It all began innocently enough on November 6, 1984, when Lisa Van Dusen, then a press assistant in the Prime Minister's Office, got a call from Edison Stewart of Canadian Press. Stewart was one of the reporters who were forever trying to catch us contradicting the leader. Lisa was no match for his guile; her chief characteristic was a disarming frankness that had made her many friends among the Press Gallery. This was just as well, too. On one occasion a reporter phoned about a huge herd of caribou that had drowned in the Caniapiscau River in northern Quebec. The area happened to be in Manicouagan riding, and the journalist wondered if the Prime Minister intended to heed a call by Liberal Senator Charlie Watts to pay an immediate visit to the site. "What does he expect him to do?" Lisa asked. "Give them mouth-to-mouth resuscitation?" A line like that in the newspapers would not have gone well; it did not appear. Stewart did not have the easy-going nature of the reporter involved in that incident, and he was pressing Lisa for details of one Elizabeth MacDonald, listed as a public employee on the payroll of 24 Sussex Drive.

After checking it out Lisa phoned back saying: "That's the nanny."

What she didn't know was that Stewart had before him the transcript of an interview with TV anchorman Tom Cherington in Hamilton, Ontario on May 7, 1984. Nannies had been a Tory hobby horse ever since Liberal Transport Minister Otto Lang had flown his in from Scotland on a government plane, and Cherington asked, "Will we have to go and pay for your nannies?"

"No, no," Mulroney replied righteously, and he added, "It seems to me that there are a number of things symbolically like that, that have to be changed, that if you are to ask people to make sacrifices and to join you, then you have to provide the leadership — that's one area."

Thunderclouds rolled up over Sussex Drive when Lisa realized how she had just been suckered. She was scheduled to accompany the leader at a public function later the next day, and timidly she asked Bill Fox what she should do.

"Just stay out of his line of vision," said Fox, ever ready with priceless advice.

Fox tried to repair the damage by putting out the line that the lady in question wasn't really a nanny as such, but by then it was too late. The story got inflated with every convoluted explanation. It was at this point that Fred Doucet, the senior adviser, decided to take the matter in hand and clarify the situation for Edison Stewart. He explained that Ms. MacDonald was one of a number of employees at 24 Sussex who "interface with the (Mulroney) children in an habitual way," and as such, not a nanny in the full meaning of the term. Well, that only made things worse. Again, the perception was fostered that we were trying to hide things.

I still wonder how a serious parliamentary correspondent can put such effort into pursuing such trivialities, but equally mysterious is why we took it as seriously as we did. Jamie Lamb, Ottawa columnist for the *Vancouver Sun*, had our number when he wrote, "If this government is going to mask a little affair with such heavy verbiage as 'interface with the children in an habitual way,' then what might it be doing about big issues?"

This perception was given another boost with the notorious public communications policy for civil servants that we unveiled at a prime ministerial press conference on November 23, 1984. This was one of Fox's strokes of genius, or so we thought it at the time. The idea was to prevent public servants from hiding behind their anonymity while giving damaging information to the media, or criticizing government policies. The move had been prompted by leaked memos within the External Affairs Department that basically told bureaucrats to avoid the media like the plague. We were convinced that our greatest enemy lurked within the bureaucracy, in the form of Liberal sympathizers wedged into the woodwork during two decades of Liberal administration; there had been incidents in which bureaucrats, speaking off the record, raked the government, to perk our paranoia. The new policy insisted that all conversations between reporters and civil servants would have to be for attribution, with the bureaucrats named. We weren't so naive as to think that this would deprive the Press Gallery of the usual "reliable sources," but we thought that at least some mandarins would think twice about embarrassing the government.

"What do you think?" asked Fox.

"Sounds great to me," I told him.

The Prime Minister wasn't so sure when we talked before his press conference, but I did my best to reassure him.

"I don't know," he said. "I think we'll get criticized for it."

"The reporters aren't going to be happy," I said. "But, on paper it's a debate that you can't lose."

We didn't lose it on paper. We lost it in the editorial boardrooms where it looked, once again, like a cover-up, to say nothing of a gag. That was not clear at once. At the press conference, the reporters squawked, but they always squawk, and if the Prime Minister was worried, Fox and I weren't. During the days that followed, we even did radio and TV interviews defending the new code we had imposed on the civil service, and never once did we mention why we had done it in the first place — our deep fear of the Liberal enemy within.

At this time, the Press Office was a powerful arm of the PMO. Fox and I spread terror among the troops. We were under the impression that nothing could stop us. When we said "no" to something, we prevailed. Neil Macdonald of the *Ottawa Citizen*, the very man who reefed us with the "old whores" during the campaign, waxed dramatic about the myth of Bill Fox and, quoting an anonymous source, said we were about to become the most powerful press office ever in Ottawa. I got a chuckle out of that one, because the anonymous source was none other than myself. I'd slipped the line to Macdonald at the Governor General's annual skating party for the Press Gallery. My reasoning was that the more powerful Fox became, the more power would accrue to me, and the greater would be the respect we would get from the Prime Minister and the media.

This was a serious misreading of the dynamics of Parliament Hill, where I had spent the past five years. I should have known better. In general, people get nervous when someone becomes too powerful, particularly someone who isn't afraid to show it. Fox had all the reticence of a rock group, and all the subtlety of a Sherman tank. He was resented, and had already been subjected to some vicious personal attacks. But he was a tough nut, and always would be, and when, later on, he tried to convince the Boys that he had changed, no one believed him.

He'd tell me that we made the perfect "good cop, bad cop" combination, he being the bad cop, I being the good. It had to be like that, because I was the one to handle most face-to-face encounters with the journalists. I was regularly dispatched to the Press Club to find out what the Boys were saying, either by the Prime Minister himself or by Fox. He preferred to limit himself to phone calls, or discreet dinners with correspondents who wouldn't feel the need to report how many glasses of wine he consumed. For a man who had in his time closed most of the bars in Ottawa and Washington, Fox was being remarkably abstemious, but if he lifted one glass too many just once, that wouldn't save him. Some of the rancour towards him was provoked by the arrogance of someone who doesn't let anyone tread on his toes, but there was also a substantial element of jealousy.

We didn't see this, didn't read it rightly. We saw ourselves as a formidable team, determined to enforce the supremacy of our law, that of the Prime Minister's Office, over the bureaucracy. We didn't understand to what point the bureaucracy had honed the fine art of survival in a government town.

Fox had some intimation. "They're laughing," he said. "They know they'll be here long after you and I are gone." But in the meantime, we were riding high. Too high. It was only a question of time, or of polls. We were too powerful, and too many people didn't like the way we threw our weight around. We were becoming the subject of news stories ourselves. Fox was frequently interviewed on TV, and came across more like a minister of the Crown than a mere employee of the PMO. Sooner or later, we'd pay for our celebrity.

Indeed, a blow was dealt to our effectiveness, not to mention a shock to our friendship, when it was decided in the fall of 1985 that we should be separated. Fox was named Communications Director, "to put his feet up and do some strategizing," as The Boss said, and he would move into an office down the hall. I was promoted Press Secretary in his place. I often thought that the idea behind the switch was to weaken us. If so, it worked. Things were never the same between us after that. I now think I should have fought the move.

However, in the fall of 1984, these squabbles were still ripening on the vine, out of sight. The Prime Minister was buoyed by his participation in a series of prestige events, including the visits to Canada by Pope John Paul II and Queen Elizabeth (the visit that Turner had postponed back in July). He also paid an early visit to Washington to signal the emergence of a new era in Canada – United States relations, and announced later that a Mulroney – Reagan summit would be held on St. Patrick's Day in Quebec City the following March.

The Shamrock Summit was to be our high-water mark, and we will come to it shortly, but to set it in context, we need to meet, first, the people who made the government run — sometimes, right off the rails — the people who came to be lumped together under the single name, "The Cronies."

79

CHAPTER EIGHT

The Cronies

So, who were these guys, the famous team of Mulroney intimates who came to be known, derisively, as "The Cronies," a term suggesting that the Prime Minister had surrounded himself with political amateurs and incompetents. Well, some were amateurs, but the most amateur of them all, in political terms, was the most competent, and any sketch of the operatives at the heart of the Mulroney government must begin with him.

Bernard Roy, the Chief of Staff and Principal Secretary to the Prime Minister, was a long-time friend of Mulroney's from law school at Laval. Then, when they were both young bachelors starting out in law in Montreal, they shared an apartment in lower Westmount. Many people were surprised to see Roy pack up his lucrative Montreal law practice to move to Ottawa, for a $100,000 a year cut in pay to work for Brian Mulroney.

Roy, a tall, fair-haired, athletic-looking man — the "jock type," as he says himself — was by no means a political pro, but there was no one Mulroney could count on to be franker with him, or more honest and loyal. He was perhaps the only man in Canada Mulroney totally admired. His greatest quality was at once his most telling defect: not only was he unfamiliar with the demands of power, he knew nothing of the tortuous byways of Ottawa. His first year was a constant series of shocks; he had trouble understanding the voracity of the media pack and the hypocrisy of the bureaucracy. He had come to do a job, never thinking that it would entail publicity, rancour and envy on the part of those who are always convinced that they can do a better job than the guy at the top. He didn't even read the newspapers, a trait that constantly exasperated the Prime Minister; he preferred his weekly hockey game or playing squash to poring over the musings of journalists, whom he dismissed as *les putains* (whores).

He wasn't one for three-hour lunches; you would often find him in the little Langevin Block cafeteria munching a hurried sandwich, and, though he was untried like the rest of us, he more than made up for this by his inexhaustible appetite for work. Finally, his most valuable quality was that he could see through the Mulroney character in filtering down the orders that emanated from The Boss, whose impetuous commands were such that, without someone like Roy to act as a buffer, half the civil service would have been fired during the first few months.

Fred Doucet, the Senior Adviser, was not so much a filter as a sounding-board. Doucet is a short, pudgy, grey-haired man with a voice like a pound of plums, and a tendency to mumble. He wouldn't hesitate to argue with The Boss, but once a decision was made, he was the perfect trooper. According to a *Saturday Night* magazine article written by Charlotte Gray, Mulroney, while looking out his office window in Montreal, once said of Doucet: "You know if I asked Fred to move that building over there one inch to the left by morning, Fred would do it, no questions." Like Roy, Doucet would never go telling tales to the media. He was perhaps Mulroney's closest confidant, and the man entrusted with the delicate task of administering his personal affairs, such as the management of 24 Sussex and his financial arrangements with the Conservative Party. Doucet was charged, for instance, with getting an evaluation for Brian's and Mila's private art collection, one Mulroney began when he was still a bachelor. ("I'd buy myself a new picture as a present every Christmas.")

When questions deemed to be "intimate" came into the press office, we would appeal to Fred. We always knew two things: he'd have an answer, and he'd be at work. He didn't take a single vacation until he remarried in the spring of 1986, and I was dismayed, but not surprised, when, after a strenuous African tour, he fainted from exhaustion in the parking lot of an Ottawa hospital where he'd gone to visit a relative.

Fred was a favourite media target, as one of Mulroney's old classmates from St. Francis Xavier University in Antigonish, Nova Scotia, and, unlike Roy, who never hesitated to fire back, he kept it all bottled up inside. Later, when I became the prey of the news-hounds, he was a source of sympathy and strength.

His basic problem was communication. In trying to follow the example of the man he admired most in the world, Brian Mulroney, and in trying to protect the leader at all cost, he produced utterances that were so convoluted, or so baffling, that it was hard to tell if he was speaking English. During a media briefing on the Shamrock Summit, he was asked what it would cost and responded, flatly, "It will cost what it will cost."

He was trying, with my advice, to keep the dollar figure obscured for the time being, so that it wouldn't become the day's lead news item, but he might have chosen a happier way to do it.

In private, he was one of the pleasantest people in the PMO, although there was much grumbling that he hoarded information to keep control. During the Africa trip, he kept the press clippings sent on from Ottawa to himself, to prevent the Prime Minister from being distracted by bad news from home. In fact, we often excised from the clippings items that might ignite the short Mulroney fuse; the difference this time was that The Boss, then trying to control his news addiction, had given permission for Fred's editing, *but* that didn't silence the complaints from other staffers.

Doucet, as the organizer of all trips until he left the PMO in March, 1987, contributed substantially to Mulroney's success on the international stage, but no one ever knew that. Like the rest of the administration, he was in the thrall of the obsession with secrecy, and managed only to get across his bad points without ever communicating his good.

Bill Fox, the Press Secretary, and later Communications Director, shared with Doucet and Roy an unwavering loyalty to Mulroney, which did not, however, keep him from being one of the few in the entourage willing to shout back at The Boss. The deep friendship between the two was based in part on the explosive temperament they shared.

Fox had a fine mind under the burly exterior of an Irish detective-sergeant, and, during the early days in power, he was the terror of the federal bureaucracy. Not only did his alley-brawler's style offend them, they knew all too well that he had the ear of a Prime Minister who would call him late at night to complain, compare notes, or just to chat. They had more than their work in common: Fox had a personal relationship with Bonnie Brownlee, Mila Mulroney's executive assistant and alter ego. The relationship never affected their work, but when the Prime Minister spoke to Fox about Mila and Bonnie, he would talk of "the girls" in the tone used by brothers-in-law who have married sisters.

Unlike Roy and Doucet, Fox was not an old school chum, but he was held in enormous regard and affection. Mulroney seemed most vexed at times when his Press Secretary was angry with him. When he'd ask me, "How's Foxie?" I knew there had been a flare-up.

In the final analysis, I think Fox, like myself, was not really cut out for the power game. I never saw him really happy except when he could cut loose with some of his old reporter buddies. After a going-away party for Bernard Descoteaux of *Le Devoir*, he said, almost wistfully, "Those are our guys."

Bonnie Brownlee held the title of Executive Assistant to Mila Mulroney, but she was also press secretary, chief of staff and I don't know what else — she did it all. I can't imagine Mila without Bonnie, a petite freckle-faced brunette, somewhere nearby. She would acompany her to all her public appearances, respond to all her letters and invitations, write her speeches, plan her trips, answer reporters' questions and do her shopping. She did everything but the sinks. She managed to accomplish all this with grace, professionalism and a sense of humour that rarely slipped — although she bristled when the Mulroneys tried to use her to tone down Fox.

Her influence was considerable because Mila had a lot of influence on her husband, and Bonnie on Mila. She was practically a member of the family. On September 3, 1985, when the Prime Minister and his wife were at the military hospital in Ottawa for the birth of Nicolas, Mulroney complained about the high, narrow hospital bed where he was to spend the night. He might fall out!

"No problem," retorted Bonnie, "we can put up the sides the way they do for little kids."

Not many in the entourage could have gotten away with such a crack.

Charley McMillan, the York University professor who as Senior Policy Adviser (as opposed to Senior Adviser, period) played a crucial role in the election and leadership campaigns, was in an unenviable position. He was responsible for getting the bureaucracy to follow all the fine principles put forward by Mulroney during his seduction of the electorate. Moving a mountain of Jello would have been easier. Amiable by nature, always in a good mood, Charley was quite simply the nicest guy in the PMO. A balding, bespectacled, professorial type, they say of him, "His brother (Tom, the Environment Minister) got the looks, and Charley got the brains." Despite a string of diplomas, he never showed a trace of arrogance. He wasn't one of Mulroney's schoolboy chums, either, although he had been one of his earliest and eagerest supporters. At times, he'd miss the morning meetings without giving notice, but that was Charley. The Boss appeared to like his distracted, nutty-professor side, his way of talking at ninety miles an hour, and of laughing delightedly at his own jokes when no one else in the room had a clue.

But if there was an agent of change in the entourage, it was Charley. He had a powerful intellect and definite ideas about how government policies should be applied. However, not even he was privy to the master plan that presumably existed in the brilliant mind of Brian Mulroney, and like many others, he grew frustrated. No one was greatly surprised when he left in the late spring of 1987.

Pat MacAdam, a member of the St. FX Mafia, was put in charge of caucus liaison which, with 210 MPs, is like being head nurse in a gigantic nursery with a million diapers to change but no more "Pampers" in the closet. A tall, bald, garrulous man, MacAdam had the sense of humour to take it all in stride; during the campaign, he was the official joker of the Prime Minister's bus. He also knew well the Ottawa political mind, having worked within the parliamentary compound for Conservative MPs for a number of years before his advent to power. He was one of the key engineers in Joe Clark's downfall and Brian Mulroney's rise in the years when such a coup d'etat was deemed impossible. He had also cultivated some media contacts and the Prime Minister would not hesitate to use him to stoke stories without advising his press spokesmen, sometimes provoking nasty confrontations within the PMO. MacAdam would get his just reward for his efforts with a diplomatic posting in the summer of 1987.

Peter White was another of the college friends, from law school in Quebec City. White, also a close associate of Canada's answer to Daddy Warbucks, Conrad Black, was in charge of "nominations," which is a polite way of saying patronage. He seemed to run his own tight ship, and for me he was something of a mystery man. Always pleasant and smiling, he tried to bring a sense of order and cohesion to the PMO, a Tower of Babel in those early days. He was one of the few who didn't adopt a bunker mentality from the outset, freely giving interviews when he thought it could be useful. He was one of the first to leave, however, gone suddenly in February, 1986 to become president of the crippled

Dominion Store chain when Black's Hollinger Corporation took over.

Peter Ohrt was another of the old chums who called the Prime Minister "Brian," and another who didn't last long in the PMO pressure-cooker. He was intimate with the Quebec "Blue Thunder" organization, but also had Ottawa experience and had served as tour organizer for the election. He continued as Mulroney's program director, but the job degenerated into drudgery. He was caught between outside pressures, mostly from the Big Blue Boys in Ontario, clamouring for appearances, and pressure within, because no on in the PMO was ever happy with all the arrangements. He left to head the MPs' services bureau, out of the direct line of fire.

Ian Anderson, the Communications Director who later became Deputy Principal Secretary, was, like Fox and myself, an ex-journalist. He was not a personal friend, and, while he had access to such highly confidential material as the budget, he didn't have the privileged access of long-time pals. The relations between his office and ours became, to say the least, strained. Fox occupied too much space, and his influence with Mulroney was too great. On the other hand, Anderson was one of the few who tried to get off on a good footing with the bureaucrats and tried to build bridges between us and them until he, too, was swept away by the wave of change in the spring of 1987.

Geoff Norquay, Director of Policy Development, was regarded with some suspicion as a "Clarkie," because he had worked in the former leader's office. However, he proved himself as a specialist in social policy when we were in opposition, and his expertise earned him a spot in the PMO. His readiness to put in long hours and his general competence were rewarded with an office next to Mulroney's on Parliament Hill, and he became a filter for information. Later, he came under suspicion for leaking to the press largely based on the fact that he was never really attacked by the media. He survived the purge of spring 1987.

Bill Pristanski and Hubert Pichet were The Boss's executive assistants, who would respond instantly to his every whim. What a pair they made! Pristanski fantasized about becoming Premier of Ontario, while Pichet's dream was to become Premier of Quebec. Who knows? Maybe someday . . .

Gerard Godbout, who had put in yeoman service on the campaign trail, stayed on as Mulroney's linguistic director. Not long after we took office, Godbout and I were summoned to meet with

Governor General Jeanne Sauvé; she was unhappy with some of the French in the upcoming Speech from the Throne, and declared, in effect, that she wouldn't be caught reading such drivel. Godbout, always accommodating, polished up the phrases that offended her, although the changes didn't amount to much.

Dalton Camp, the Tory mastermind, was never far from the telephone when The Boss would seek out his wisdom, and would only come on board officially two years later. As for his brother-in-law, the ever-smooth conductor of the Big Blue Machine, Norm Atkins, he would come back into our lives after being appointed to the Senate in July 1986.

Including the support staff, there were more than 100 people officially assigned to the Prime Minister's Office in 1984, but these were the key players. This was the original team that was put together to meet the challenges of the years to come. Some of the challenges they conquered, some of them they didn't.

CHAPTER NINE

The Cracks Begin to Show

As winter approached, the formidable Convervative machine, so smooth-running during the election campaign, began to show signs of being under the control of a gaggle of amateurs. These were not the staining scandals that would mark us later, but a series of blunders that would make the voters wonder, "Are these the guys we elected?"

The first miscue came from Finance Minister Michael Wilson, the Bay Street business whiz who was going to restore order to the nation's finances. In early November, just after Wilson delivered a preliminary economic statement, the Prime Minister met his provincial counterparts for the first time over lunch at 24 Sussex Drive and announced that a first ministers' conference on the economy would be held in Regina on February 14. Quebec Premier René Lévesque cracked, "I have some good news and some bad news. The good news is that we're having an economic conference; the bad news is that it's going to be in Regina."

For us, it was all good news, the beginning of the process of national reconciliation through open dealing with the provinces. The most contentious issue at the upcoming meeting would be, as usual, transfer payments. This was boring to everyone but Michael Wilson, anxious to reduce the deficit, and the provincial governments, anxious that he not do so out of their pockets. Part of the groundwork for the meeting was a trip by Wilson to the provincial capitals, and, during his visit to Manitoba, someone in his entourage left his attaché case in a Winnipeg hotel lobby. A reporter from the *Winnipeg Free Press* went through the case and came up with a strategy paper prepared by the federal bureaucracy, suggesting how Wilson should handle himself in preparing Manitoba for a cut in the payments. The opposition naturally had a field day with the document, as an example of the federal government's "underhanded tactics." That was gaffe number one.

Two days later, NDP MP Rod Murphy, no doubt tipped off by fellow NDPers in Winnipeg, charged in the House of Commons that Wilson had tried to tape a private meeting with the Manitoba Finance Minister. One of Wilson's assistants, either on purpose or by accident, had started his tape recorder and — as I had already discovered — when the tape runs out on these things, an alarm sounds. This one went off in the middle of the Manitoba conflab, to the consternation of all present. Eyebrows began to rise.

They shot up a notch further a few days later when a member of the staff of Joe Clark, another of our cabinet stars, sent a tape to a radio station which was supposed to, and did, contain a quote from Clark, and which was not supposed to, but also did, contain confidential information about an embassy-opening. This was a memo Clark had dictated, but which somehow hadn't been erased. When this one broke, The Boss said, "I don't know whether to laugh or cry."

Clark did better than that. He said, "I've tried to a find a way to demonstrate that this government isn't perfect, and I've been finding some success at it."

This laid-back style was one of the qualities that got Clark over a shaky start in the new government. It was a quality we might have emulated, but we didn't. We couldn't seem to realize that the election was over, and the Liberals beaten. In early December, questions were raised about the installation of a hot tub and a satellite dish at the Prime Minister's country place, Harrington Lake in the Gatineau Hills. The hot tub was your basic Jacuzzi, not terribly extravagant, and the dish was needed to monitor newscasts. Mulroney paid for both out of his own pocket, but the opposition still made hay of them, to the Prime Minister's intense irritation.

With his full knowledge, we orchestrated a leak of documents to James Rusk of the *Globe and Mail*. The material was channelled through the then Transport Minister Don Mazankowski, and concerned his predecessor, Liberal MP Lloyd Axworthy, whom The Boss particularly despised. The leaks showed that, in his last year of office, Axworthy had overspent his office budget of $1.2 million by a staggering $900,000, and employed a staff of 75, almost as many people as there were in the entire PMO. Rusk dutifully wrote several stories, and Axworthy cried blue murder about what he called our "smear campaign."

We were rubbing our hands with glee, but what was this getting us? We had 211 seats in the Commons, we were four years away from an election, and still we were preoccupied with trampling an enemy we had already trashed soundly.

It was at this point, in mid-December, that Michael Wilson put his foot in it again, with the out-loud musings already mentioned in Chapter Six about the universality of social programs. He compounded the embarrassment by saying that we had avoided the subject during the election campaign for fear that the Liberals would distort our good intentions. Mulroney had spoken of the "sacred trust"; Wilson was in effect saying that it wasn't a binding commitment. The whole affair degenerated into confusion as the opposition raked the government mercilessly. They had found the chink in Mulroney's armour — his credibility. In late December, Parliament adjourned amid a mounting political storm, and the Prime Minister told me that Wilson, an outstanding minister, with intelligence and integrity, "totally lacked political instinct."

I've always thought there was something symbolic in the snowstorm which, about this time, followed us to Baie Comeau and back, and nearly dumped us in a drift. We were going to Manicouagan via Quebec City, where there would be an important meeting with Premier Lévesque. Because it was snowing so hard that day, I knew commercial carriers were out and hired a press plane to take the fifteen-odd reporters and cameramen along. Our man for these purposes was Max Pelt of Bradley Air Services, who had never let us down before. So there we were in the little private air terminal at Uplands, waiting, patiently at first, for the leased Convair to be brought up from Montreal. It never arrived, and Max recommended, instead, two Citation business jets that would just hold our number, but they were in Carp, up the Ottawa Valley. The Prime Minister had already left on the government jet, but we decided that we would follow; even if we were too late for the meeting, we would be there for the following press conference — the only thing that mattered to the press, anyway. That was fine, except that there was still no sign of those damn jets. When they finally arrived, I shouted at the pilots, "Quebec! Full speed ahead!"

At Ancienne Lorette airport, the snowstorm, which had been merely bad in Ottawa, was truly fearsome. Still, our local organization had managed to find cabs, and we headed for downtown Quebec. Dishevelled, out of breath, and covered with snow, I burst into the room where Lévesque and Mulroney were waiting. They had delayed the press conference for our arrival. And so, my little band of reporters brushed off their clothes and stilled their beating hearts to observe, for the first time, an *independantiste* premier in joyful company with a federal prime minister. Trudeau and Lévesque had hated each other. Whoever would have predicted something like this? But then, this was quintessential Mulroney. He had succeeded in snaring the support of nationalist Liberals as well as Parti Québécois members during the federal election; now he was continuing the dangerous balancing act by charming Lévesque, while opening a line of communication and friendship with Quebec Liberal Leader, soon to be Premier, Robert Bourassa.

Once the press conference was over, we hustled back to the airport for the trip to Baie Comeau, the Prime Minister in his Challenger, a CBC phalanx in their own rented planes, and our two Citations. Fox baptized our little fleet, "Air Gratton."

The storm was still mean at Baie Comeau, and the press bus was stuck in a drift on the steep hill leading to our motel, so we struggled through the snow with our luggage and camera gear like an Everest expedition and made it to the lobby, where we discovered that some idiot had cancelled half our reservations, and the place was fully booked. I launched into a tirade at the desk, and in the end, we found a bed for everyone. I then stayed in the shower, not moving, for twenty minutes, before joining the Boys at the town's best restaurant, where we demolished the local stock of Beaujolais Nouveau.

It was, as I say, a time of storms, and, even though we were still ahead in the polls — we had hit an astonishing sixty per cent of decided voters in October — when Parliament met again in early 1985, we managed to continue to find ways to make life uncomfortable.

On February 12, Robert Coates, Minister of National Defence, resigned after the *Ottawa Citizen* ran an account of a visit he and two staffers had paid to a tacky strip club — now a Canadian tourist attraction — near the Canadian Forces base at Lahr, in West Germany. Coates insisted that the story contained major errors, and he wanted to leave office to pursue the *Citizen* for libel. Mulroney advised him to "go see Erik," the then Deputy

Prime Minister Nielsen, old Velcro-lips, but Coates insisted on resigning that very afternoon.

It was a difficult moment for the Prime Minister; Coates had been one of the first in the Tory caucus to support his leadership aspirations, at a time when most party MPs treated him like a pariah. Now, in Coates's time of trouble, Mulroney showed one of his finest qualities, loyalty, as he escorted the heartbroken Coates through the crush in the Commons lobby, down the stairs and out to his car, where the two embraced before Coates climbed in for the long ride home to Nova Scotia. This instinct, to give those close to him the benefit of the doubt, would later come to haunt the Prime Minister.

Most of the PM's advisers had much less sympathy for the wretched Coates. They told themselves that all we'd lost was a cabinet minister whose weakness showed in a tenuous grasp of his portfolio, and who had already earned the suspicions of the Press Gallery by his extensive junketing to Taiwan and South Korea while he was in opposition.

Besides, we were already preoccupied by the love-in to come in Regina on Valentine's Day when Mulroney would participate in his first full-dress first ministers' conference. We liked our odds here; seven of the premiers were Tories, and not one was a Liberal. The run-up to this meeting had its moments, for me.

The advance team from the federal-provincial provinces secretariat had decided to hold the conference in the basement of the Saskatchewan Centre for the Performing Arts, and when I saw photos of the site, I hit the roof.

"The Prime Minister of Canada is going to meet ten premiers in a community hall basement?" I raged. "You've got to be kidding!"

So a team of us from the PMO went out, and, when I saw the proposed meeting room I was convinced that it would never work; the leaders would be broiled like capons by the TV lights under such a low ceiling. We ordered everything moved upstairs to the main theatre, to the consternation of the secretariat functionaries.

"Down here, it's a meeting. Up there it's a show!" one of them complained.

I replied, "What do you think it's supposed to be?"

And it was some show, with the stage festooned with great blue banners and the crests of the provinces, along with the Canadian coat of arms. The scene inspired Ian MacDonald, then

91

of the *Montreal Gazette*, to remark, "Gratton, what you've done here reminds me of the Nazi rallies at Nuremberg."

Well, if it was a trifle overdone, it was good theatre, and the Prime Minister thanked me for it. It was both a political and public relations triumph, and brought forth a fountain of praise for the new and constructive atmosphere the Mulroney government had fostered to replace the bitter confrontations of the Trudeau years. That wouldn't last.

The only tense moment in Regina happened, fortunately, behind closed doors. The Prime Minister was in the temporary office assigned to him at the Centre, watching a press conference with Frank Miller, then the Ontario premier. The questioner was asking Miller to reply to comments from Mulroney that Mulroney had never uttered. The Boss went into one of his crimson rages, and started yelling at Fox to rush right in there and set this fool straight. Fox replied, "Sir, I can't just go in there and pull the plug."

How could a man as smart as Mulroney imagine that Fox could get away with bursting on camera to interrupt a press conference on those grounds?

But this was all off-stage. Out front, Regina was a triumph. Now we were ready for the international scene, the big leagues. Less than ten days later, we were aboard an Armed Forces 707 on our way to the Carib-Can conference, attended by Canada and Caribbean members of the British Commonwealth.

Here, Mulroney was at his best, making friends, absorbing information, and building the ties that would help him later to exert Canada's influence on such international issues as the approach to South Africa. That was not the only good news to come out of this trip. We learned that Mila Mulroney was pregnant with her fourth child. Bonnie Brownlee had denied rumours to this effect, to protect Mila in case of a miscarriage, but the truth got out before we returned to Ottawa. After that, whenever the question of a fifth child arose, I'd say jokingly, in front of her, "You'll have to ask Bonnie."

The successes at Regina and Kingston, Jamaica, were only dress rehearsals, in fact, for the really big show we were planning in conjunction with the Americans in Quebec City on March 17: the Shamrock Summit.

CHAPTER TEN

The View from the Shamrock Summit

ichael Deaver knew exactly what he wanted. As his team
of thirty-odd staffers from Ronald Reagan's White House
hustled down the ramp of the government jet that had
brought them from Washington to the Quebec City airport, the
President's communications guru could apparently already
envisage the images that would flash across America's TV screens
from the Shamrock Summit on St. Patrick's Day, 1985.

We were a bedraggled half-dozen, by comparison, who had
come up from Ottawa under the leadership of Fred Doucet to
confront this impressive troop of Americans, hardened by two
presidential campaigns and numerous expeditions abroad. For
those of us at the PMO, it was our baptism of summit fire, and
it turned out to be a scorcher. Our job was to ensure that neither
we nor the Prime Minister would be eclipsed by our state visitor
and his organization. We'd been warned. The Americans always
wind up getting whatever they want, wherever they go in the
world. They fuss about the minutest details, and leave nothing
to chance. They always have the upper hand, and treat everyone
else like underlings.

Still, for Ron Lemieux of the External Affairs department's
protocol shop, who had been through the drill with the Americans a few times, Reagan's guys were at least a tad less over-
bearing than Jimmy Carter's crew. The night before we were to

93

meet Deaver's Army, Lemieux told me about how one of Carter's people had discussed the formation of the motorcade that would go from Uplands Airport to downtown Ottawa on a presidential visit (the visit was cancelled at the last moment by the Iran Embassy crisis). The man from the White House had opened his briefcase, produced a set of little toy cars and lined them up on the table in the decreed order, to make sure his Canadian counterpart could fully understand what he was getting at.

We were determined not to let ourselves be treated like country bumpkins. After all, weren't we the boys from the machine that had swept all before it, from one end of the land to the other, just the year before? We were intent on accomplishing, in three months of preparation, what would normally take twice that long, so the pressure was on. But we could do it. We hoped.

In the end, the St. Patrick's Day summit was, without doubt, the apogee of the first half of Brian Mulroney's mandate as Prime Minister. The whole team scored a smashing triumph, and I've rarely seen the Prime Minister more confident and more serene than after his meeting with Reagan. However, there were times . . .

The exercise began here, at Ancienne Lorette airport, on the chilly morning of December 17. We were surprised even to be here. Peter Ohrt, who was responsible for logistics on our side, had been on a ski hill in Bromont, Quebec, when he was fetched back by a panic call from Fred Doucet and informed that we were all to rush up to Quebec City to meet the "Pre-Advance" — not "Advance," that would come later — team from Washington. We came by commercial aircraft, the Americans in their own jet, and together, we did the rounds.

As we rushed from the airport to the Château Frontenac, to the Grand Theatre, to the Citadel, and back to the hotel, we realized that the visitors, with the help of their local consulate, were running a very tight operation. We, on the other hand, were not. It was a bit embarrassing, for example, when we went to check out one of the rooms suggested as a possible site for a summit session, and found it full of broken glasses and the general sticky debris of a party the night before. Nor were the Americans terribly impressed by the floor of the hotel where the Presidential suite was to be; it had to be redone from top to bottom before the visit. But they were delighted with the terrace on the Citadel above the sweeping height of Cape Diamond, with the St. Lawrence River as a backdrop. For them, this was it. The picture they wanted from the visit would be staged here. Still, they weren't satisfied.

94

"We need something for St. Patrick's Day," said Michael Deaver.

At this point, nobody had any real idea what to do about that. A few of us talked of having the Prime Minister take the President to an Irish pub, but the Irish still left in Quebec City now live mostly in the suburbs, and the only place close to an authentic Irish pub was in Ste. Foy, a lengthy trip we knew the US Secret Service would never okay. For the next few days, we let our imaginations run riot with St. Patrick's Day scenarios — at one point, we had a huge choir in the picture, but it came to nothing.

Deaver also wanted the President to be able to speak to the Canadian people; it was a major preoccupation at this first meeting. He kept repeating, "Yes, but how will he speak to the Canadian people?"

We were to find out later why he was so insistent.

Deaver was also fascinated by the famous "Vindouze," as the Americans called the celebrated 22e Regiment stationed at the Citadel. They would make fine picture fodder; we had to make sure of them.

That first trip, touring the sights that would serve as the summit decor, only lasted a few hours, but it was long enough for us to notice, by their manner, that they felt more at home here than we did, and to suspect what lay in store for us three months down the road, when the main event would take place.

The Advance team, lagging behind the Pre-Advance boys, descended on Quebec a month later. This team, naturally, was larger; there were about sixty of them, led by Bill Henkel, later to be promoted within the White House upon Deaver's departure. Our ranks, meanwhile, had also swollen. We were up to about a dozen, so they only outnumbered us about five-to-one.

The Americans arrived at the Quebec airport in their own government jet; we came in our own plane this time, too — an old, prop-driven DC-3, a real museum piece, that we stashed out of sight behind a hangar before the visitors deplaned. We could hide our ancient aircraft, but not the fact that, at every turn, they outnumbered us by a wide margin. When the actual summit got underway, I discovered that there were at least ten people on the American side doing basically the same job I was doing alone for our side. They had, for instance, a guy named Barney, whose sole responsibility was to look after media buses. Not the media, just the buses. We were the ones who rented the buses and told the drivers where to go and how to get there, but every day, Barney would be there, harassing me about my buses.

They had the numbers and the money. We were consumed with envy as we watched the American operation. We knew that if we ever mustered as much, in proportion, as they did for an international visit, our media puritans, particularly from English Canada, would crucify us for our presidential aspirations. The Americans were proud of the comfort and support their president enjoyed on trips abroad; perhaps they realized more than our media, the enormity of the responsibility that weighs on every leader of a front-rank state.

In any event, one of the major preoccupations of our Canadian journalists covering the summit was just how much this "giant photo opportunity," as they called it, was going to cost our taxpayers. But our orders, as transmitted by Fred Doucet, said that this time, there would be no rubbing nickels together. We were to go all out for the big score.

It was up to us to meet and match the Americans in expertise, and, as it turned out, their professionalism was, in the end, a source of inspiration. It made us work harder, and it made us push back. I had my first run-in with them during the Advance visit.

The Americans were unhappy with the press centre we were offering their side, in the old Quebec Court House, just opposite a Château Frontenac that had been spiffed up to Presidential standards. It seemed like an ideal location, since most of the American media representatives were billeted at the Château, and most of the bilateral meetings would be held there. The provincial government had come through with exemplary co-operation in offering to let us have the old Court House, then conveniently empty, and awaiting renovation, but the Americans wanted no part of it for some reason. Very well, we said, it will be the Canadian press centre, instead. At once, they switched sides, and began agitating furiously to have it for themselves. When I suggested that we could share it, they reluctantly agreed, but insisted upon occupying the first floor, grumbling all the while that it really wasn't up to their standards. We told them we'd give them a wonderful press room elsewhere that would satisfy all their needs and lay on a bus service to and from the Château, and we left it at that. In the end, we wound up sharing the first and second floors.

Bill Fox and I went back to Ottawa happy in the thought that we'd won the first round with the White House heavyweights. But we also suspected that they'd be laying for us from now on.

After the Pre-Advance and Advance waves of Americans came the Advance-Advance wave, a full-dress invasion of Reagan shock troops, led by the Secret Service contingent, two weeks before the event. Before we could get to the scene with our brave little band of PMO staffers, they were well installed and well embarked on what our crack advance man on his first big assignment, Stewart Murray, called a "strong-arm job" on the Château Frontenac. They had literally taken the place over, installing a parallel White House operation, as they do everywhere the President travels. They even had business cards printed giving the phone number for what they called "The Quebec City White House." They had installed special cables and telephone lines for their electronic gear, which they had first lifted in through the windows with a ten-storey crane. The lines were then run down one of the emergency stairwells in the hotel, when the Secret Service deemed that that wasn't secure enough, because someone could come along and chop through the wires with an axe, so they were moved to chop-proof safety.

We began, in turn, to learn what it is to be leaned on when the joint meetings between the PMO and White House media personnel were convened. Chief leaner was an enormous Irishman named Rick O'Hearn, head of the White House advance operation. The meetings took place every day, usually late at night, and every day, the Americans brought in a fresh demand for something we thought had already been settled.

We ought, therefore — but we weren't — to have been prepared for the Great Teleprompter Coup that they hit us with forty-eight hours before the President's arrival. During one of our evening meetings, big O'Hearn announced, with false sheepishness, that Reagan would need his teleprompter to read his speech during the Monday noon banquet in the Château Frontenac ballroom.

The teleprompter allows an announcer to read his lines from a screen in such a way that it looks to the audience as though he's memorized his lines. That's the ordinary teleprompter — pretty primitive compared to the rig Ronald Reagan had. He had *two* teleprompters, one for each side of the podium, and they were both practically transparent. From the floor, they looked like two windows, each about a foot square, supported by a microphone stand whose base was a small box containing the transmitter. The teleprompter operators were hidden in another room, scrolling the speech as Reagan spoke. The President, a Hollywood veteran, had the technique down cold; he would turn first to his right, then to his left with a movement that looked perfectly natural. He also had a printed text in front of him, but he would rarely refer to it, except when quoting someone else — which, again, seemed natural. And the best part was that the two screens virtually disappear from the televised image, and the impression transmitted would be that here is a president who, at his age, can easily learn a fifteen-minute speech by heart.

The Americans suddenly sprang this bit of technological magic on us almost on the eve of the visit, when we were neither prepared for it, nor anxious to have the President using technology we wouldn't be able to match for our man. It would look as if Reagan had memorized his talk, while Mulroney had to depend on a text. When they unrolled their magic for us, along with a demand that we rearrange all the tables and change the colour of the tablecloths for television, I was both humiliated by my ignorance and furious with their arrogance. They advanced the explanation that this had to be sprung at the last minute because the President had just found out his speech was going to be longer than six or seven minutes — which he might have faked — and he could not do without mechanical aids. The President could shove his teleprompter, as far as I was concerned.

That was not the only row over the Monday banquet speech. The CBC was to televise the event and had already made special arrangements for lighting. This, too, would have to be changed, to accommodate the teleprompter. Again, I said there was no question of making such a change at this late date. We left it at that for the evening. The next day, we got a call from Ottawa reporting that the White House had complained about an individual in the Prime Minister's Office who was refusing to let the President have his teleprompter. The battle was over, right there. I had to give way, and the CBC had to re-arrange its lighting; I could only offer my apologies. One of the White House press officers, Gary Foster, a friendly Texan, told me he had passed the word along to his superiors that they ought not to have sprung all this at the last moment, but I always suspected they did it on purpose, just to show us who was in charge.

Then there was the matter of the positioning of Air Force One, which suddenly erupted into a major controversy when we were at the Quebec airport on Saturday, March 16, for a final inspection. I was checking out media installations — platforms and camera emplacements — while a mixed group of Canadians and Americans were talking over details in one of the airport offices.

By pure chance, I ran into someone who told me that I was supposed to be at this impromptu meeting, and I knew there was a problem when I walked in the door and a chorus of voices announced, "Aha! There he is."

It had rained that day. The American expert assigned to check the runway where Air Force One, the presidential plane, would land, had noted that the water didn't stay on the surface of the runway at the spot where the plane was to stop. He consulted a geologist and was told that the ground in the area was porous. So he concluded that Air Force One was in danger of sinking into the tarmac. It would have to be moved — which, of course, meant moving the platforms and camera positions and starting all over again.

This the night before the meeting! I couldn't believe my ears. We had already accommodated one American demand when we allowed them to park the plane several hundred feet from the hangar where the welcoming was to take place. They insisted that this was a necessary security measure; it seems the presidential plane always has to be in a position to take off in case the need arises — such as, I guess, the event of a nuclear strike against Quebec. Again, we had no choice but to give way. Air Force One was given a new berth, and all the camera positions replotted, but these constant last-minute changes were getting on our nerves.

Finally, came the big day, March 17. Mulroney had arrived without incident the night before and was awaiting his moment of glory. After what we'd been through, I was expecting the worst, and clung to the comfort of the words of Jacques Grilli, one of the veteran RCMP security people: "When it starts, you know it's on the way to being over."

As a matter of fact, it started badly. Everybody, particularly Peter Ohrt, who was from Quebec City, had told me that the town usually gets hit by one of the worst snowstorms of the winter precisely on March 17. When I got up at about 6:00 a.m. on St. Patrick's Day and opened the curtains in my room at the Quebec Hilton, it was snowing so hard that I couldn't even see the city lights below me. This is it, I thought. The arrival was going to turn into a nightmare, compounded by traffic chaos. I went back to bed, and when I woke up again, two hours later, the storm was over and the sun was shining. The luck of the Irish.

The hour was approaching. I made my way to the airport where I was in charge of herding around the cameramen, photographers and reporters assigned to pool positions close to the action. I also wanted to make sure of the arrangements for the motorcade and the media mini-buses that would follow it downtown. These included a special mini-bus laid on for the Americans, who always have to have a "death watch" pool close to the President, in case somebody blows his head off. No kidding; it's a standard rule for the White House press corps.

When I got to the airport, about twenty minutes before the President's plane was due, I couldn't see the mini-buses, so I got on my walkie-talkie to Art Lyon, a veteran tour co-ordinator on loan from External Affairs.

"Where are the mini-buses for the reporters?" I asked.

"We don't have any mini-buses," Art replied.

My American friend, Gary Foster, who was standing beside me, said, "I'll pretend I didn't hear that."

"Art," I said, trying to keep the panic out of my voice, "find the mini-buses!"

"I'm doing my best," he radioed back.

Two minutes before the scheduled touch-down, two mini-buses rolled onto the tarmac, and I thought my problems were over. Foolish me.

The President's arrival was grandiose. Ron and Brian, followed by Nancy and Mila, walked together to the hangar where the ceremony would take place. In brilliant sunshine, they ambled between two rows of red-coated Mounties; Reagan must have thought he'd stumbled into a re-make of Rose Marie.

Governor General Jeanne Sauvé, our constitutional head of state, had been informed by the PMO that her presence wasn't necessary here because this was a "working visit," as opposed to a full-dress State visit, so she wound up watching it on TV at Rideau Hall, in Ottawa. She let everybody know of her displeasure in no uncertain terms afterwards, because as head of state, she should have been the first to greet the Reagans on Canadian soil. But for us, it was mission accomplished. Our "pony" was the star of the show, and this was precisely what we had intended. There was nothing personal in the decision to freeze out the Governor General; Mulroney often expressed admiration for her talents. But this was our rink and our puck, and we were playing by our rules. We weren't about to let picayune protocol details spoil our show.

The arrival went without a hitch — the national anthems, the welcoming speeches, the inspection of the glittering Royal 22e honour guard — all went as choreographed. Then things began to come apart. I was supposed to escort, on the run, the group of pool reporters designated to ride in the presidential motorcade aboard the famous mini-buses. We bolted for the buses like the field coming out of the gate at the Preakness, and piled inside. I jumped into the lead bus, where I found the young driver cowering like a frightened doe.

"Pull out!" I ordered him, as I saw the motorcade begin to move. But he was frozen in his seat. I may even have sworn at him, just a little.

"Where? Where? Where?" he whimpered.

"What do you mean, where?" I shouted, "Follow that motorcade!"

He was totally petrified, and he was also blocking the bus behind us, which was ready to roll. I could hear the Americans beginning to yap in agitation. Finally, he got the vehicle moving, but not fast enough to close the gap between us and the vanishing motorcade.

"Move it!" I bellowed, "we're going to lose them!"

"I didn't know it was going to be like this," he whined. The poor guy had been told to "pick up a few reporters" at the airport. He had no idea he was going to be part of a Presidential and Prime Ministerial motorcade.

"I think I'm going to be sick," he whimpered.

Now I was starting to get scared; we'd just left the airport and had a twenty-minute drive ahead of us, and this guy was going to be sick on us. The RCMP agent with us on the mini-bus reacted to this announcement by getting on his cohorts in the escort cars ahead and saying, "I think we're going to have to stop. We have a problem."

"Stop!" I said incredulously. "No way! You," I said to the driver, "stay behind the wheel, don't move; and piss in your pants if you have to!"

It was one of the longest bus trips of my life, but it must have seemed even longer for the poor driver, who longed for the cargo of docile tourists he was used to. When we got to the Château, he bolted from the bus as if the devil was at his heels and ran through the hotel doors before even the Secret Service men could react. I don't know what he was doing in the washroom, but I knew he was in a hurry for something.

As for the Americans, they were outraged because, at the last minute, we left the motorcade and took a different route to the Château than the Presidential limousine. My reasoning was that, if we'd stayed behind, we'd have been blocked off by traffic at the Porte St. Louis, and the President would arrive at the hotel while we, who were supposed to be covering the great descent, would still be blocks away. I was right, but that didn't help — the Americans were still sore at me. And the day had just begun.

After a photo session for the first bilateral meeting, from which the leaders emerged with an agreement on acid rain, we had to think about the evening's gala at the Grand Theatre. This is where we had planned our big coup; we had decided to meet the St. Patrick's Day challenge by having Ron and Brian and Nancy and Mila come down from their boxes to the stage for the last number of the gala which would be — there was never any question otherwise — "When Irish Eyes Are Smiling." All of this would be broadcast across Canada by the CBC, and clips would be offered to the American news networks.

The concert hall of the Grand Theatre was bulging at the seams with Conservative Party bigwigs and hangers-on disguised as ordinary folk. According to a system worked out with the Prime Minister, every Member of Parliament was allotted a number of guests. To even things out slightly, we also invited members of the provincial government and eminent persons not directly connected to the party; but with those few exceptions, just about everyone else was a party loyalist — we weren't worried about being booed that night.

The show went beautifully, with the additional bonus that, thanks to Mila Mulroney, this marked the big break for the Famous People Players, a troupe of handicapped young Canadians who, two years later, would find themselves on Broadway. They were a smash, and so was everything else about the show. When the moment for the big finale arrived, the two leadership couples appeared on stage to render Irish Eyes with the entertainers, led by acclaimed singer Maureen Forrester. When they hit the final refrain, Forrester did something totally unexpected, passing the microphone to Mulroney, who sang the last words by himself: "Sure they'll steal your heart away . . . " in a true clear voice.

The Tories were proud of their boy. Most of them had heard stories of his vocal prowess; it turned out as advertised. I was beaming. We'd taken the round. Reagan had barely moved his lips. We'd beaten the Great Communicator at his own game — showmanship.

The curtain came down and the two couples offered congratulations to the performers, shaking hands with everyone. A special CBC camera unit we had arranged beforehand followed the

President's every move. Then, suddenly, there was another camera, an American one, which had not been arranged. Backstage was becoming a little clogged with cameras, and that set off a shouting match between big Rick O'Hearn and myself.

"That camera!" shouted O'Hearn, towering over me. "What's it doing there? You didn't tell us the President would have a camera up his nose!"

"Well, what's *your* camera doing there?" I yelled back.

"It's for the archives," he replied.

"Ah, so. And how are our guys supposed to know that? Are they supposed to guess?"

While the camera crews threshed around in the Presidential wake, O'Hearn and I discussed the matter in language somewhat removed from the normal diplomatic lexicon, but I didn't care any more. I'd just about had it with these damn pushy Yanks. O'Hearn stomped off in a giant huff — and that wasn't to be the end of it.

The Americans swore that, for the next day's events, including the Château banquet, they would get rid of the CBC tracking camera, which was feeding the national network with exceptional footage. They claimed that this state-of-the-art machinery was distorting the images they were getting with their equipment. CBC producer Gilles Thibault assured me that this could not be the case, so I was determined to stand my ground. As far as I was concerned, what bothered the Americans was that they hadn't made a deal with the CBC for the pictures from their special camera and only now realized that they were missing the best shots. So, remembering the little affair of the teleprompter, I refused to budge.

That is, until the next morning, when Lee Richardson, then Fred Doucet's assistant, came to see me. "The old man himself" — meaning the President — had complained to the Prime Minister about the Canadian camera that was following him everywhere. Once again, that was the ballgame. I went to tell Gilles Thibault the bad news. He took it with a smile; we both realized, by then, how far the Americans were willing to go to make their point, even over something so insignificant.

That morning was marked by another alarm. The American Secretary of Defence, Caspar Weinberger, gave an interview to CTV's *Canada AM* show, in which he said that the North American Air Defence Agreement (NORAD), which we were poised to renew that very afternoon, did not exclude the possibility of placing American nuclear missiles on Canadian soil.

What was he trying to pull? The presence of American weapons on Canadian soil had been a contentious issue years ago in the Diefenbaker era; were we to go through all that again? We were convinced the Americans had done this on purpose, knowing what would happen if they unleashed their loose cannon on Canadian television. We had to begin damage control immediately, starting with an internal request for clarification, if not rectification, from the Americans. Presidential Spokesman Larry Speakes co-operated part way, fudging the issue as only he could, but when our Secretary of State for External Affairs, Joe Clark, tried the same evasiveness, he got a rude mauling from the American reporters during that day's briefing at the press centre.

Amid the *brouhaha*, the show had to go on. Stewart Murray rushed about performing miracles to prepare the Château ballroom for all the changes required to accommodate the Reagan teleprompters, while I shepherded the media mob to a photo session between the two leaders. As a courtesy, I always let the American journalists go first on joint events; the Canadians formed "the second wave." When the Americans cleared out, and the Canadians took over, Paul Chiasson of Canadian Press called out to the two leaders to shake hands across the table, which, being the instinctive performers they are, they immediately did. Thus, the Canadians got a better shot than the American wave. I wasn't sorry. Then a few minutes later, Lee Richardson scurried up to tell me that the Americans were complaining that they "got fucked" because the Canadians had a picture they didn't have and maybe we should give them our picture. (Incidentally, the Canadian picture would be available to them off the CP wire, but it wouldn't be "theirs.")

"They're getting nothing from me!" I told Richardson. He seemed a little dazed by my fury, but it didn't seem wise to press the point.

By now, we were only a few minutes away from The Teleprompter Speech, where Reagan would, in the words Michael Deaver had kept repeating last December, "speak to the Canadian people." We listened with dismay as he gave his modified Evil Empire oration, vaunting his Star Wars defence initiative and clawing away at the image of the brutish and untrustworthy Soviets. There was nothing new in the rhetoric, but we had hoped he might hold back on the cold war dramatics a bit while on Canadian soil.

As for the celebrated teleprompter, despite all the rancour it provoked, it was indeed a marvellous device, that allowed Reagan to perform with startling aplomb. Nor did it escape the Prime Minister's attention. Bill Fox and I, dazzled by the instrument, started agitating to get one for Canada, but Mulroney held back, arguing that the Canadian people, and in particular the Canadian Press corps, weren't ready for such stuff.

Round Two to Reagan and his heavies. But then, a tie against the Americans is as good as a win.

All that remained was the final photo session at the Citadel, the fortress built by the English after the fall of Quebec, and now the Governor General's summer residence. Everything had to be right here; this was the shot that was going into the history books. In reality, the signing ceremony was merely a formality to justify the glorious photo opportunity we had arranged overlooking the river, on the terrace where Mackenzie King, Franklin D. Roosevelt and Winston Churchill had posed for a famous photo forty one years earlier.

The Prime Minister had even visited the site to make sure it wouldn't affect his equilibrium, and the picture that came out of the session was so perfect that I suggested we make posters of it. But then I almost spoiled everything, right there in the middle of the session.

The Americans had promised us that there would be no one around the two stars not necessary to the event, so as to have a minimum number of bodies in the way of photographers' lenses. But when we got there, who should I see blocking half the skyline in front of the President? None other than my old buddy, Rick O'Hearn, of the White House advance corps.

I shouted at one of his assistants, Stephen Hart, standing next to me, "I thought there wasn't to be anybody!" We were about twenty feet away from the two leaders at this point.

"They're guys from Security," he said.

"Security, my ass! What's Rick O'Hearn doing there?"

"Listen, Michel . . . "

I ended the conversation with a brusque "Fuck off" as a startled Bill Fox and Bill Henkel, of the American team, rolled their eyes. Hart told Fox later that I was totally "unfair" in flying off the handle. He was right; first of all, it wasn't the time for it — I risked blowing my own show — and secondly, the reporters standing by heard the exchange. Fortunately, nothing much was made of it. But I was boiling at the way the Americans always conducted themselves, and I may have conveyed that feeling to them. I know that a year later when Bill Fox was setting out for Washington to organize the second Mulroney–Reagan summit, and I asked him if my presence would be required, he explained that he was going to keep me in reserve, instead. "If they don't play along with us, we'll threaten to send down the Tasmanian devil," he said.

Finally, it was all over. After this, I wasn't going to be impressed by anything any more. After the summit, the Prime Minister was happier than at any time I saw him during three years, except the day Nicolas was born. He never again felt so in control. The media could write it off as one giant, costly photo session, but we knew we had won the PR battle. We were never stronger than we were then, and the Prime Minister was never so proud of his team.

The next Gallup poll had us at 54 per cent. We were all geniuses, starting with The Boss.

We found out a few months later to what extent the summit strategy paid off. One night, we were at the Quebec Coliseum for a play-off game between the Nordiques and the Philadelphia Flyers, as guests of Nordiques' president, Marcel Aubut. Just before the game, the team's public relations man told me that they planned to introduce the Prime Minister to the crowd. I was taken aback — there is nothing more dangerous for a politician than to put himself at the mercy of sports fans — but I was assured that the greeting would be friendly. Despite nagging doubts, I said to go ahead; then I almost choked when I discovered that this was to be live on national television. By then, it was too late to draw back. A few minutes later, I was in the CTV studio, negotiating a between-periods interview with the Prime Minister, when I heard the rink announcer begin his introduction. I held my breath. Then, to my amazement, the crowd rose as one, with a resounding, standing ovation.

The Boss, who was totally unaware of the heart-failure I nearly went through, was radiant. I'm glad he enjoyed it. In the months to come, standing ovations would become something of a rarity.

PART THREE

The Slide
Begins

"This is a difficult country to govern."

Sir Wilfrid Laurier to Sir John Nillison, 1905

CHAPTER ELEVEN

Rampaging Through Europe

I t was only a matter of time before our enormous self-confidence, often bordering on arrogance, would boomerang and come back to hit us squarely in the face. It happened during an official visit to London in late April and May 1985, that was followed immediately by the Western Economic Summit in Bonn, West Germany. Like the scandals, pratfalls on international trips were to become a trademark for this government, more renowned for its escapades than its policies.

I was to go to London two days before the Prime Minister's arrival to make sure that all the necessary media installations were in place. Bill Fox had already advanced the visit, compiling a schedule that included meetings with Prime Minister Margaret Thatcher and the Queen.

At his best, Fox doesn't exactly fit the mould of the diplomat, in the classic British sense; for that matter, neither do I. Fox's rocky journey through London's diplomatic channels came to the attention of the Southam News correspondent in London who wrote a story that received great play in Canada, to the effect that Fox's boorish behaviour had grievously offended the delicate sensibilities of the gentlemen in the British Foreign Office.

Knowing Fox, I was sure that there were moments when he became somewhat impatient with the genteel Lords of London;

but I knew he was too intelligent to have disgraced himself totally. He had simply, as always, carried the Prime Minister's interests foremost in his mind and was trying to make the visit as effective as possible. He was, in fact, trying to make things as easy and as interesting as he could for the Canadian media, knowing well that they are considerably more docile when well-nourished with material. However, as is often the case, his best efforts were turned against him.

The crux of the affair was a photo session that Fox had the temerity to try to arrange with Her Majesty and the Prime Minister. Apparently, this is something that just isn't done. Fox had insisted that it ought to be done, saying he couldn't understand why the Queen would pose for pictures with the meanest foreign royalty, but would refuse to do so with the Prime Minister of Canada because he wasn't the official head of state, simply the head of government. Okay for Jeanne Sauvé, not for Brian Mulroney.

By the time I got to London, we had already come to the realization that we'd never get the cameras into Buckingham Palace. But we had also arranged a meeting with the Queen Mother, and Fox decided to try to persuade her to participate in a photo session. It was my job to make the arrangements. Lee Richardson, Stewart Murray and I showed up at the Queen Mother's residence, Clarence House, at 11:00 a.m. Richardson was a cowboy from Alberta, Murray a farm lad from a place called, no kidding, Punnichy, Saskatchewan, and I was a franco from Vanier. The Three Stooges were launched on a less outrageous premise.

The Queen Mother's personal secretary met us at the door, a grand septuagenarian who gushed, in the perfect British manner, "So glad to see you! Frightfully good to see you!"

He seemed perturbed by a call he had received from a certain "Dr. Doucet," in Ottawa.

"Oh, that's Fred," blurted Richardson.

The secretary couldn't figure out why Dr. Doucet would call him, and didn't know if he should return the call. Richardson explained that Doucet probably wanted the same thing we did, to set up a photo opportunity with the Queen Mother and the Prime Minister.

"No, no, no, no," the secretary said, with the air of a father admonishing a thick-headed child. I dared to ask as politely as I could, why not?

"It's not done," he blustered. "It's never been done and it never will be done."

And that was it for the explanation. I couldn't believe these crazy Englishmen. We might as well have asked them to move the Tower of London. Having disposed of the formalities, and with Murray, Richardson and me still in a state of bewilderment, the secretary invited us into the next room for a drink. There, among others, stood my counterpart, the Queen Mother's Press Secretary, who looked well past the age of foolishness.

"You'll have something to drink, won't you?" he asked. "A gin and tonic, perhaps?"

It was eleven o'clock in the morning! Speechless, all three of us took a gin and tonic. The Press Secretary, whose job it obviously was to make conversation with me, asked, "And so, how is my good friend John Turner?"

"Not bad, I suppose," I replied neutrally, wondering if he thought Turner was still Prime Minister of Canada.

"Yes, yes, yes," he said. "He went and did a little bit of non-sense, didn't he?"

I had another gin and tonic.

We left the Queen Mother's empty-handed, with no photo op in the bag, but slightly bagged ourselves from the gin and tonics. We'd been had.

That afternoon, we went to Westminster Abbey, where the Prime Minister was scheduled to place a wreath at the tomb of the Unknown Soldier. While we were there, I asked the Foreign Office type who was with us if it would be possible to put camera platforms on either side of the tomb, so that the cameramen could get a better view of the proceedings.

"Oh, no!" she said, straight away. "They'd never allow that," she added, alluding to the senior clergy who administered the Abbey. Still, I summoned the audacity to ask if I could speak to the man in charge to see if it could be arranged.

"Of course, no problem," he said, while the Foreign Office functionary looked on, slack-jawed. Later, the Canadian media would report that we had wanted to shuffle the furniture around in Westminster Abbey, but there wasn't so much as a hymn book where I installed the risers with the blessings of the Abbey's good fathers.

The Pastor then took us on a guided tour of the Abbey, a veritable treasure trove of British history, where the Empire's greatest heroes, military, literary, artistic and scientific, are entombed. Finally, he stopped proudly before one particular monument, explaining that this part was the "Canadian content" element of the tour. It was the tomb of James Wolfe, the conqueror of Quebec. Richardson and Murray started snickering when I looked the Pastor in the eye and told him, without cracking a smile, that Mr. Wolfe had killed my ancestors. He didn't linger on the Canadian content.

As though I hadn't put her through enough that day, I had to make another request of our Foreign Office escort. I wanted a double-decker bus, as there were many of them around London, one without a roof. The idea was to use the second storey as a rolling platform for the cameramen, who would have an unobstructed view of various sites along the route. The lady from the Foreign Office thought I was crazy. She had, she said, two spanking new, modern buses for us. The old double-deckers were hard to manoeuvre in traffic.

"But, they're all over the place," I protested.

She didn't understand why I was so insistent, but she gave way in the end. The next day, she was astounded to see practically the entire forty-member Canadian press contingent seated on the top deck of "my bus," even though the weather was sub-Arctic by London standards, while her lovely modern vehicle sat empty at the curb.

"They're all on your bus," she said. "I'd forgotten that you're used to this kind of weather in Canada."

She'd also forgotten that the media boys and girls will always go for the most extravagant and amusing alternative.

Among other locations, my double-decker bus was to be used in front of the Commodities Market where Mulroney was scheduled to make a visit to see the modern electronic Canadian-made tote board. I parked my bus on the wide sidewalk in front of the building. We had to get special permission from the City to do this and our London contact from the Commodities Market assured me we had it. As I stood there with my media bunch awaiting the Prime Minister's arrival, two "Bobbies" came walking by and stopped to inspect my bus suspiciously. I walked over to them asking, "Is there a problem, officers?"

"This is your bus?" asked one of them. "It's not supposed to be here." I explained diplomatically that I was told that we had obtained permission from the City to park it there. "The problem is," he continued, "that the ground underneath is hollow . . . "

"Hollow?" I gasped.

"Yes . . . The subway runs under this sidewalk." Then, seeing my horrified look he added without flinching, "Yes, in two minutes, your bus could become a northbound train!"

Bill Fox had already given the media a store of material on the way over on the Prime Minister's plane. Talking about the problems he had lining up photo opportunities, he said, with his unerring instinct for hyperbole, "The King of Oogabooga can get his picture taken with the Queen, but not the Prime Minister of Canada!"

I knew something was up when I saw the TV cameras following Fox's every movement, from the time he got off the plane, looking menacing behind his sunglasses. They even zeroed-in on a private conversation he was trying to have with me. He was afraid that he'd gone a little too far in his banter with the reporters; but I thought nothing of it. To amuse the troops on the press bus, I even distributed pictures of the Royal family, saying in a fake British falsetto that I'd be around to sign autographs later on. And I told everyone about our adventure at the Queen Mother's.

The next day, there were stories in the Canadian papers quoting Fox's reference to the King of Oogabooga, and some accounts added that a member of the Prime Minister's staff had mimicked the Queen while distributing photos.

"Who was imitating the Queen?" a furious Mulroney asked Fox. I don't think Fox dared tell him. Fred Doucet, the delegation chief, was terribly upset over all the bad publicity, and Fox moaned, "I could be going down on this one."

It had all turned sour, and that was most unfortunate, because he'd carefully scouted our locations and the arrangements for once were perfect. However, we had committed the capital error of becoming the story. Through us the media were able to attack the Prime Minister; it was a technique they would apply repeatedly in the months to come, carrying on a guerrilla war against the PMO, rather than venturing a frontal attack.

Otherwise, the two-day visit was a great success. Logistically speaking, it was impeccable; we had succeeded in obtaining the ultimate goal of a communications strategy by effectively lending substance with pretty pictures. But the tone set at the beginning of the trip, making us look like bootless louts assaulting the most cherished traditions and institutions of the British motherland, would follow us to the Economic Summit at Bonn, and beyond.

The capital of West Germany had been transformed into an armed camp for the occasion, as had unfortunately become the case at all meetings of the seven major western trading nations, in light of the international terrorist threat. Everywhere there were soldiers and policemen, all armed to the teeth. They had firm orders to let no one pass who was not accredited as a Summit participant or observer. When the orders were confused, or the guardians too intransigent, it led to problems.

Moreover, every time a motorcade went through the city, and that included not only the leaders, but their senior ministers, everything stopped. Our difficulty was that the reporters had to move during, or just before, the motorcades, to get to where events were taking place. The result was that we were frequently trapped between two cordons of soldiers who didn't or wouldn't understand. And you don't argue too long with a machine-gun staring you in the face. As even Idi Amin recognized, "You can't run faster than a bullet."

My frustration mounted by the hour and with each obstinate guard I had to deal with. I was being told, even though I was a full-fledged member of the Canadian delegation, that I didn't have the proper authorization to go where I was supposed to be leading the reporters to do their work. I finally exploded.

It happened just before the official arrival ceremony at the West German parliament, the Bundestag. I was with a small group of reporters, including Bob Hepburn of the *Toronto Star*, one of the black sheep of the Press Gallery, as far as we were concerned, ever since the election campaign.

That day, we had made it through the barrier on the way to the opening ceremonies. It was raining buckets and we were on foot, hurrying through the downpour. For one reason or another the second cordon of soldiers, most of whom spoke only German, refused categorically to let us past and told us to go back where we had come from.

"We're not going anywhere," I shouted defiantly. "We're not moving."

The German soldier looked as if he had been pushed a little too far, but I was sure he wasn't about to machine-gun us on the spot. I asked him his rank, and told him rudely, "If you have a rank, you won't have it tomorrow!"

During this skirmish, the reporters behind me were busy taking notes. Then, after a long standoff while the Prime Minister's car passed right under our noses, we were allowed to go ahead, thanks to the intervention of a German civil servant, who spoke to the soldiers. She was later attached to my person as a special

114

escort, and I was fascinated by the fact that she insisted on referring to the "talkie-walkie" we used to communicate.

The next day, I got a squawk from Fox on my walkie-talkie.

"Michel, I've got good news and bad news for you."

"What happened?" I asked worriedly.

"Your run-in with the German police made the front page of the *Toronto Star*," he said.

"And what's the good news?"

"The good news is that they said it was me!"

"It couldn't happen to a nicer guy," I chortled.

But there was nothing funny about it. Once again, this news story, insignificant as it was, showed how the press office, and Fox in particular, had become news objects. In this case, he hadn't even done anything — he wasn't even close to the scene. When I ran into Hepburn that day, I sarcastically thanked him for not having named me in his story. He claimed he had had nothing to do with the use of Fox's name. Someone on the desk, he said, had simply assumed that the "representative of the Prime Minister's press office" he referred to in his copy must be Bill Fox, their former colleague. There was nothing anybody could do about it. The damage was done.

Why should a story like this rate front page play in the biggest newspaper in the country? Because, for the media, the incident was further proof of the arrogance of the PMO and, by extension, Brian Mulroney himself. This was part of their revenge for the bunker mentality we had adopted in the early months of the administration. They were starting to make us pay for it, and they did so with stories that were easy for ordinary readers to understand. Slowly, but surely, the base on which the public would build its negative perception of the Mulroney government was being moved into place.

The Prime Minister would be the next victim. He was under no illusions; he knew he wasn't one of the summit's big players. He didn't hesitate to say privately that the United States could hold a summit all by itself, so greatly did the Americans dominate the event. So, he deliberately tried to play the mediator's role, using his natural charm and his professional background as a conciliator. The difference this time is that he didn't hesitate to do it before the cameras.

During one of the photo sessions, the Prime Minister could be seen flitting from one leader to another trying to get an agreement on the final communiqué, which was being blocked by French President François Mitterand. I thought the pictures were going to be good for us; there was the Prime Minister negotiating with the major world leaders and the TV cameras recording the action. Unfortunately, his efforts failed to bear fruit. But no matter, I was convinced, after talking to a few Canadian reporters, that The Boss's initiative had been well perceived.

Just before the press conference, the Prime Minister called me aside, and I told him, "You've won this one. Now go for the home run!"

He did, and struck out.

Asked about "Your efforts at forging a compromise," Mulroney responded:

"Yes, I can tell you that, yes, we are deeply involved in that and that on two occasions today, on two separate go-arounds today that I made I think lengthy and I think helpful — I hope, anyway — interventions in this regard putting Canada's view forward."

Later, he pressed the point even further:

"The French staked out their position very clearly and announced it to the world. We were all aware of the American position. So it was quite an exercise to bring two large nations to a mutually acceptable agreement within the parameters that you are aware of. And we played, I think Mr. Wilson and Mr. Clark and I throughout — from both on the telephone, telephone conversations yet unreported, but with President Reagan and other leaders throughout ongoing private meetings and tête-à-têtes and direct bilaterals. I think we played I hope a helpful role in bringing this about."

Even the most serious and friendliest members of our press contingent concluded that the Prime Minister had gone overboard in trying to blow his own horn; they felt he ought to have been more becomingly modest about his place in the international scheme of things. I was stunned. The whole trip, despite our best efforts to be helpful, despite the efficiency of our logistics, had turned into near catastrophe. On the way back to Ottawa, the Prime Minister called me into his private cabin at the front of the plane.

"So, what are the Boys saying?"

"I'm starting to wonder if we're doing more harm than good," I replied.

At this point, he was more commiserative than anything else. We've worked hard, he said; we still had to work hard and we had to keep on working. Personally, I was contemplating resignation. I had offered my resignation once, two months earlier, on a day when I had simply had enough. Fox and Bernard Roy had convinced me to stay, and I promised to do the Quebec Summit and the Economic Summit before leaving.

Now I was feeling the burden of power. We'd been through crises before, but things had always somehow turned out right in the end. The London–Bonn trip marked an important turning point in my perception of what we were making of the Mulroney administration.

Without knowing it, we had begun our slide into the abyss.

CHAPTER TWELVE

The Granny Revolution

W hen the Prime Minister phoned me at home one night near mid-June, 1985, to ask me what I thought of this business of de-indexing old-age pensions, I knew we were about to beat a retreat. After ten months in power, the Mulroney administration was going to learn its first really hard political lesson. The Prime Minister was about to come under a personal attack that would colour the public's perception of him for the years to come.

We all thought when Michael Wilson brought down his first full budget on May 23, 1985, that his proposal to de-index pensions would require delicate handling. Under the arrangement then prevailing, Old Age Security payments, then running at $263.78 per month for individuals, and the Guaranteed Income Supplement, then at $265.60, were re-adjusted every three months in line with increases in the Cost-of-Living tables — thus, indexed. This had been a matter of controversy for some time, particularly when the indexing was limited to six per cent and five per cent by the Trudeau government, in the battle against inflation. During the election, Mulroney had spoken of the nation's social security system as a "sacred trust," and most Canadians took that to mean, no fooling around.

However, Wilson proposed to funnel more money from the well-to-do to the poorer sectors of society, and to get the funds required — and, also as an anti-inflation measure — announced in his budget speech that henceforth, pensions would be partially de-indexed. They would not rise fully with the cost-of-living. The Finance Minister produced elaborate charts to show that this wouldn't mean much to the average pensioner, at least not for the present, but he had no charts to show how a sacred trust could become a negotiable budget item once the ballots had all been counted. During PMO strategy meetings in the days leading up to the budget presentation, Bill Fox stressed that it was crucial that we bring on Health Minister Jake Epp to face the cameras and microphones immediately after Wilson spoke, to calm the fears of the old folks. As it turned out, that was a task that would have daunted Mother Theresa.

All of us, starting with The Boss, had badly underestimated the negative impact of the de-indexation proposal. In fact, when the Finance Minister sat down after his budget speech, the Prime Minister was proud of his performance.

"Look at Wilson," he said. "You'd trust him with your mother's will."

Unless your mother happened to be a pensioner. The opposition, of course, jumped on the issue after doing some simple arithmetic that showed just how much the seniors would be losing in the years to come. However, the greatest pressure came from outside Parliament, from a group that was usually quite docile. This time, the old folks weren't taking it sitting down.

At the beginning of June, the Prime Minister declared categorically that he did not intend to change the policy.

"There will be no change," he told the Commons.

But already Mulroney's instincts must have been telling him that this was more serious than he originally thought, because he immediately added, "We will monitor this very closely and, at the earliest possible moment, discuss it in the House. We will continue to monitor it to ensure to the extent humanly possible and as quickly as finances permit, that no difficulty is sustained by our elderly in Canada."

From then on the government was torn between the credibility of its budget and, by extension, the Minister of Finance, and the potential extent of the political damage. As he had often done before, Mulroney preferred to wait before doing anything rash. The upshot was that our eventual retreat was telegraphed so clearly that any positive impact or element of surprise was dissipated beforehand. By June 10, Mulroney was talking about de-indexing as something that might only be a temporary measure; on June 12 it became a "proposal" that would not come into effect before April 1986; at his June 14 press conference he said, with breathtaking understatement, that "we have the beginning of an uproar" on our hands, and that erroneous concerns that anyone would be immediately affected by the measure should be rectified.

"It is an erroneous conclusion," he said, "but it is there, and I think we have to deal with it. That is not the fault of the elderly. That is not their fault. Nor is it their responsibility. It is mine and the responsibility of my colleagues and so we have to deal with it. Perception sometimes becomes reality, and we have to deal with that as well."

He was basically admitting that the public relations battle had been lost, but still the government made no decision. Michael Wilson was digging in his heels, fearful that any concession would destroy the credibility of his entire maiden budget. And the Prime Minister still agreed with him. I was also worried about our credibility, but one of the things I'd learned from watching the Liberals for five years was that you don't mess with the senior citizens.

The question was finally settled for us by a woman named Solange Denis, who wasn't quite five feet tall in her heels. Clearly, Brian Mulroney had no idea of what was about to hit him when he went over to talk to a group of elderly people protesting de-indexation in front of the Centre Block. Usually Canadians are polite, even if they're demonstrating, and they usually react amiably when the Prime Minister goes over to them. Most wind up shaking his hand, instead of hurling insults. Solange Denis, alas, wasn't versed in the niceties. The woman from Ottawa planted herself in front of the Prime Minister, her nose roughly at the level of his belt buckle, and declared in French, "You lied to us! You made us vote for you, and then goodbye Charlie Brown. If you do anything (on pension de-indexing) you won't get back in three years."

"I'm listening to you, Madame," said Mulroney, aware of the TV cameras attracted by the little scene.

"Well Madame is damn angry!" she retorted.

For once he didn't have to ask what the Boys were saying that day. We all knew that we'd just absorbed a fearsome pounding. The TV clips were devastating. That tiny woman, shaking her fist at the Prime Minister and calling him a liar to his face. If Brian Mulroney didn't know how serious the situation was before, he certainly understood now. Sure enough, at the Press Club they were talking about nothing else. "Goodbye Charlie Brown" became the rallying cry of a media pack that smelled blood.

A week later, on June 27, just before Parliament adjourned for the summer, Michael Wilson, who had to be worked on until the last minute, conceded defeat. He grimly announced that the government had abandoned its de-indexation plan. We were the government that listened to the people instead of giving them the finger, said the Prime Minister.

But once again we couldn't get our act together. While Wilson delivered his speech, the Prime Minister was seated by his side, a graveyard expression on his face. At one point, his eyes strayed to the Press Gallery above the Speaker's chair, and he noticed that most of the reporters were doubled over with laughter. What was going on? He turned around, and there behind Wilson, and thus within the camera angle, he saw what at first he thought was an apparition. But no, it really was Tom Siddon, the Minister for Science and Technology, decked out in a flowing graduation gown, complete with doctoral hood. The Boss erupted.

"Siddon," he hissed, "get the fuck out of here!"

The Prime Minister couldn't get over Siddon's insensitivity for days afterward. He talked about it openly, even with a group of reporters on one of his rare visits to the Press Club, where, in an off-the-record chat, he clearly insinuated that Siddon wasn't long for the Cabinet. I was surprised, not to mention slightly terrified, by his candour. But he just couldn't believe that one of his ministers would have the gall to pull a stunt like that. I don't know how, but Siddon survived not only that summer's shuffle, but the major one a year later.

The pension climb-down was not our only disaster that summer. Soon after Parliament rose, the American icebreaker "Polar Sea" sailed unmolested, and without official Canadian permission, through the Northwest Passage, which we claimed as our territorial waters, thereby adding one more conundrum to the items already on the negotiating table with the Americans. The Prime Minister assured us that the White House had nothing to do with the "Polar Sea" affair, insisting that our friends in the Reagan administration were still on our side. That didn't help when it came to explaining what good it was to have a friendly White House if the State Department — which was supposed to be under White House control — could order the violation of Canadian sovereignty.

The "Polar Sea" voyage may not have meant much in the grand scheme of the universe, but it showed, once more, that what we said — the Arctic is ours — and what happened — no it isn't — were two different things. The strongest government in Canadian history was beginning to look like a wimp, and a vacillating wimp, at that.

We were taking a pounding in the press, and, as September approached, the media talked more about our embarrassments than our achievements. The *Globe and Mail*, for example, ran a series called "The Perils of Power" that did nothing to polish our image. Still, with some lurches, we continued to sit comfortably atop the public opinion polls. The poll released on August 15, which had been taken between July 11 and 13, right after the indexation capitulation, reduced our lead to forty per cent of decided voters, with thirty-three per cent for the Liberals. Then we floated back up to forty-six per cent, and, later in September, we were comfortably out in front, with forty-eight per cent. This moved the Prime Minister to say that, as usual, the Boys didn't know what they were talking about.

What was happening, although we didn't realize it at the time, was that the perception of incompetence and deceit which would plague us later was just beginning to sink in. We still believed ourselves to be invincible, but we were not — far from it. The honeymoon was coming to an end; our glory days were finished, and the delicious irony of it is that, despite the humiliation of the de-indexation tussle, we still didn't get it.

We soon would.

CHAPTER THIRTEEN

Tuna, and Other Big Stinks

T he fall of 1985 began for us with the birth of the Mulroneys' fourth child, Nicolas, who arrived, with exquisite timing, on the first anniversary of the glorious Fourth of September, 1984. Who would have thought that this is where the really rough sledding was about to begin? Certainly not us. We were aware that there were tensions building up that would have to be defused in due course, but no one expected in these last sweet, melancholy days of the fading summer that we were about to step on another land-mine. It all started so prosaically, with a can of tuna. At least the Fall of Troy was precipitated by a struggle over the heart of a woman; we were about to be undone by a can of fish.

I was at the National Press Club the night of September 17 when Justin de Beaucamp, then Press Secretary to Flora MacDonald, came by to tell me that the CBC's public affairs show, *fifth estate*, was just about to air a report that would be most damaging for the government.

"What's it about?" I asked him.

"It's about John Fraser (the Fisheries minister)," he said. "He might have to resign."

There were few people left at the Press Club, so I tuned into *fifth estate* in time to catch the report. It maintained that, against the advice of the Fisheries department inspectors, the minister

123

had authorized the distribution of close to a million cans of tuna to the nation's supermarkets. According to the CBC, the tuna was rancid and in a state of decomposition; it was, according to prevailing standards, unfit for human consumption. The company involved was Star Kist Canada, Inc. of New Brunswick. The *fifth estate* segment also included an interview with Fraser in which he said that he was trying to give the struggling company a break when he overruled the inspectors. "Perhaps they were being too severe," he said. "And I gave the benefit of the doubt to the company."

It didn't take a doctorate in political science to know that we had a problem. My first reaction was to phone the Prime Minister directly. But I held back — better to phone Bill Fox first; he was better at breaking these things.

"Bill," I told him, "I think this one's serious. Maybe you should talk to The Boss."

According to what he told me later, Bill had called him that night. "I told him we can't fool around with this," he said, "that it was a question of the public health."

In our minds, the minister would have to resign. If he had indeed gone against the inspectors in favour of the company, it amounted to a political battle we couldn't hope to win. But the Prime Minister didn't agree. As he told me, "It's unthinkable that John Fraser would do something that would endanger public health."

I didn't know Fraser personally, but I was aware of his reputation as a competent and compassionate individual. If everything I had heard about him was true, then Brian Mulroney was right. However, I also knew that we'd never win this one in the court of public opinion; so better to amputate the diseased limb before it infected the rest of the body.

On the day after the story broke, we had a war council in the second floor boardroom of the Langevin Block. From the outset, most of Mulroney's advisers were telling him to dump Fraser, but Bernard Roy was inclined to wait before doing anything so rash — although he communicated the majority's view to The Boss. For him, always sensitive to the human factor, there was a man's life involved here.

Just the same, John Fraser was only part of the problem. Remembering the lessons of Watergate that I'd learned as a reporter, I said at one tense moment during the discussion, "One thing we have to be clear on is that nobody here knew about this before yesterday, right?"

I asked the question because I knew this was going to be the thrust of the opposition attack: what did the Prime Minister know and when did he know it? There was a short but heavy silence around the table. Then, taking off his glasses with a despondent gesture, Bernard's assistant Ian Anderson said: "I knew." A butterfly winging across the room would have sounded like a 747. "Yes, I knew," Anderson repeated.

Fox and I exchanged glances. We both knew we were cooked.

The story of Ian Anderson and the tuna affair is one of the saddest of my stay in the PMO. He made a mistake, a purely human mistake, and the consequences were incalculable.

Anderson, who at the time was Director of Communications, had been visited two months earlier by two officials from the Fisheries Department who were worried that a report on the tuna business would be aired by the CTV network that night. They could have come at a better time. Anderson suffered from chronic back pain that had kept him in bed most of that day. He listened to their story and told them to find a spokesman in the department to defend the minister's decision, if necessary. Then, the report they were worried about never appeared (it was withheld on the advice of CTV's lawyers), and Anderson told himself that they'd gotten excited over nothing. No more than John Fraser, who made the fateful decision to release the questionable tuna on the market, did Ian Anderson think for one minute that he was endangering the public's health. And he didn't mention the matter to anyone else in the Prime Minister's Office.

Bernard Roy was particularly vigorous in Anderson's defence. Still, we all knew that his knowledge of the essential facts of the matter two months earlier was surely going to cause problems for us.

"Did anyone else know?" I asked desperately.

We would find out later that Pat MacAdam, responsible for liaison between the Conservative caucus and the PMO, had heard rumours about the tuna business, which began with a ministerial directive issued on April 29, long before Ian Anderson had even heard about it. MacAdam has been haunting the corridors and byways of Parliament Hill for so many years that he hears everything that's talked about. But to survive here you also have to know that all the stories you hear aren't true, or exactly as told. I'm sure he has heard much worse things than the tuna rumour before and after September 1985, over which he didn't necessarily feel the need to raise a national alert.

There was much more to come. Even though most of his advisers told Mulroney to call for Fraser's resignation, Mulroney obstinately declined. He refused to believe there was really anything serious in this business. I don't know if I admired his loyalty more than I deplored his stubbornness, but I knew he was too smart not to realize that hanging in with Fraser would put him at a political disadvantage. If he was ready to run the risk, then, as I always said, it was his head on the block.

On Wednesday, the 18th, the opposition focus, as we'd expected, was squarely on tuna, with both opposition parties demanding John Fraser's head. Fraser and Mulroney insisted there was no danger to the public health from the cans of tuna in question and refused to recall the shipment from the supermarket shelves. Later that afternoon, however, Fraser got a direct order from Mulroney to do precisely that. The next day, the Prime Minister told the Commons that he had reversed his position to calm mounting anxiety among the population about the rancid fish. Fraser said, in my presence in Erik Nielsen's office, that he was prepared to do whatever he was told. And the Prime Minister continued to support him, in private as in public.

By then, some supermarkets had already begun clearing their shelves of Star Kist tuna. The federal order to remove the rest was issued by Health Minister Jake Epp, officially at Fraser's request. This is the way it was choreographed by the PMO.

On Friday September 20, the Prime Minister told a press conference that it was "pretty damn obvious" that the cans of tuna in question should never have been released for distribution. He added that he had them recalled as soon as he heard about the matter. During the Question Period that followed, Fraser was confronted with a statement by the Productivity Research Council of New Brunswick, saying that the minister had released the shipment of tainted tuna before the council had submitted its final conclusions on whether the tuna was edible. Fraser had been basing his defence on the council's report all week long.

As if that wasn't enough, Fraser, who later explained himself by saying that he never avoided reporters in his life, said in the vortex of a rowdy scrum outside the Commons that the Prime Minister's Office had known about the tainted tuna shipment for weeks and that he, not Mulroney, had ordered the recall. The Prime Minister had not been consulted.

He was flat-out contradicting the Prime Minister on not one, but two counts. I spent the rest of Friday afternoon trying to figure out a way to put a favourable face on what Fraser had blurted out. But the transcript of the scrum was quite categorical, and it couldn't be erased. The Prime Minister wondered how Fraser could let himself blunder into a pack of hungry reporters after he had already been feeble in his Commons responses.

The first thing to do was to demand a correction from Fraser. But this was difficult because he was essentially telling the truth. Someone in the Prime Minister's Office had known of the affair since July, even though it hadn't been brought to Mulroney's attention before it blew up on TV two months later. And the Prime Minister himself may not have ordered Fraser to recall the shipment of tuna, but as Mulroney said when he heard about Fraser's scrum: "When Erik or Bernard tells him something, it's like he's talking to me!"

John Fraser's hours as a minister of the Crown were numbered. This time, as Fox said, the Prime Minister couldn't let a member of his cabinet contradict him in public. Fraser had already said he'd do anything we asked, so on the weekend, the Prime Minister asked for his resignation. It became official on Monday, September 23, 1985.

But that didn't put an end to it. Now the opposition trained its guns on the head of the government who had twiddled his thumbs, even as his staff was aware of the problem. Overnight, John Fraser went from villain to martyr, having paid the price for the government's incompetence. Brian Mulroney was beside himself. He hadn't lied and had acted honourably at all times; he had tried to understand his staff and he had tried to understand his minister. Yet, his personal credibility was gurgling down the drain.

We were still up to our nostrils in rancid tuna when, two days after Fraser's resignation, the volcano heaved again. I was on an advance trip outside Ottawa that day, September 25, when I called the PMO for a routine check-in. I was told that Communications Minister Marcel Masse was about to resign from cabinet. Masse had apparently learned that he was under investigation by the RCMP, as were a number of other members from both sides of the House, on the suspicion that his election spending during the last campaign exceeded the legal amount. Masse's resignation statement came at the end of an unruly Question Period dominated by the Fraser resignation, so when Masse dropped his bomb the entire House, along with the Press Gallery, was stupefied.

"What the hell is going on back there?" I said to myself as I hung up the phone.

Masse wasn't just a minister. He was, with Roch La Salle, the only Quebec cabinet member reasonably well known outside his immediate family. After tuna, this was a big fish to swallow. The Prime Minister had heard about it only the night before when Bernard Roy broke the news without mentioning the name of the minister in question. I never had any reason to believe that Mulroney knew anything about the Masse affair before Tuesday, September 24th. If anyone in the office was aware of the investigation, he was extraordinarily discreet. An RCMP investigation is somewhat more serious than a possible report on CTV on cans of tuna. An investigation into Marcel Masse wouldn't have been merely a rumour.

The next day, Jerry Lampert, the national director of the Progressive Conservative Party, gave an interview to Canadian Press. Asked when he first heard about the Masse investigation, he said, according to the CP transcript, "Informally, by conversation, it was probably a couple of months ago that I was informed."

"That it had been turned over to the RCMP?" probed the CP reporter.

"That it had been turned over to the RCMP for investigation, that's right," said Lampert. "I think it was probably a couple of months ago, but that's at best a guess on my part."

The interview continued:

Q: Did you inform the leader of the party, or are you under some legal stricture not to?

A: I am not under any legal stricture, (I) did not inform the leader, but had discussions with people in the Prime Minister's Office, so that they were aware.

Q: And who would you have informed in the PMO?

A: Well, you know, there may have been a couple of people, but I don't want to put anybody on the spot, you know, with respect to that. That would not be fair.

Q: Mr. (Pat) MacAdam?

A: No, it would not have been MacAdam.

Q: Was it the Principal Secretary?

A: I can't recall if it was Bernard Roy or whether it may have been some other person as well. I'd have to go back and try to

128

Me, Bonnie and Fox during happier times on the campaign
plane "Manicouagan I."
Scott Grant

The Prime Minister with Ministers Robert de Cotret and
Michael Wilson at the First Ministers' Conference in Regina.
Fred Doucet and I are in on the conversation.

Prime Minister Brian Mulroney with Bernard Roy (centre) and
Lucien Bouchard in Quebec City.

The Boss congratulating me after the Quebec summit.
Peter Bregg

The Mulroneys with Helmut Kohl. Mila is sporting her babushka look.

Bill Fox and Brian Mulroney with Ronald Reagan. (I'm in the background.)

With John Paul II
Foto Felici

Stewart Murray, Marc Lortie and me at the Vatican.
Mike Duffy

The Boys, in the desert of Senegal.
Mike Duffy

A typical "organized" scrum.
Andy Clark

The Prime Minister bantering with the Boys during the campaign: Peter Moser, from Southam; Pierre April, from Presse Canadienne; Maurice Jannard, from *La Presse*; Maurice Godin, from Radio Canada. *Globe and Mail* columnist, Geoff Simpson is in the background.

Scott Grant

The Langevin second-floor boardroom. Charley McMillan, Bill Fox, Scott Norquay, me, and Fred Doucet with his back turned.

Andy Clark

Here are Fox, myself, Les Richardson (with glasses), and Peter Bregg, then official photographer.

Bill McCarthy

Brian and I at a hot dog stand in Chatham, Ontario.

Andy Clark

The Boss with my three daughters Marie-France, Valérie and
Brigitte.

Andy Clark

Bonnie and me.

recall, and I just don't know.

Q: But these were senior people?

A: Oh yes, senior people in the PMO, yeah, yeah.

The clear impression was of another coverup. Now, I will never know if Jerry Lampert just went off his rocker that day or whether the "senior people" he was talking about refused to stand up and be counted. But I remember that when Bernard Roy was asked the question directly, he shrugged his shoulders.

"He never told me that," he said.

We tried to find out if anyone had heard so much as a hint of a rumour about it two months earlier, or even the week before. No one had heard a thing. I don't believe Bernard Roy is capable of telling a lie, and I don't believe that anyone around the table that day, and that included most of the senior PMO staffers, had any reason to lie. And as far as I know, Lampert never identified anyone, in public or in private.

Why would Jerry Lampert say such a thing? Who knows? In the end, Masse was cleared and rejoined the Cabinet, but in the meantime we all suffered.

Then, along came Fred McCain, the MP for Carleton–Charlotte in New Brunswick, the riding where the ill-fated Star Kist plant was situated. McCain, who has spent just about all of his time as an MP in Ottawa in total obscurity, told Canadian Press reporter Bob Fife on September 25 that he had raised the tuna matter at the Conservative national caucus a week before the news broke and that the Prime Minister had been present. In other words, the Prime Minister knew earlier than he'd admitted about the stink in Fraser's office. Fred McCain was never for a second regarded as cabinet material by anyone but himself, but he was an elected representative and a member of our caucus who was contradicting the Prime Minister, even though, as he said later, he wasn't aware of the contradiction when he spoke to Fife.

It was totally absurd. There's no way the Prime Minister could have pretended not to have heard about the matter if it had been raised in caucus a week before, with 210 MPs (potentially) as witnesses. Somebody would have talked, and Mulroney isn't foolish enough to expose himself to that kind of risk. But as Bob Fife told me: "What do you expect me to do? He said it to me."

And so he had, and Fife couldn't help but write it. I would have done exactly the same thing.

Throughout this tempest, Mulroney would say that it would blow itself out soon, that people soon forget things like this in politics. "In a year it'll have been forgotten," he said.

But he was getting fed up with being called a liar. It was a hard position from which to defend himself; he couldn't stand up and say, "I am not a liar." Lampert, like Fraser before him, issued a denial, as did Fred McCain, though he admitted that between his original statement and his denial later on, he had talked to Pat MacAdam, Mulroney's caucus watchdog. In each case, the opposition escalated its accusations by charging that the Prime Minister had not only lied, but had put pressure on those who tried to set the record straight. This thing was growing like a cancer; we were starting to wonder where it would all stop. The Liberals, we thought, would never have fallen over each other, the way we were doing, when they were in power.

On Friday September 27, the Prime Minister was scheduled to give a press conference. I was still Deputy Press Secretary at the time, and it was one of those rare times when I was to accompany Mulroney to the National Press Theatre. On the way over in the car Mulroney asked me pensively what I thought of the Fraser business. I told him I was moved by the human drama of the whole affair, by a man who, while absolutely sincere, lacked judgement and paid the price by losing an office to which he long aspired. I still remember John Fraser's face when he shook my hand after the resignation, thanking me for the help I'd been to him during the affair. He wasn't trying to be sarcastic in any way, and I felt small, knowing I'd been one of the people who had called for his resignation from the first day.

"He's a sincerely nice guy," said Mulroney of Fraser. "He'd never do anything to hurt anybody."

Mulroney asked me if I remembered John Boccabella, a catcher for the Montreal Expos in the early days of the franchise. I said I remembered him well. And he told a story of how Boccabella, in a game back at old Jarry Park, struck out three times in four appearances at the plate. When the reporters thundered into the dressing room after the game, one of them asked Boc how he felt.

"I feel good," he replied, "but I don't think I did too well."

As though he had been a tick in the upholstery at that moment, the reporter who asked the first question at the news conference wanted to know precisely that. How does it feel, he asked, having gone through the last two weeks? Of course Mulroney had the Boccabella anecdote handy. He seemed natural and at ease, even humble in the face of fate. He was at his best when confronted with adversity, something he would have ample opportunity to prove as early as the next week.

The week began with the announcement that the Northland Bank of Calgary had gone belly up. The Canadian Commercial Bank of Edmonton had done the same at the beginning of September. The government had to announce that it would cost the taxpayers more than $1 billion to reimburse uninsured depositors. This was far worse than the putrid tuna or the investigation into Marcel Masse's campaign spending. Two Canadian financial institutions had just gone bankrupt in the space of a month. One never gets used to seeing banks fail. Talk to those who lived through the Depression. But I remember saying to the Prime Minister that I'd rather see the opposition hammer away at the bank failures than the tainted tuna. "Bad fish is something the average guy can understand instantly. Banks are complicated things that most people don't really understand."

I included myself in this analysis, of course. Mulroney was evidently more nervous, although he believed that even if the opposition attacked him for the billion-dollar reimbursement, he'd look good in the eyes of westerners, who were unused to getting that kind of benefit from their central government.

The minister responsible for financial institutions, Barbara McDougall, stood up to the opposition attacks in the House like an old pro. I was convinced we weren't losing this debate. Yet, in the context of the other "scandals" it helped the pundits, who were describing us as a government whose rudder had snapped.

Ah, but there was more to come. Suzanne Blais-Grenier had not been a great success as Environment Minister, but she turned out to be quite some traveller, and the matter of her limo bills soon deepened our misery. Two days after the second bank closed, Blais-Grenier became the target of the opposition wolves in the wake of an item by veteran Southam columnist Chris Young, whose credentials and sources were impeccable. The column charged that the minister had abused her authority by wasting tens of thousands of taxpayer dollars on frivolous trips abroad. There was a visit to Paris the previous Easter, followed by a jaunt to Stockholm, and another continental tour in July that took her to France, Finland and the USSR. The second trip also included a thirteen-day vacation in Corsica, for which the minister paid out of her own pocket. The final tally for her trips, compiled by the media through Access to Information laws, came to more than $30,000, of which $4,000 was for limousine service.

Since Blais-Grenier was never very good in the House of Commons, the Deputy Prime Minister, "Yukon" Erik, undertook to weather the opposition attack in Question Period. And what a show he put on! Everybody on the floor of the Commons was stupefied and the reporters practically fell out of the Press Gallery when he made his reply. Nielsen claimed that Blais-Grenier had been the victim of a racist attack. The Prime Minister wasn't in the House, and I was watching the proceedings at the Langevin Block. I almost gagged when I heard Nielsen's answer.

Speaking of the reporter, Chris Young, the Deputy Prime Minister said: " . . . One who I have regarded at some time as having some professional integrity, but, after having read the column and the article yesterday in that newspaper and the manner in which it was followed up today, I ask myself the question as to whether the motivation wasn't to arouse some kind of racism here."

How could Nielsen think anyone would take him seriously? Who did he think he was attacking? Not someone from the opposition, but a top journalist like Chris Young. It didn't take long before I was inundated with calls from my former Quebec colleagues. They didn't want information so much as to laugh in my face. The worst of it was that even if Nielsen's tactic was not directly choreographed by the Prime Minister, it was certainly inspired by him. He had alluded to the same thing in private conversations in remarking on the vehemence with which the hounds had set off on Blais-Grenier's trail. He had also made a reference to this a month earlier on *Le Point*, the CBC French network's version of *The Journal*, where he had told interviewer Pierre Nadeau that "notwithstanding the opinions of certain anglophones," Blais-Grenier had turned in an "historic" performance in the environment department.

Though he demonstrated exemplary solidarity and angelic patience with Blais-Grenier in public, inside he was boiling. What he couldn't forgive was that Blais-Grenier took her trips while the government was having its first serious problems with the row over de-indexing old age pensions. He had already been strict about foreign trips by cabinet ministers, and he became even stricter after that. "If they want to travel, let them travel inside the country," he said.

What he didn't know at the time was that the Blais-Grenier episode set a precedent that would come to haunt us. For the first time ever, expense accounts for ministers' travels would be made freely available to the media under the Access to Information machinery that came into operation after we took power. We would remember Suzanne Blais-Grenier when the media seized on his and his wife's expenses on subsequent trips to France and Asia.

Our troubles continued. Two more of our cabinet ministers contributed to our black fall with statements that reflected poorly on the administration.

The first was Justice Minister John Crosbie, who told a radio interviewer that the Prime Minister's office personnel wasn't up to scratch.

"Perhaps you could say they aren't as politically astute or as politically attuned as they should be," he said.

Crosbie, whose verbal flights, often ill-considered, we were starting to get used to, subsequently said he didn't mean to say what he'd said.

Then there was James Kelleher, the Minister for International Trade, who told a group of reporters in Halifax that free trade wouldn't hurt the province's textile industry, thinking Nova Scotia didn't have one.

"I won't be too concerned," he said, "I don't think Nova Scotia has a textile industry." Nova Scotia's industrial development minister, Ross Thornhill, standing beside Kelleher while he made his statement, rolled his eyes toward the heavens as the minister planted his foot in his mouth.

"I'll have Stanfield's call him tonight," he said, referring to the long-established Nova Scotia textile firm whose founder was none other than the father of our former party leader, Robert Stanfield. Textiles were, in fact, the major industry of three of the province's cities.

On October 8, the Prime Minister attended the first game of the play-off series between the Toronto Blue Jays and the Kansas City Royals at Exhibition Stadium. He threw out the traditional first ball and was warmly applauded by the crowd, much to our delight and relief. But part-way through the game, as he made his way to a radio booth, some fans spotted him and started up a swelling chant: "Tu-na, tu-na, tu-na."

I had to force myself not to laugh, but I didn't find it so funny when one guy, his courage fed by beer, shouted "You're a bum, Mulroney!"

The Prime Minister kept smiling throughout the episode, but if he had any illusions about the political consequences of the last few weeks, he was rudely disabused that night.

CHAPTER FOURTEEN

Back on Track

W e needed a miracle, and fast! The opposition was cutting us to ribbons in Question Period, day after day. The spate of ministerial resignations, the scandals, patronage, and our inability to project our good intentions all added up to the picture of a government squandering the biggest majority in Canadian history. We were haunted by the ghost of John Diefenbaker. Was it possible that history could repeat itself? Could we be going through the disintegration that beset the Conservatives the last time they won big, in 1958? Maybe we were really the natural opposition party, put into office every twenty years only because the electorate sometimes gets bored with the Liberals.

The Nassau trip was coming at us like a freight train. It was to be the first Commonwealth conference for the Prime Minister. I was terrified by the very thought of going. After the tempest back home, what would we look like encamped on the beaches of Nassau for ten days in October at a conference for the feeble vestiges of the British Empire? How could we feed our contingent of media wolves with positive material for such a long time?

What I saw in Nassau on an advance trip with Stewart Murray (by this time we'd become an inseparable combination) was hardly reassuring. Media relations there were in the hands of one Bill Kalis, whose credentials included a stint at the *New York Times*; but Bill, now in his sixties, had been on the islands for some time and had come to adopt the island pace of life. In Nassau, as in most of the Caribbean, people work on two speeds: slow and stop. Nothing seems to excite anyone. Life proceeds according to the rhythm of the waves, kissed by the perpetual sunshine, and in town there was a flourishing drug trade that did nothing for local efficiency.

Three weeks before the conference, Bill Kalis still couldn't tell me how the pool system for the media would function. (A media pool, you will recall, is a reduced press contingent that covers events where there isn't room for the whole mob.) Since pool reporters are supposed to share their information with their colleagues, they are particularly useful for the TV crews, who can exchange cassettes. When I asked Kalis if the pool passes would have their own numbering system, he said, "It's an idea that should be looked at."

At the protocol office they couldn't tell us who was going to speak at the conference opening, and, of course, we had no idea of the order in which the leaders would speak. Or even if there was going to be a formal closing ceremony. All of this may seem insignificant now, but these were things that had to be looked after, and at this point we had enough problems back home that we didn't have time to tear our hair out over the details of a conference for which we weren't even responsible. We couldn't believe that the people in Nassau were being so calm about it all. Maybe we should have taken a few lessons from them.

It occurred to me that we should try to take control of the media relations process at the conference. I had to get a press room for the Canadian media apart from the rest. I felt it was the only way to control our media contingent, to peddle them our line without having them distracted by too many outside influences. Our plan was to take over two whole floors of the media hotel, the Ambassador Beach, and to use the presidential suite at one end of one of the floors as our press centre. That way we could keep the Boys amused, fed, and happy, just a few steps from their hotel rooms.

Kalis, along with the other Bahamians, couldn't understand why we were insisting so firmly on being apart from the others, trying to explain to us that in the Commonwealth, all countries are equal. In the end they let us have what we wanted, although there were stories reminiscent of the London–Bonn adventure — that they found us hard to deal with. But they were very happy to take us up on our offer to lend them two armour-plated limousines to meet the security requirements for British Prime Minister Margaret Thatcher and Indian Prime Minister Rajiv Gandhi. There was no such thing as an armoured limo on the island.

The conference took place in the Cable Beach Hotel, a fairly new establishment on the outskirts of the capital, and our media contingent couldn't have been better behaved at the nearby Ambassador Beach. We could always tell which camera crew was on duty by checking the beach. If the crews from Global and CTV were there, it was the CBC's turn to shoot the stock footage. And it wasn't hard to keep track of the reporters. They were mostly in their rooms, in the press centre, on the golf course, or around the pool demolishing "Bahama Mamas," a delightful rum concoction, as they waited for the daily Commonwealth and Canadian briefings. Because most of the conference agenda, except the opening and the photo ops, unfolded behind closed doors, they had little to do for most of the day. To my great relief, most of them made the most of the local diversions instead of climbing up our backs.

The Prime Minister, meanwhile, was working morning, noon and night to convince Margaret Thatcher to support sanctions against South Africa. It was a little like trying to sell girdles to an anorexic. But in trying, Mulroney forged a close bond with India's Rajiv Gandhi. The Boss was greatly impressed by the serenity Gandhi projected, even though his mother had been assassinated not long before. This is also where he got close to the leaders of the African front-line states, people like President Kenneth Kaunda of Zambia, who became an ardent supporter. "He's a good man, Brian," I remember him saying. Mulroney's comportment at the Nassau conference was of crucial importance a year-and-a-half later, when he himself went to visit the front-line states to preach against apartheid. His credentials for the Africa trip were forged at the Nassau conference.

It wasn't easy to resist the temptation to compete with Australia's flamboyant Prime Minister, Bob Hawke, who tried day after day to steal the spotlight with proposals that were bound to be unacceptable to Britain. But Mulroney told us that Hawke's proposals weren't going anywhere and that we should stick to our strategy.

I was convinced that a good part of the battle could be won with logistics. If the media were well served, if they knew exactly what was going on, if we were available to answer questions, then we had a chance to make them forget, momentarily, the disaster we had left behind us at home. I got up every day at 6:00 a.m., no matter what time I got to bed, and padded through the empty hotel corridors to the Commonwealth conference secretariat to get the pick of the pool passes for that day's events. It meant our reporters would get the choice spots, and they'd love us for it. And I was lucky. The guy in charge of handing out pool passes was a Canadian from Toronto, working on contract. I didn't have to explain to him what the CBC was. He got so used to seeing me in the morning that he'd lay out my pool passes before I got there. He even created new pools, just for our benefit.

"I thought there wasn't going to be a pool for this event," I told him one day.

"Well there is one now," he said with a smile.

Now, I'm not going to pretend I didn't down my share of "Bahama Mamas" on this trip. There are too many living witnesses for that. Still, I never worked so hard as I did on that trip. The days that started at 6:00 a.m. rarely finished before midnight. That was the work part. The pressure and our desire to please were constant. In the end it paid off. On the evening of October 20, our dedication to organization allowed us to pull off the coup of the conference.

The Commonwealth leaders had cloistered themselves at Lyford Cay. It was part of the tradition of these conferences that the leaders would leave the rest of the world behind for what was called the "weekend retreat." It was here, while the rest of us slipped into tourist gear, that the other leaders planned to put the heat on Britain to sign the final communiqué that included sanctions against South Africa. It was here where Brian Mulroney's talents as a negotiator came to the fore.

When, late Sunday night, they came to an agreement, Bill Fox called me from Lyford Cay. "We've got an agreement on South Africa," he said. "Don't tell anybody. Andy Clark (the PM's official photographer) is going to bring over a bootlegged copy of the agreement. Make copies. The Boss will be there within an hour to give a press conference."

Suddenly everything was happening at once. An agreement, The Boss, a press conference . . . now! And on top of that Fox wanted my hotel room to park The Boss while he waited for the press conference to start.

"You know, he might want to go to the washroom or something like that," said Fox.

"But in my room!" I wailed.

I hated to think of what or who he'd find there, because I hadn't had time to tidy up for a few days now. So I got out of the proposal by saying that my room was just a few steps from the press room, and it wasn't a good idea to expose The Boss to the media before the press conference. Better to use a room on the floor below.

Andy Clark arrived with the clandestine copy of the agreement, which proposed modified economic sanctions. We had insisted on having our own photocopier flown in from Miami. When the Prime Minister started his press conference, we distributed the copies. The reporters remarked that the paper they were printed on was still warm. The Commonwealth authorities, on the other hand, were beside themselves. In their press room, word got around that the Canadians were already distributing copies of the agreement. So, the reporters from all the Commonwealth countries descended on our press room where we happily handed out copies to them. Meanwhile, the Commonwealth press people were wondering how we'd done it; they were able to get our copies only an hour later. We had pulled a "White House"; it was a lesson from the Shamrock summit that had borne fruit.

The Bonn lesson had been learned, too; at the news conference, Brian Mulroney showed exemplary humility. The *Globe and Mail* later editorialized:

"Brian Mulroney went to the Nassau summit without preconceptions that the Commonwealth was an anachronism, but he had other lessons to absorb. His debut in the leaders' league had been the Bonn summit of industrialized nations last May, and on that occasion Mr. Mulroney reaped ridicule with his inflated public accounts of his skills as a mediator between the United States and France.

"At Nassau, by contrast, Mr. Mulroney has understood that effective diplomacy can mean quiet diplomacy. He has shown some modesty in his claims of credit for the compromise."

On his way back to Ottawa, the Prime Minister stopped off in New York to deliver his maiden speech to the United Nations, then celebrating its fortieth anniversary. Advised by his ambassador to the United Nations, Stephen Lewis, the ex-leader of the Ontario NDP, Mulroney eloquently pursued his attack against the racist regime in South Africa, with the result that leaders from a dozen African nations rose to shake his hand afterward. He was on Cloud Nine that day. He needed something like this to lift his spirits.

When we finally got back aboard the Armed Forces 707 that would take us back to the frozen North, I felt like celebrating. We were heading back to winter, but the two weeks of Nassau summer had been invigorating. When I asked for a beer, I was told there was none. Bill Fox told me there was nothing to drink on board except cases of champagne. The Boss and Fox were reluctant to break it out because they worried about what the scribes would think of our modesty if we turned the trip home into a champagne flight.

"What kind of champagne is it?" I asked him.

"Ontario bubbly," he replied.

"Break it out," I said. "That's not champagne!"

Better to serve them that than nothing, I thought. But I was wrong. Sure enough, a few of the anglo reporters with a Calvinist bent had to remark on the "champagne" on the homeward flight in subsequent stories. Fox commented, "You've got to realize that, for the anglos, Ontario champagne is champagne."

There was something symbolic in the fact that the beverage with which we celebrated our Nassau victory was not the real thing; we would soon be up to our hips in trouble again.

CHAPTER FIFTEEN

Down Again

I could never forget this scene.

We were in downtown Edmonton, before a vacant lot where the mud had frozen in patterns that made it look like a lunar surface. A snowstorm was just starting. Barely 250 people, half of them demonstrators, had come to see and hear the Prime Minister of Canada. Brian and Mila Mulroney were seated, flanked by local and federal dignitaries, on a covered stage built in the middle of nowhere specially for this event. Mila, with a scarf over her head against the cold, looked as if she had stepped straight out of *Dr. Zhivago*. And what was the occasion? The sod-turning ceremony for a new $200 million federal government building that was to bear the startlingly original name "Canada Place."

So here was the Prime Minister, sitting straight backed on this wind-whipped stage at the start of a snowstorm, confronted by demonstrators who mocked the tan he had picked up in Nassau. When he noted in his speech that this was "a unique occasion," we understood for whom the message was intended. It would be a frosty Friday before we ever laid on a sod-turning ceremony again.

I recount this episode by way of showing how we were constantly frustrated in our image-building efforts, unable to score points even when the odds were rigged in our favour. Here the Prime Minister was announcing the start of construction on a long-promised project, one that would create jobs in the area, yet the day's headline from the event was about how he was greeted by demonstrators. Then there was the depressing picture that ran in the local paper showing the Mulroneys huddled together in their seats, like two turkeys trapped in a snowstorm, he with his tongue sticking out of his mouth, and she in what had come to be known as her "Babushka look." In this black fall of 1985 it seemed that everything we touched turned into disaster and derision.

In Quebec, for example, Pierre-Marc Johnson had succeeded René Lévesque as premier and leader of the Parti Québécois. Soon after, he had called a provincial election, and now he was running against the needle-nosed phoenix, Robert Bourassa, risen from the ashes of defeat.

Mulroney knew both men well. Bourassa was a personal friend of many years' standing, and though The Boss never said outright how he'd vote, he was convinced from the start that Bourassa and the Liberals would win. He was convinced that with Bourassa in power in Quebec, great things could be accomplished. But there was a problem. Having no provincial Conservative party, Mulroney had drawn support from both nationalist provincial Liberals and Parti Québécois workers during the last federal election. It was risky to tilt in favour of either side, for fear of offending the other to the point where it would hurt us in the next federal campaign. He was so intent on remaining neutral that he even refused to endorse a fledgling provincial Conservative party, under the leadership of André Asselin.

But while neutrality looks good on paper, it's hard to practise. The provincial parties watched our every move, as did the media, prepared to jump on the slightest sign of favouritism. The best example of our inability to walk the tightrope was the announcement that Hyundai would build a new car assembly plant in Quebec at Bromont — the perfect example of what not to do in public relations.

Hyundai was one of Mulroney's babies. "The auto industry is perfect," he'd say. "It doesn't pollute, it never stops and it creates lots of jobs. They're laughing in Southern Ontario."

With most of the auto industry's infrastructure centred in Ontario, it was difficult to give Quebec a leg up into the business. Hyundai was the break that Mulroney had been waiting for. Weren't Quebeckers the biggest buyers of Korean cars in the country? So why shouldn't the factory be in Quebec? For the Prime Minister this was incontrovertible logic. He told me what he'd told then Industry Minister Sinclair Stevens, when he went to negotiate the car plant deal with the Koreans.

"I told him," he said, "to come back with a plant for Quebec or not to come back at all."

The Parti Québécois, of course, was also keenly interested in the car plant negotiations. A $300 million plant announcement in the middle of an election campaign would be about as welcome as a case of Dom Perignon at a midnight choir session. The PQ, which had been battered against the ropes by Robert Bourassa and was on the verge of losing the election, began to lobby furiously with us to speed the announcement of the Hyundai plant. At the PMO, the Prime Minister's advisers were divided; some favoured the Liberals, others the PQ, and all were keenly aware of the dangers involved.

As only we could, we wound up getting all the blame and none of the credit when the announcement finally came. Pierre-Marc Johnson, accompanied by Hyundai officials, announced in mid-November that the plant would be built in Quebec's verdant Eastern Townships. On the Prime Minister's orders, no federal minister was present. It was as though we had no part in the deal, yet we were sharing the cost of the $100 million subsidy offered the company to locate in Quebec. And to put the cherry on the sundae, the opposition, as well as Ontario's Liberal Industry Minister, Hugh O'Neil, accused us of helping out the separatist Péquistes at the expense of the Liberals. It was a textbook bungle. We had transformed what should have been good news into bad news. We were trapped by our own indecision, consumed with arguments over standing room as the parade passed us by.

Nor was the Prime Minister pleased with our talents as communicators when, two days after the Quebec election, which Bourassa won handily, he travelled to Chicago to give a speech on liberalized trade at the invitation of *Time* Magazine. The speech made headlines back in Canada, but there was a sliver of a story in the *Chicago Tribune*, buried inside, and no mention at all, save for *Time*, of course, in the rest of the American media. Mulroney was furious; he couldn't understand how we could have failed to sell his message to the American media. He also let his unhappiness be known the next day when he met with the *Tribune's* editorial board at his hotel. It was useless for us to try to explain that the American media don't put themselves out for anything.

But if the Hyundai episode and the Chicago speech showed our weaknesses on the PR side, it was the privatization of the Toronto aircraft manufacturer, de Havilland, that same fall, that best showed how banalities and family quarrels can scupper the best communications strategy.

It all began when the Prime Minister's Office decided to get involved in the affair. We were about to announce the sale of de Havilland, then a money-losing federal Crown corporation, to the American aircraft giant, Boeing Corporation. It was a good deal from a business standpoint, but we knew the opposition was going to attack us for selling out to the evil Americans. Sinclair Stevens, at this time Minister of Regional Economic Expansion, knew more than anyone else about the sale, and his office had prepared a communications strategy. But at the PMO, we weren't persuaded that the department's strategy would convince the media — and hence the public — of the deal's positive aspects. We also needed a francophone spokesman, since Stevens didn't speak any French, a problem that haunted us with a number of unilingual ministers. Treasury Board Chairman Robert de Cotret, who would be directly responsible for the privatization, was selected. However, it seemed Stevens, just coming back from a major surgical operation, didn't like us tinkering with his communications strategy and didn't want to share the spotlight with de Cotret.

The result was that the Treasury Board President went to face the media alone, while Stevens sulked. De Cotret had been well briefed, but it was Stevens who really knew what it was all about and would have made it all go more smoothly. Instead, he stood us up.

The upshot was that de Cotret was stuck defending the de Havilland sale in the Commons for the next two weeks, and he refused steadfastly to submit the arrangement to a Parliamentary committee for detailed study. Then, on December 19, Stevens returned to the House to announce that he had no objection to the deal being brought before a committee; and so it was. This was a total humiliation for de Cotret, and for the government, it was another messy retreat. The de Havilland sale, which might have done us some good, was instead another communications failure.

De Cotret exacted swift revenge. As part of a complicated deal involving major oil companies, Gulf Canada Limited sold its major refinery in Montreal to Ultramar Canada Ltd., a British firm. Ultramar was only buying the refinery to shut it down, which would have the effect of wiping out 400 jobs. Stevens was going to have to take the heat for this at a Montreal press conference and de Cotret pointedly refused even to appear at the conference. It got worse. To ease the pain in Montreal, Stevens announced a $55 million subsidy to the Petromont refinery, and Industry Minister Daniel Johnson, of the new Liberal government, turned up to take some of the bows. It wasn't merely poor foresight not to have a French-speaking federal representative on hand for an announcement of such importance to Quebec, it was sheer insanity.

As though she hadn't done enough for us already, Suzanne Blais-Grenier announced her resignation from Cabinet to protest the Gulf sale, on the day before New Year's. Her days in cabinet were numbered anyway. Our line in the press office about Blais-Grenier was, "You can't fire me, I quit." But the joke didn't calm Mulroney's anger. Here she was stabbing him in the back after he'd carried her through her troubles with travel not long before.

So our black fall ended the way it had begun, with a minister's resignation. At least by then Marcel Masse had returned to Cabinet, the RCMP having concluded they had no case against him. None the less, his resignation was still always included in the tally that the media were keeping of cabinet heads that had rolled.

We were all thoroughly exhausted. Not only had I been taking the blows like everybody else, but I was constantly on the road. Since I was assigned to do much of the advance work, I wound up going to a lot of places twice. From Brussels, where I advanced a two-day visit to NATO headquarters, to Manicouagan, to Halifax for a first ministers' conference, to Chicago and Edmonton, not to forget Nassau. It was a wicked pace.

Along with all this, we were taking a beating in the polls. The November Gallup showed the Liberals dangerously close to erasing our lead; we had forty per cent, but they were up to thirty-six. At the beginning of January the publication of a poll taken during the first week of December put John Turner and the Liberals ahead, thirty-eight per cent to thirty-seven, for the first time since the September 4 election.

The national political picture had changed considerably; we were far from the St. Valentine's Day love-in at Regina, where Mulroney was the darling of the provincial premiers. He got on well with the new Quebec premier, Bourassa, and that was a plus, but Bourassa was a Liberal, and there was a new Liberal premier in Ontario as well — David Peterson, elected in June, 1985. We had to start worrying about a Quebec City–Toronto axis. What's more, The Boss, who knew him well, was put off by Peterson, complaining that the new leader would say one thing behind closed doors and something else in public. He quickly and derisively named Peterson "Red Tie," for his favourite neckwear.

Grant Devine, in Saskatchewan, was always a loyal Tory, but next door in Alberta, Peter Lougheed — feisty, but friendly — had been replaced by Don Getty, who was a Conservative, all right, but much more of an Ottawa-basher than Lougheed had been since Trudeau left the prime ministership. The Boss never hid his displeasure for some of the statements Getty had made on his road to the premier's chair.

The cooing that had emerged from Regina was turning to, at best, frosty smiles and at worst, outright snarls, and our "national reconciliation" plank was beginning to splinter. Added to our scandals and Cabinet disarray, it did not make a pretty picture.

Never mind; The Boss was going to set things right — or, at least give it a hell of a try.

PART FOUR

On The Road Again

"The two big tricks of the 20th Century are: technology instead of grace, and information instead of virtue."

Ulysee Comtois, 1971

CHAPTER SIXTEEN

Do Or Die
Or Fly

This was the first time I'd heard Brian Mulroney talk in this tone. It was January 9, 1986, and we were gathered in the second floor conference room at the Langevin Block. There was Bernard Roy, Fred Doucet, Bill Fox, Pat MacAdam and about half a dozen others, including me.

"I hate whiners and back-biters," began the Prime Minister, leaving no doubt that he was talking about the infighting within his own office. "If some of you want to leave, then leave; now's the time. I won't be mad at you; I'll give you a hand and I'll throw you a going-away party, if you want. But don't stay here if you don't want to.

"There are going to be days, as you know, where it's going to be very difficult," he continued. "God knows we're not doing this for the money. But remember this: when people see you getting off the Prime Minister's plane, they'd all like to be in your place. They all want to know what it's really like to be there. And maybe you're finding it hard now, but when you haven't got it any more, you'll miss it.

"What we need," he said, getting down to the nub of his lecture, "is a communications strategy. The Liberals have a strategy. I know they have one. But they can't get us unless we do ourselves in. I'll do what you want me to do. Prepare me and present me with a communications strategy. I'll go anywhere. We've got the means to deliver our message, but we haven't done it very well so far.

"As for John Turner, God bless him, I hope they keep him. He's our biggest ally."

For us this was the speech to get the team back on its game. The pep talk from the coach in the dressing-room between the second and third periods. Afterward, when I found myself alone with the Prime Minister, he looked at me with a smile at the corner of his mouth, and said, "So?"

"That was pretty good," I told him.

I meant it. He'd finally said a few things I'd been hoping to hear. Not that I considered myself a complete innocent. But I was tired of watching internal quarrels tear us apart. And it was depressing to see that when the going got tough, the team tended to fall apart instead of pulling together. We weren't elected by any voters; we weren't civil servants; we were named by the Prime Minister to see that his will prevailed. It was time to get our act together.

Maybe he hadn't felt the need to tell us straight to our faces before now, thinking we'd manage with the means at our disposal. One of our problems, to be sure, was that we didn't know and never really had known what exactly it was he wanted, but at least this time he'd opened up more than usual with his advisers. He showed some emotion other than the anger we were used to. That day he was the guy we all liked. I remember Bill Fox among others, applauding at the end, even though that wasn't what the speech was intended to elicit.

At that time, the situation hadn't yet reached catastrophic proportions. There had been the January Gallup that put us behind the Liberals, with thirty-eight per cent for them, thirty-seven for us, and twenty-four for the NDP. But the February poll put us back in front, forty-one per cent to thirty-six for the Liberals. The NDP had slipped back to twenty-three per cent.

But we weren't about to let that one poll fool us. We knew, starting with the Prime Minister, that our slide had been steady for some months now. A single poll means little, but a trend is telling. In the absence of divine or other outside intervention, chances were that we'd keep sliding.

The temptation was great at that point to deviate from Mulroney's original plan to give all his ministers until June 1986 to master their portfolios. This period of grace was particularly important for the Quebec ministers who, with the exception of Marcel Masse, Bob de Cotret and Roch La Salle, were totally inexperienced in the devious art of politics as it's played at the cabinet level.

There had been a small shuffle in August, but it was strictly minor, with no important players affected. It had been like pulling a tooth when what was needed was a cardiac bypass. Near the end of our black fall, the Prime Minister was leaning so much in favour of a cabinet shuffle early in the year that he made allusions to it in a year-end interview with David Halton and Peter Mansbridge of the CBC. I don't know what finally made him decide against it. In cases like this the Prime Minister would talk to a lot of people, but you rarely got the impression that he was soliciting direct advice. He'd talk about everything and nothing, and somewhere along the line, something that might seem insignificant to you would turn out to be just what he was trying to get at. When that happened, he wouldn't tell you, but at that moment his face would change expression and he'd sit up as though to better absorb what you were saying. With time we learned how to read his body language such as when he'd blink his eyes rapidly. It wasn't only a sign that he was nervous, but often it was a signal that he was barely containing profound anger.

At this time, Mulroney was under intense pressure not only to shuffle the cabinet, but also to conduct a housecleaning in his own office. At caucus, a number of members suggested publicly that heads should roll at the PMO. Fox and myself were prominent among the names mentioned. Our problems, it seems, could all be traced to our inability to communicate, hence the cancer to be excised lay in the Press Office. Never mind John Fraser's tuna, Bob Coates' bad taste in night spots and Suzanne Blais-Grenier's junketing. We were the guilty parties. We should be making them look good.

After that caucus meeting, Mulroney decided to take charge of the communications strategy himself. Without telling anyone, certainly not us in the Press Office, he led off with a frontal assault on the Press Gallery. He claimed that the Gallery was being "fairly negative," on the whole, about his government and not paying attention to the administration's genuine accomplishments. "Our tremendous record," as he put it.

"We know what we're up against," he told a group of reporters. "We're not a bunch of children. We understand your obligations and we accept our own. And we've got to get our message out and we're going to do it."

Asked if a change in the Cabinet might relieve the pressure on the government, Mulroney replied, "A change in the Press Gallery might."

Fox and I wondered if it was that smart to put so much of the blame for our failure on the Gallery. Not the Prime Minister, however. He quoted Dalton Camp, the veteran Tory backroom wizard, "Camp told me that it was like tossing a grenade into the Gallery," he said. "If I was a reporter, I'd think twice." It was an expression he'd often use: If I was a reporter, I'd write this or I'd write that, or I'd think such and such. It was his way of telling us what message he wanted carried to the Boys.

The new strategy we implemented in January, 1986 took us outside Ottawa almost every week. Not only would we take the message directly to the people in the remotest hamlets of the land, but the strategy also called for maximum use of local media in each region. This tactic became quickly evident to the Press Gallery, and the national media types didn't like it one bit. The word spread that Mulroney preferred to deal with reporters from outside Ottawa because they were more docile. The fact is that sometimes the effect was precisely the opposite.

I remember a TV interview in Kitchener where the interviewer asked the Prime Minister of Canada, in so many words, if it was true that he had once made off with David Peterson's girlfriend. Mulroney, who was trying to reel off his list of happy statistics about the drop in unemployment and interest rates and the increase in employment and productivity, was not amused.

What Mulroney was doing was following the strategy that had served him so well while he was opposition leader during the Liberal leadership campaign, when the front pages carried nothing but John Turner and Jean Chrétien. He was relying on his greatest strength, his talent as a campaigner. And we had the ideal instrument, he told us, meaning the Challenger, which, with its capacity to fly a thousand miles in two hours, put most of Canada in easy reach.

We also had our secret weapon: Mila. As Bernard Roy said, "Thank God we've got her." Through all our tribulations, Mila Mulroney's popularity had never wilted. She had been on the campaign trail with her husband since 1983 when he ran for the leadership, yet she never flagged, her fetching smile eliciting adulation wherever she went. While watching the tape of an interview Mila did with the abrasive Jack Webster in Vancouver, Mulroney said with admiration: "How would you like to be a candidate running against her?"

It wasn't just an act for the peasantry. In private, Mila was even more pleasant and animated than in public where, if anything, she was a better campaigner than her husband. Loquacious by nature, she loved to chat about anything at all with everybody on the staff as well as with her husband. She'd often slip out of her seat in the front of the Challenger and come to the back with us plebes while The Boss worked on his papers up front.

I rarely heard her interfere in any matter of public policy, even though she must have had her own opinions about some of the issues, but she had a great influence on how her husband comported himself in public. She was about the only one he'd listen to about little things he should or shouldn't do, or words he should avoid.

Mila was also human, and she had her prickly moments, when the many miles travelled and the thousands of hands shaken, often with no one but Bonnie Brownlee and a bodyguard for company, began taking their toll on her composure. She had just about had her fill of these hinterland jaunts, and was beginning to doubt they were worth the strain.

Yet, she also told us that she probably wouldn't have it any other way. Being away from the children is what bothered her most, and often she insisted that they come along on trips. Yes there was a nanny, an undoubted nanny, and undoubtedly paid for by the Mulroneys; she became indispensable, particularly after Nicolas was born (the earlier employee, the one who interfaced with the kids, had left). But I've also seen Mila change a nauseating diaper without so much as a grimace while we were aboard the mini-train at the Canadian National Exhibition in Toronto. That also reminds me of the time she told an interviewer that the Prime Minister often changed the diapers because he had no sense of smell. She insisted afterward, when we kidded her about it in private, that it was absolutely true, that Brian changed more diapers than she did. This little revelation provoked one of the funniest political cartoons of my tenure in the press office. It was by Aislin and it had Mulroney about to tuck into a plate of something saying: "Great! Tuna for lunch!!"

The Mulroney children were perfectly normal for youngsters their age. The two eldest, Caroline and Benedict, were unfailingly polite; they almost made me behave the same way when they were around. Caroline had inherited her mother's eyes and her father's sense of humour. In one of our rare conversations she quoted the political adage to the effect that "In television, sincerity is everything; if you can fake that, you've got it made."

Mark, the third child, was also a polite youngster, but much more of a live wire. One day during the election campaign I couldn't find my shoes. I looked everywhere before I noticed that I'd left the door open. Out in the corridor I found Mark Mulroney parading around with my shoes flapping on his feet. As for Nicolas, he was the happiest baby I've ever seen in my life. You would have thought he'd been born on a campaign plane and briefed on the thoughts of Dalton Camp before taking his first spoonful of solid food.

During these trips, the rest of us became extensions of the family. I didn't have much to do with the children, having enough on my hands with the crybabies in the press room. But Stewart Murray would often volunteer to babysit, telling them stories and making them laugh, and amusing the Prime Minister at the same time. There was the time, for instance, when we visited Expo 86 in Vancouver. The Mulroney children had gone to the fair with their parents that afternoon, but they couldn't do much of what kids like to do at fairs with the mob of camera crews around at all times, so that night, even though he'd already put in a long hard day, Stewart took them back for a low-profile visit.

The travel strategy paid off, and by the beginning of 1986, the dark days appeared to be behind us. Or so we thought. As always, there was something lurking in the bushes. A few days later none other than Erik Nielsen, the Deputy Prime Minister, took his turn in embarrassing the government. As Mulroney said later: "Erik Nielsen gives his first interview in twenty years, and look what happens!"

The minister had talked once too often — thirteen years earlier, as it turned out, long before this administration, he had told reporter Peter Stursberg that during the 1960s he and his caucus colleagues would regularly eavesdrop on Liberal caucus meetings. It seems that they didn't actually go so far as to plant bugs in the Liberal caucus room, but somehow the phone lines on the Hill had got crossed in such a way that it was possible to overhear what was going on at the Liberal meetings if you knew which buttons to press. This thirteen-year-old interview suddenly re-surfaced as a hot news item.

It was an old story from another era that had no place in the Parliamentary debate of the '80s, but for the first time ever, the opposition found their Number One Enemy suddenly vulnerable. Nielsen, who had led the charge that destroyed half a dozen reputations in Lester Pearson's cabinet was about to get a taste of his own medicine.

On Friday, January 31, Nielsen stonewalled all the opposition's questions. It was hard to tell if they were out for his resignation, a public inquiry, or simply an apology. But, through the normal unofficial channels, the NDP let us know that they'd be happy with an apology.

That weekend, the Prime Minister was scheduled to speak at the provincial Conservative convention in Nova Scotia. A substantial mob from Ottawa followed us down East, not the least bit interested in what Mulroney had to say at the Convention. What they wanted was a scrum on the Nielsen affair. We had become a government of affairs, not policies. The Prime Minister was determined to avoid the microphones, and the result was one of the worst media mob scenes I've ever witnessed as the security guards shoved their way through the crowd of insistent reporters.

John Crosbie, the ever-helpful John Crosbie, did his bit by telling an interviewer that if he'd been Nielsen, he would have spied on the Liberal caucus meetings, too. Crosbie was echoing the sentiment of quite a few of the hardliners in the Cabinet, particularly the western contingent, led by Don Mazankowski, who were insisting on sticking with Yukon Erik to the end.

Happily, it all ended almost as quickly as it began. The next Monday Nielsen and the voluble Crosbie offered formal apologies in the Commons.

Another crawl-down; it was a great way, I thought, to kick off our new communications strategy. And no doubt the conclusion would be that the Prime Minister's staff had screwed up once more. The Cabinet, of course, had nothing to do with it.

CHAPTER SEVENTEEN

A Canadian In Paris

P aris.
The name itself is magic. And it was pure chance that our departure for the City of Light was scheduled for St. Valentine's Day, the day for lovers. We were off to the first francophone summit meeting, made possible in large part by Brian Mulroney, the Prime Minister of national reconciliation, and a miraculously favourable alignment of the planets. For Mulroney, the very fact that the meeting was taking place was a triumph. The French, despite their public declarations of brotherhood, weren't all that convinced of the necessity of such a summit that risked, among other things, opening doors into France's former colonies for powerful economic forces like Canada. Canadians, particularly English-speaking Canadians, were also skeptical. Seeing the Prime Minister seated at the same table as Quebec Premier Robert Bourassa, they wondered who was speaking for Canada at this klatsch. And what was Richard Hatfield, Premier of New Brunswick, who had instituted bilingualism in his province but was himself unilingually English, doing here being about as participatory as a plant in the President of France's elegant salons? Why create another Commonwealth when the Commonwealth we had was a rickety creature at best? But Brian Mulroney and Lucien Bouchard, his indefatigable ambassador to France and long-time friend, were determined to convince the rest of the world.

The summit began on February 16 with a subtly engineered silence. The Prime Minister, Bourassa and Hatfield held a preliminary meeting to plot strategy and to synchronize their watches, and afterward they submitted to a press conference at the residence of the Canadian ambassador in Paris. What we were most worried about was that someone would ask Richard Hatfield a question in French. I was the one put in charge of singling out the reporters who would ask the questions, and my strategy was simple: I crossed my fingers and prayed to God that the image of Hatfield declaiming in his polyester tourist French wouldn't embarrass the entire summit. Naturally, the leading questions were for Mulroney and Bourassa. There was nothing they didn't handle with ease, and I thought it best to cut it off while everything was going well, so I announced that the next question would be the last. Just then I heard a voice from the back of the room, calling out in French: "A question for Mr. Hatfield! A question for Mr. Hatfield!" But out of the corner of my eye, I saw Bernard Descoteaux of *Le Devoir* and recognized him immediately. He then put a question to Mulroney and Bourassa, knowing there was nothing of substance to be gotten from Hatfield. The guy in the back was still yelling for Hatfield when I announced that the press conference was over. The Canadian reporters had seen immediately what had gone on and didn't hesitate to accuse me of manipulation. But then I didn't really regret having spared Canadians, and the francophone world, the sound of Richard Hatfield mangling the language of Molière.

The next day, The Boss was nervous. The summit had opened amid the splendid opulence of the Palace of Versailles, and he was one of the leaders scheduled to speak. Mulroney was always sensitive about the quality of his French, and he'd rehearse his French speeches much more intensely than those mostly in English. He was also about to commit what would, for some, be interpreted as an act of supreme *lèse majesté* by including a paragraph in English in his speech, under the very nose of François Mitterand. But then it would be useless to try to explain to all these francophone leaders that whenever he spoke in English anywhere in the world, including deepest anglo Canada and the Commonwealth, he always made sure he said something in French. With the situation reversed, he could hardly do otherwise.

President Mitterand had a bemused smile on his face when Mulroney spoke in English. But in the end he got through it without damage.

The hairiest moments for us were yet to come. Later that afternoon, the Premier of Quebec decided to "pull a Bourassa" on us, threatening, in one fell swoop, the fragile harmony achieved between Quebec and Canada established by the agreement that made the conference possible. It happened without warning. After the opening ceremonies, which were held in public, the leaders went into closed session at the Centre Kléber. Afterward, while Mulroney unsuspectingly went back to his hotel, Bourassa turned to his Press Secretary, Ronald Poupart, and said, "Come on, let's go see the Boys."

The Boys, of course, were the reporters. In the little office reserved for the Quebec delegation, just next door to ours, Bourassa, while our backs were turned, told the furiously scribbling reporters that he had made the most of the first closed-door session by suggesting a new form of "Marshall Plan" designed to distribute western agricultural surpluses to African nations suffering famine. He had discussed the idea with Jacques Delors, President of the European Economic Community's governing council, who had previously suggested something along those lines. The reporters naturally asked him if he had consulted the Prime Minister, in accordance with the agreement governing Quebec's participation at the summit. A Canadian reporter told me later that Bourassa had smiled like a Cheshire cat that had just swallowed a sparrow when he said no, he hadn't mentioned his proposal to his good friend Brian. For his part, Quebec's Minister of International and Intergovernmental Relations, Gil Rémillard, had given a radio interview in which he said that Bourassa had emerged as the second most important francophone leader at the conference, after François Mitterand, because he had been appointed the conference's official "reporter," who would compile a summary of the in-camera proceedings at the end of the meeting. When we learned about Bourassa's statement and Rémillard's commentaries, I quickly alerted the Prime Minister and told him we might have a problem. Mulroney, however, wouldn't hear of it.

"He didn't say anything," he said, referring to Bourassa's speech during the closed-door session. "You were there, Fred . . . it was nothing."

Unfortunately Fred Doucet had left the room a moment before. I told the Prime Minister that the media were saying that Bourassa did it on purpose, to make himself look important, and that Rémillard had probably been behind it. Whether we were right or wrong, we pinned most of the blame on Bourassa's minister. Mulroney said, "Rémillard had better get out of the way because the big trucks are coming down the road."

We finally got out of the situation by saying that we had known about the Quebec agricultural proposal all along, because it had been included in the pre-conference briefing papers. The term "Marshall Plan" was even included in the documentation. But that was merely a convenient exit. We knew exactly what Bourassa had tried to pull, and it led the Prime Minister to issue a thinly veiled warning at his closing press conference, "Blindside me once and you'll never do it again."

We were happy to see the Quebec delegation leave town two days later, while we stayed on for an official bilateral visit. It's not that we didn't like them, it's just that having them around meant one more thing to deal with, and we'd already amply demonstrated that we didn't need any help making problems for ourselves.

The rest of the Paris visit was much more relaxed, with the exception of the scary, high-speed motorcades through the congested Paris traffic led by daredevil motorcycle cops who made the Hell's Angels look like Beaver Scouts on tricycles. Give a Frenchman a uniform and a motorcycle and he's instantly transformed into Evel Knievel. The biker gendarmes, members of a special squad, were assigned to clear a way for us through the virtual gridlock so that we could reach our destinations in time. I'm not sure if it was courage or temerity or sheer folly on their part, but every time out they put on a show that left us breathless. They would drive through the traffic at incredible speed, their hands off the handlebars, smacking cars left and right to clear the ones not moving out of the way fast enough. When they saw a hole they'd hit it at full speed, like a fullback running off tackle. And we had to follow them or we'd lose them.

Ask Joel Ruimy, assigned to cover the summit for the *Toronto Star*. Ruimy was running late one day and had missed the press bus for the Académie Française where Mulroney had been invited — a signal honour for an Irish kid from Baie Comeau. I'd been delayed at the hotel myself, because as usual the copies of the speech weren't ready. My chauffeur, Pierre, hired for the summit by the embassy, was waiting, along with a motorcycle escort. I offered Ruimy a lift, saying, "You sit in the suicide seat," meaning the front passenger seat. "Hold on to your hat, as The Boss used to say, you're in for a hell of a ride!"

After a few minutes of racing hell-bent through the flashing traffic, I tapped him on the shoulder and said, "I'm going to make you regret all those negative stories about us in the *Star*."

Terrified, he cried, "Enough, enough! I take it all back."

When we got to the Académie he was a fishbelly white. Ann Charron, my assistant, who had also come with us, was shaking so badly she could barely climb out of the car. By then I was getting used to the drill, and the combination of Ruimy's terror and Pierre's delight at flooring it through midtown with the complicity of the "flics" had me laughing all the way there.

As it turned out the drivers were helpful in other ways. I'll never forget the scene in the coatroom of the Chamber of Commerce building in Paris. As often happened, there was a word in his speech that the Prime Minister didn't like, so he changed it a few minutes before he spoke. We thought the change was so insignificant that it didn't justify redoing the whole text. And besides, it was too late. We could never get enough copies printed in time. The Boss made an exception this time and authorized us to change the texts we had by hand. So there in the Chamber of Commerce coatroom, a few minutes before the speech, Bill Fox, Marc Lortie, Ann Charron and two of our French chauffeurs stood there correcting the hundred or so copies of the speech, one by one. This was life in the fast lane, PMO style.

It was during the same lunch that the master of ceremonies rose to announce that we shouldn't be alarmed if we heard an explosion. The security service had discovered a mysterious briefcase, he said, and it would have to be detonated in case it contained explosives. I didn't hear the explosion, but we saw the famous briefcase afterward — that is what was left of it. All it contained were the morning newspapers. I would have liked to see the owner's reaction.

I would have liked to have seen Paris. Thanks to Pierre and the outriders, all I saw were shadows flashing past. Ann Charron is probably the only person in history to tour the Louvre in fifteen minutes. As was the case with most of our foreign trips, the working days started early and ended late. The best times I had were in the late-night restaurants where the waiters were quintessentially Parisian. I asked one one night in my most cultured accent if he was serving our table. He looked at me, he looked at the table, then he said, "Yes," and walked off without waiting to hear if I wanted anything.

I got my revenge the next day when I confronted a particularly impolite policeman.

"Are you Parisian?" I asked him.

"No," he answered.

"Then how is it that you're so obnoxious?"

It was the first time I've ever seen a Frenchman dumbstruck.

The Prime Minister adored France. He'd often visited the country starting when he was still a bachelor. One time he and his friend, now a Senator, Jean Bazin, travelled to Corsica to try to trace Napoleon's ancestors. One of his most pleasant memories of the 1986 trip came when President Mitterand, in what was apparently an unprecedented gesture, invited him to "come see something." The something was the room where Napoleon had signed his abdication. Mulroney often talked about it afterward; it was the finest present Mitterand could have given him. It was well that he enjoyed it because, from Paris, we flew back to Ottawa, where cold Canadian reality awaited us.

CHAPTER EIGHTEEN

Sondra's Slap and Champagne's Follies

Alan Gotlieb, our ambassador to the United States, had the look of a condemned man. It was the morning of March 20, 1986, and we were in the Prime Minister's suite at the Hotel Madison in Washington. I'd just come from the Vista Hotel, a few doors down the street, where the media were staying. The blow had landed the night before at the ambassador's elegant residence.

In the Prime Minister's suite were Bruce Phillips, formerly a prominent CTV commentator, now the ambassador's press secretary, the PM's senior adviser, Fred Doucet and Communications Director Bill Fox. The atmosphere was funereal.

The night before, on the occasion of a lavish dinner in honour of US Vice-President George Bush, Sondra Gotlieb, the ambassador's wife, had slapped her social secretary, Connie Connor. Not only that, she did it on the steps of the embassy, in full view of the reporters waiting out front. Fortunately, there were no photos or film of the incident, but it was nevertheless the slap that was heard across the continent. A photo taken later, after everyone had recovered composure, showed Sondra and Connie arm-in-arm, but if you looked closely, one of Connie's earrings was missing, knocked off when Sondra let fly.

This could only happen to us. The Prime Minister's visit to Washington had otherwise been a smash on all counts. Not only were the TV pictures pretty, but there was also substance, particularly on acid rain. From expressing the view a few years before that acid rain was caused by trees, Ronald Reagan had now come around to a commitment to invest seriously in pollution control measures. Mulroney was also able to do some high level lobbying on behalf of trade liberalization with key members of Congress.

The days preceding the Washington visit had been sufficiently eventful that Sondra's slap was really just par for the course. Our first major outing after our return from France was Michael Wilson's second budget. This time the Prime Minister's instructions had been specific. Above all, he wanted a "no mistakes" budget. He didn't want anything the opposition could make us eat. He didn't want pensioners or widows or anyone like that on our backs. Wilson's subsequent masterpiece, while somewhat colourless, was nevertheless "saleable"; we thought it might be a useful tool for our climb out of the popularity pits.

The next day, Jean Chrétien, the most popular Liberal in the land, announced that he was leaving politics. For us this meant that the Liberals were having internal problems. If Chrétien was leaving, it was so he could better fight Turner, whose leadership he'd never truly accepted in that dogged heart of his.

Was fortune about to smile on us at last?

Not really.

At the beginning of March, yet another of our ministers landed in hot water. This time it was Andrée Champagne, who, because of her TV career in Quebec, was one of the best known Quebeckers in the Cabinet, after Roch La Salle and Marcel Masse, according to our in-house polls. The Youth Minister, whose $17 million budget had been axed by the Wilson budget, was accused of having used public funds to recruit young people for the Progressive Conservative Party. The charges were based on a confidential letter signed by the minister, in support of a $7.5 million program to assist young people throughout the country. The key phrase was the following: "Support for the recruitment efforts of the PC Youth Federation will be a pre-writ (i.e., pre-election) priority for the government."

The affair was first trundled out by Howard McCurdy of the NDP on Thursday, March 6, when he revealed the existence of the letter. Champagne then blundered spectacularly, refusing to admit that the signature on the letter was hers. She insisted that the signature must either have been forged, or else the letter had been pasted together with scissors and glue in such a way as to incriminate her. In my seven years on Parliament Hill I've never heard anything so ludicrous come out of the mouth of a cabinet minister. The letter in itself was damaging enough, without trying to make the world swallow this tale that smacked of evil gnomes at work during the night in the minister's office.

The very next day, she settled down and admitted that it was indeed her signature and apologized to the Commons, saying that she should simply have changed the word "government" in the contested quote to "party," as was the letter's intent. But once again, the damage had been done.

At the time, I was out of town with the Prime Minister on a western swing. I don't remember if he talked to me about Andrée Champagne, but there was no doubt in my mind that she had just signed her political death warrant, effective the next cabinet shuffle.

In keeping with our new campaign-style strategy, after stops in Regina and Vancouver, we went on to Prince George, where we spent a night, then on to Penticton, an enchanted spot deep in the Rocky Mountains. But as so often happened, our best efforts to regain the electorate's confidence were undermined by things that happened in Ottawa or elsewhere in the country.

In Winnipeg, for instance, John Laschinger, who had been John Crosbie's campaign manager for the 1983 Conservative leadership race, and now was directing the provincial election campaign for PC leader Gary Filmon, told reporters that when the Prime Minister offered his help in the campaign, he had refused the offer. This was a direct insult to Mulroney — not only to refuse his help, but to talk about it in public.

Then, on March 10, the Monday after we got back to Ottawa, Jacques Hébert, a Liberal Senator and Pierre Trudeau intimate, began a hunger strike in Parliament's Centre Block to protest the government's decision to eliminate the Katimavik youth training program. Hébert's hunger strike was to last twenty-one days. Throughout the episode, the Prime Minister insisted on holding the line. Bernard Roy was particularly incensed by what he regarded as the Senator's attempt to blackmail the administration. But from the Privy Council Office headed by the senior bureaucrat in Ottawa, Paul Tellier, there were suggestions that we should make a concession. Never mind public opinion — and we were sure most people disagreed with Hébert's tactic — we didn't want him dying on our hands. But it all petered out uneventfully. Hébert started eating again and stopped sacking out in the Senate lobby after Jean Chrétien and a group of businessmen pledged to try and raise the money needed for Katimavik from the private sector.

It was against this backdrop that we set off for our second Prime Ministerial visit to Washington. Thanks to some fancy preparatory footwork in Washington's inner sanctums by Fred Doucet and Alan Gotlieb, the Prime Minister was able to extract a substantial acid rain agreement from the encounter with Reagan. The pictures from the visit were superb as usual, particularly the footage from the visit to Arlington Cemetery, which overlooks Washington, giving a spectacular view of the American capital.

Fortunately, the Prime Minister's closing press conference was held before the fiasco at the embassy. For once we decided to hold it, not at the very end of the visit, as was the custom, but at the end of the second day, just hours before the reception that made the history books. I was presiding over the press conference, and at one point the Prime Minister became exasperated by the fact that I was recognizing only Canadian reporters, so he did something he'd never done before and never did again. He turned to me and said brusquely, "Let's hear some Americans!"

The trouble was that none of the Americans had raised a hand. I mean, I couldn't force them to ask questions. Finally, I noticed an elderly lady, festooned with trinkets that made her look like a fortune teller, who had her hand up. She must be an American, I thought, and if the Secret Service had let her in she must be a bonafide reporter. When I recognized her, she jumped happily out of her seat and began a rambling speech about how she adored the Prime Minister because he was a genius. She could tell, she said, from the marvellous lines in his expressive hands. Mulroney couldn't help but laugh.

The lady in question was apparently a long-time correspondent, accredited to the White House press corps for as long as anyone could remember. She probably knew Herbert Hoover. When she finally finished, I turned to the Prime Minister with a smile to say, "You want more Americans?"

He pretended not to understand, but in the first few rows I saw some of the correspondents shaking with laughter. Afterward, I got to meet the lady myself and she took the trouble to read my palm, and wouldn't you know it, I was a genius too! I told the Prime Minister, hoping he wasn't too let down by this blow to his fan's credibility.

That and the time one of the Congressmen referred to the Prime Minister as "Mr. Muldoon" instead of Mr. Mulroney were the worst moments of the trip up to then. Nothing dramatic, so far. Fortunately slugger Sondra only pulled her act that night and it took awhile before the Canadian media were able to get the full details.

To distance the whole episode from the Prime Minister's Office, Bruce Phillips was assigned to respond to all media questions. Phillips, in turn, composed a statement which he then repeated to every caller:

"I am informed that an incident of a purely personal character occurred last night before the embassy dinner," it said. "The incident was immediately regretted, an apology extended and at once accepted, and the issue was immediately resolved."

The Prime Minister didn't mention the incident when we boarded the Challenger for the homeward flight. Nor did I see him raise it with the ambassador while I was in his hotel suite, though it must have come up before my arrival, judging from the long faces around the room. However, Gotlieb was still Ambassador when the 1987 Canada–US summit rolled around, and there was never any question of demanding his resignation because of his wife's colossal breach of etiquette.

None the less, her slap is probably what most Canadians will remember about the March '86 summit. All the months of work in preparation had largely gone by the board. The government had absolutely nothing to do with it, but by this time we'd become like the tar baby: everything stuck to us.

CHAPTER NINETEEN

Sinc, Sank, Sunk

"**D**on't worry about it. We're leaving the country. In a few days nobody'll be talking about it."

This was the Prime Minister talking, and I think he was making a profession of faith, rather than stating fact. We were on the eve of a trip that would take us to the Far East for three weeks. He was referring to a series of stories in the *Globe and Mail* that week about the business dealings of Sinclair Stevens, that had already sparked several stormy Question Periods.

Sinc, as everybody called him, was the Industry Minister and he had himself pleaded innocence before the Prime Minister, who thus was inclined to think there was nothing serious in the allegations which charged Stevens with a conflict of interest. He believed that in his absence, and most of us agreed with him, the affair would quickly play itself out and the opposition would move on to other things.

It had all begun with a story in the *Globe* on Tuesday, April 29. Written by Michael Harris and David Stewart-Patterson, the article said that in May, 1985 Stevens' wife had negotiated a $2.6 million loan to refinance some of her husband's business ventures that had run into trouble. The loan, according to the *Globe*, came from a source recommended to Noreen Stevens by Frank Stronach, President of Magna International Corp., who had himself been approached by Mrs. Stevens, but declined to get further involved. Instead, Anton Czapka, a co-founder and former officer of Magna, gave her the five-year loan, deferring the first year's interest. Under the Liberals, Magna had received about $30 million in grants and interest-free loans from Ottawa, and the help had continued under Stevens.

The opposition, of course, was incensed. They demanded the minister's immediate resignation and a public inquiry. The government's defence was weak. Stevens had indeed complied with the guidelines regarding ministerial assets by placing all his holdings in a blind trust, so technically he was on safe ground if it was true that, as he maintained, he had no knowledge of the loan. But appearances, as a pro like Sinc should have known, mean everything in politics, and this deal appeared mighty fishy. To accept Stevens' story, it was necessary to believe that he and his wife never discussed this extraordinary loan to his floundering company. It was possible, of course, but would require saint-like reticence. By this time the rest of the national media had joined the pursuit with as much fervour as the opposition, and Sinc was doing badly on both fronts.

The Prime Minister let it be known that he was personally disgusted by the savagery with which the media were persecuting poor Stevens. Particularly when someone asked Stevens if he talked to his wife when he saw her at night. At a news conference on May 2, Mulroney was generally evasive on the affair. He tried at once to protect his own flank, while at the same time sticking up for his minister, with the result that he didn't really answer the questions that were asked.

After that we were glad to climb aboard the plane that would take us to Expo 86 in Vancouver, and then across the Pacific for the annual summit of the Big Seven western economic powers in Tokyo. After the summit, the Prime Minister would stay for an official visit to Japan, then travel to Beijing, China, and Seoul, in South Korea.

Instead of using the aging Armed Forces Boeing 707, we leased a Lockheed 1011 from Air Canada. We had three reasons for preferring the mammoth Lockheed, which is just a shade smaller than a 747 Jumbo. First of all, we got a good price from Air Canada; as well, the roomy Lockheed would allow everyone, including our forty-odd media contingent, to stretch out and sleep on the long night flights; and, finally, some of us were getting worried that the creaky old 707 was going to fall apart from strain one of these days with us aboard eight miles up.

The Prime Minister disagreed. "If a 707 is good enough for President Reagan," he said, "it's good enough for me."

It took us weeks to get him to change his mind and let us have the Lockheed. But we made a big mistake from the outset when we had the plane outfitted for the trip. Along with a special compartment for the Prime Minister, there was a section of first class seats for government officials, while the media crew was consigned to economy. There were enough seats so that everyone had a row to himself, but we still looked like extravagant parvenus, something the media were quick to pick up on. From the start, they complained about the two classes of travellers on this trip. At the beginning, I thought they were kidding, but it wasn't long before it was obvious that they were taking this seriously. This was something we really didn't need. My worry-meter shot up when I saw that one of those criticizing us for the seating arrangement was David Halton, the CBC's senior political correspondent, a tough but fair reporter who had been around the world a few times and thus wasn't the type to posture about trivialities.

The journalists became even more furious when we landed in Anchorage, Alaska, for a brief refuelling stop, and wouldn't let them off the plane to stretch their legs. Only the Prime Minister was to get off the plane. Nobody in our group thought this any great inconvenience, but the reporters were huddled in the back of the plane, buzzing like hornets, crying that not even Trudeau ever treated them like this. A few, like John Ferguson of Southam News, went so far as to march to the front of the plane to use the ramp provided for the Prime Minister, and I had to go bring him back. Number one rule for the perfect press secretary is to keep the media wolves in a good mood, and this pack was distinctly unhappy. It was an evil premonition for the rest of the trip.

Oh, well, at least people's minds were off Sinc Stevens.

Upon arrival in Tokyo, it was immediately obvious that this is where the Big Seven were meeting. The police and the army were everywhere; our hotel, the New Otani, where the leaders were staying, had been transformed into a veritable fortress — with good reason.

On the very first day, terrorist mortar shells hit close to the Akasaka Palace where the summit discussions were held. Two of the projectiles struck close to the Canadian embassy. Since they were not explosive projectiles, the damage was minimal; but when news of the attack first reached us at the hotel there was a general panic in the entourage, not to mention among the Japanese security services, which had miscalculated the range of the terrorists' weapons. It was obviously the story of the day; nothing we could do would top it. The summit talks that day

169

were certainly much less exciting. When our ambassador to Japan, Barry Steers, was asked what the terrorists were aiming at, he replied, "I think it was the newspapers."

The Prime Minister told us about how the attack had come up in the summit discussions. "Somebody said that the missiles hadn't been aimed at the Canadian Embassy; and Reagan said, 'How do you know?' "

The rocket attacks prompted the security forces to redouble their efforts. But it was nevertheless possible for a pair of covert terrorists like Marc Lortie and myself to slip through their ranks. We were in one of the upper stories of the New Otani, having just come from one of our delegation's working sessions. Lortie and I were waiting for the elevator which was surrounded by a dozen security types in plain clothes. You could always distinguish them, be they Japanese or Canadian, by the wire running out of one of their ears and their curious habit of talking into their sleeves. When a leader was on the move, all the other elevators were frozen. Nobody else moved.

One of the elevators opened and out came a hostess in traditional costume, with a smile so unflinching that it could have been made of ceramic. I asked her in English if we could take the elevator to go down, and she said something in Japanese that I took to mean yes.

"Come on," I said to Lortie.

We stepped into the elevator past the hostess, whose smile suddenly crumbled, and immediately the thing filled up with bodyguards. A tall, heavy-set man then got on, and the doors closed. It was Helmut Kohl, Chancellor of West Germany. The Japanese security types started giving the two of us penetrating looks, while talking animatedly among themselves and into their sleeves. But there was nothing they could do right then, the elevator was on its way. Lortie and I tried not to giggle for the duration of the ride, which must have seemed like an eternity to the security boys. With all their manpower, two crashers had slipped into a space as intimate as an elevator along with a leader of the western world.

We saw Kohl, not a man preoccupied by appearances, again the next day. Lortie and I encountered him alone in the corridor outside his suite, strolling along in slippers and shirt-sleeves. We said hello to him and he said hello to us.

The summit was a political success. Canada and Italy were admitted to the Group of Five, making it now the Group of Seven, which basically controls the Western economy. Until then, the

Big Five — the United States, Great Britain, France, Germany and Japan — had systematically rebuffed proposals to enlarge the membership. We had to twist a few arms in the media crew to convince them that our admission was really serious, but Marc Lortie's determination and savvy carried the day.

Once the summit was over, the cops and soldiers melted away as though by magic, and Tokyo took on its everyday rhythm. The major event remaining for us was the speech the Prime Minister was scheduled to deliver to the Japanese Parliament.

Maybe they forgot to notify the Japanese parliamentarians that this was a special occasion. The chamber, which had been packed for an appearance by Ronald Reagan not long before, was two-thirds empty when Mulroney arrived to speak. I could already see the next day's headlines which would be all about the poor attendance — 200 to 300 of the 750 members — instead of the content of the speech. Flustered, I started asking the Japanese representatives if this was normal. The Japanese, phlegmatic as ever, couldn't seem to fathom my anxiety. And sure enough, the headlines I'd imagined hit the streets in Canada the next day. The event had backfired on us. The Japanese tried to placate us, saying that Mulroney had not, in fact, been deliberately boycotted by anyone the way the communist parliamentarians had pointedly snubbed Reagan. But our media took it as an affront to the Prime Minister.

The next day, I had one of my best moments during my time in the government. The Prime Minister was giving a press conference at the Japanese National Press Club. Japanese reporters, it turned out, have a tradition that astonished our media contingent: they applaud politicians, something the Ottawa Gallery would never be caught doing in public. So when the press conference chairman introduced Mulroney, the Japanese reporters clapped furiously, while our crew sat on their hands. But, as the Prime Minister's Press Secretary, I got to be introduced as well, and when my turn came, the Japanese clapped as they had done before, but this time our group, finding it all very hilarious, joined in with hoots and hollers, much to the astonishment of the Toyko reporters, who wondered who I was, getting twice as big a hand as the Prime Minister. Mulroney couldn't help laughing.

Later that day we left for China. Despite everything, spirits were good aboard the plane, thanks in part to our crew which treated us to a spectacular overflight of Mount Fuji before turning toward Beijing. Everyone was anxious to see China; most of us knew that it would probably be the first and last time we would have a chance to set foot there.

It was in China that I heard news of Sinclair Stevens for the first time on the trip. James Rusk, the *Globe and Mail's* Beijing correspondent, approached me discreetly.

"I can understand that the Prime Minister might not want to answer questions about it," he said, "but my desk in Toronto tells me that the Stevens affair is going badly for the government." There was talk that André Bissonnette, then Minister for Small Business, had punched John Nunziata after a committee meeting about the matter on the Hill.

I wondered if I'd heard right. Punched John Nunziata? I bit my tongue and didn't blurt out that if it was true, Bissonnette deserved a medal for greasing one of the most savage members of the Liberals' infamous "Rat Pack." Later on, the Prime Minister would tell me that this was his first reaction as well. As it turned out, the story was not true. At worst there had been a shoving match between Bissonnette and Nunziata. I told Rusk that the Prime Minister had other things on his mind right then. But the alarm had sounded. During the days that followed, there were numerous long distance calls between Canada and China. Practically the entire PMO was on the other side of the world while the house was on fire back home. Ian Anderson was standing in as the PMO goaltender, and he was having trouble trying to handle the pucks flying at him from all directions at once. Bernard Roy, the Principal Secretary, Fred Doucet, the Senior Adviser, Charley McMillan and Geoff Norquay, two other senior advisers, Bill Fox, the Director of Communications and myself were all in the Orient while Ottawa burned. The subsequent decision to order a judicial inquiry into the affair was taken thousands of miles away, by people who hadn't been there for the week's developments.

The fateful meeting of the Prime Minister's advisers was held in Beijing on May 11, a day that had originally been set aside as a non-working day for everyone. I wasn't there at the meeting, having been detained at the media hotel, some miles away from the diplomatic compound where the Prime Minister was lodged. But I heard enough about it afterward.

At lunch, Geoff Norquay excused himself, saying he had arranged a meeting with Jim Rusk of the *Globe*. The decision had been made that Stevens would have to resign, but the group was still trying to work out the details of a judicial inquiry. It was vital that it be kept secret until it could be announced in

Parliament, because this was the only chance we had of catching the opposition by surprise, and perhaps pulling the rug out from under their feet. A judicial inquiry, which would shed light on the whole affair, would please everyone, and the Prime Minister would be seen as having acted in the national interest.

It was a brilliant strategy, until it all came apart.

The next day, we left China for Korea after a farewell news conference on Monday morning. However, it was still Sunday in Canada, and during the flight one of the PMO staffers told Bob Hurst of CTV that something big was going to happen in Question Period, leaving no doubt that it was Sinc's resignation. The staffer in question — Hurst never said who it was — didn't know that the CTV correspondent still had time to get in touch with his desk and have the scoop broadcast on the network's *Canada AM* show Monday morning. And this is exactly what he did the moment we reached the Seoul Hilton.

Meanwhile, back in China, Jim Rusk was filing a devastating piece for the *Globe* that began, "Prime Minister Brian Mulroney appears to be on the verge of a decision to cut loose his beleaguered Industry Minister, Sinclair Stevens.

"While the Prime Minister rested yesterday after a hectic week in Japan and China, his entourage, which includes almost all of Mulroney's senior political advisers, discussed what must be done to limit the damage from the Stevens affair."

Back in Canada, Stevens, who had docilely agreed to go along with the strategy up to now, hit the roof and threatened to refuse to resign. In Seoul, the Prime Minister was thoroughly disgusted. What hope was there for the government if he couldn't hold a staff meeting on an important matter in Beijing, China, without having a detailed report splattered all over the front page of the *Globe* the next day? I agreed with Bill Fox that, in the Prime Minister's eyes, this was the nail in the coffin of the PMO.

When I saw The Boss in his suite that night, he was still white with rage. He was so angry that words failed him.

Still, we had to decide what we'd do the next day in Seoul, where there would have to be some form of press conference. Bernard Roy and I were of the opinion that we should go all the way, not merely relying on a statement by the Prime Minister, but taking on questioners as well. The questions would come sooner or later, anyway. Mulroney wasn't in the mood to talk about it that night.

I got to the media hotel at about midnight where I was accosted by Brian Kelleher of CBC radio, who was in a more aggressive state than I'd ever seen him. He insisted that the Prime Minister should submit to questioning then and now, and wouldn't be put off when I pointed out that it was the time of day when everybody should be tucked into bed. During my three years in the Press Office, it was one of the most difficult encounters I've ever had with a reporter. I had a lot of respect for Kelleher, but I also thought he was being totally unreasonable. When he started waving his microphone under my nose, I turned on my heel and went off to my room, where I set about phoning the rest of the Canadian reporters to notify them that a bus would take them to the Prime Minister's hotel where he would make a statement on the Stevens affair early the next morning.

I'd rarely seen the Prime Minister so tense as he was when the next morning came. He was still upset about the treason of the day before. Looking grave, and slightly grey around the gills, standing behind his podium, he read a statement, which said in part: "It is my belief that Mr. Stevens will be fully vindicated and will return to the cabinet he has served with such competence and distinction."

When he finished reading the text, in both French and English, he pretended not to notice the shouted questions from the pack and instead took off as though hellhounds were on his trail. Then suddenly, through the din, he distinctly heard the blunt question yelled by Derik Hodgson of the *Toronto Sun*: "Are you afraid to go back and face it?"

He stopped momentarily, turned abruptly to me and barked, "Who said that?"

I'd never seen such an expression on his face. His eyes were on fire and his features were hard as granite. He was clearly enraged. You can accuse Brian Mulroney of a lot of things, but not of being a coward. At that moment, I didn't know what he was going to do. Right then I didn't know the man before me; it wasn't the Brian Mulroney whose demeanour in public was normally so smooth you could skate on it. Seeing my horrified expression, he picked up his step and strode toward the elevator that swallowed him up to our great relief. Still, it had been a public relations disaster.

And it was one we could surely have spared ourselves. Two days later, at the trip-ending news conference, the PM was in good form when the questions came. He dealt with them smartly and appeared in command of the situation. When asked why there had been a delay in the submission of Stevens' resignation, he replied, "If you act immediately when an allegation is raised, you'll properly be accused of condemning the guy without a trial."

But, as was often the case, it was too late by then. The damage had been done. And it was on this sour note that we would arrive back home after an arduous trip that had been, in all other respects, a triumphal procession. The Prime Minister sadly summed it up on the flight home, "You see, Michel," he said, "we're accomplishing all these things, we're working hard, but on the news at night it's always the second item. Stevens is number one."

Events had confirmed his theory that if we could stop shooting ourselves in the foot, the opposition wouldn't be able to touch us.

A month later, during a Friday afternoon round of golf at the Outaouais Club in Rockland, about fifty miles from Ottawa, former Liberal leadership candidate Jean Chrétien told me, "The judicial inquiry was a mistake. A big mistake."

"How come?" I asked him.

"Now it's going to be in the papers every day for three months," he said.

He was wrong. It was in the papers for much longer than that, and, as this is written, we still await the results of the inquiry.

By way of a welcome home special, we were greeted at Uplands Airport by great screaming headlines proclaiming that one of our Quebec Members, Michel Gravel, the MP for Gamelin, had been charged with no less than fifty counts of influence peddling, fraud and abuse of power following an RCMP investigation. It didn't come as a complete surprise. It was Bernard Roy himself, after checking out some persistent rumours on his own, who had initiated the police investigation in late 1985. He'd told me about it back then, just in case, and we'd been waiting six months for the other shoe to drop.

Earlier in the week, our caucus had suffered another blow when Robert Toupin, the MP for Terrebonne, who would eventually join the NDP, crossed the floor. From our point of view it was good riddance; from now on he'd be Ed Broadbent's problem. Toupin had never been considered one of the caucus heavyweights. Nevertheless, his departure contributed to the growing perception that the administration was adrift in a sea of misfortune.

CHAPTER TWENTY
The "Maz" Shuffle

W hen?
We knew it was going to be soon, but like an army poised to attack, needing only the signal to charge from the commander-in-chief, we awaited the Cabinet shuffle of the summer of 1986. It was highly unusual that we should be consulted, but this time we were. Bernard Roy called all the senior people in the PMO together for a special meeting to get our opinion on Cabinet changes we thought necessary at this point of our mandate. This was definitely a new way of doing things. From time to time the Prime Minister would take us aside individually to get our opinions on this or that person, but never to my knowledge had there been an official meeting called by the Principal Secretary to sound out the whole group on something like this.

Only two people present didn't speak: Bernard Roy and Fred Doucet. They both had privileged access, and everyone knew that if they expressed firm opinions they would be echoing the Prime Minister. A few names were on just about everybody's hit list. Walter McLean, Minister of State for Immigration; Bob Layton, Minister of State for Mines; Jack Murta, Minister of State for Tourism; and Andrée Champagne, the Youth Minister, were the most obvious victims. And sure enough all four were out on June 30.

McLean had been controversial, and didn't seem to be getting along with his senior minister, Flora MacDonald. Layton, the English Quebecker in the Cabinet, hadn't really ingratiated himself with the community he was supposed to represent. His portfolio, mines, didn't give him much chance to shine. Champagne had been a dubious commodity all along, and her strange behaviour in March, when she had embarrassed the government, sealed her fate. As for Murta, I didn't know him and I didn't know why he'd earned the wrath of my colleagues. The other three, however, were on my list.

These were small fry, politically speaking. The big fish was Erik Nielsen. And I wasn't the only one, or even the first, to say that the powerful Erik had become a liability. But how do you fire a Deputy Prime Minister? There was one basic reason for dumping Erik: on the public relations front, lately, he had been a consistent disaster. He had contributed greatly to the image of this government as one that refuses to answer questions, that prefers to operate secretively and retreat into intrigue. I always believed that Erik merely followed orders, like the good old fighter pilot and loyal Conservative that he was. But, paradoxically, his unwavering loyalty to a leader who commissioned his strong-arm jobs, was, by the summer of 1986, his great weakness. I was personally concerned about the image Erik, like Sinc Stevens, projected in Quebec. Our polls showed that our stock was falling drastically in the province where, according to Brian Mulroney, the next election would be won or lost. Nielsen and Stevens, both unilingual anglophones, weren't going to do much to bolster our fortunes there.

In Erik's case it was easy. He had told the Prime Minister some time before that he wanted out of the Cabinet when the shuffle came. I had no reason to believe that that version was untrue. I couldn't imagine the alternative, that Mulroney could simply ditch a man who had become a legend in the party during his lifetime. I never spoke to Erik, but he didn't talk to many people in Ottawa, and then never for very long. On June 30, Nielsen left the Mulroney Cabinet.

Duff Roblin, the Government Leader in the Senate, was the other major victim. He was another one who left me indifferent, but he was ousted mainly to open the way for young Lowell Murray to enter the Cabinet, essentially as the minister responsible for federal – provincial relations, to pilot the constitutional talks. No one around the table had suggested that as part of Murray's new responsibilities. It must have been one of Mulroney's strokes of genius, and given the results of the Meech Lake conference less than a year later, the Prime Minister was bang on.

So much for those who bit the dust.

The task of letting them know their cruel fate was arduous for The Boss. There is always, as the columnists never fail to underline, the conceit that you're somehow diminished by the act of firing people you yourself have put in place. But for Mulroney what mattered most was the human factor. It's not easy putting an abrupt end to a cabinet career, particularly since it's all so public. You have to think not of the people directly involved, but their families, their friends, and even their enemies. Mulroney once confided that he had discussed the question of cabinet shuffle with his predecessor, Pierre Trudeau. He said Trudeau told him that he found it so hard that there were times when he was simply incapable of doing it.

In fact, none of Trudeau's shuffles, during sixteen years in office, was as extensive as the one Brian Mulroney announced on June 30, 1986. More heads could easily have rolled. André Bissonnette, for instance, was on the Prime Minister's hit list, but Bernard Roy, among others, persuaded him to give Bissonnette another chance. I myself was aware of Bissonnette's limitations, but I found him a likeable guy, and I hesitated to say that he should be dropped. I still don't understand how Tom Siddon survived. A year earlier the Prime Minister was ready to have him lynched.

Also, on the list that I saw the night before the announcement — only a handful of us knew then because Mulroney detested leaks — Pat Carney and John Crosbie weren't assigned the portfolios they eventually wound up with. Crosbie was listed as taking over international trade, which would have made him responsible for the free trade negotiations, while Carney was slated to go to transport. Finally, however, it was the other way around. I never got any official explanation of the last-minute switch, but the unofficial version had it that the flamboyant Newfoundlander had flat-out refused to become a "subaltern" to External Affairs Minister Joe Clark. Of the eight new faces in cabinet, four of them from Quebec, Mulroney would later express special satisfaction with the new Youth Minister, Jean Charest, the youngest-ever member of Cabinet at age twenty-eight, and Pierre Cadieux, the new Labour Minister, whose natural aplomb got him over a strong aversion to the media.

There were three guiding principles behind the midterm shuffle. The first two were to put Quebeckers into key economic portfolios, and to politicize the Cabinet by naming, for example, someone like David Crombie, the popular ex-mayor of cosmopolitan Toronto, as Multiculturalism Minister. Crombie's task was much more electoral than ministerial. It was obviously a gamble naming Marcel Masse to the energy portfolio, where, as he had done in communications, he insisted, in a department that was overwhelmingly anglo and very western-oriented, that all communication with him be in French. But part of the plan was to give him a strong deputy minister, to allow him to devote much of his time to his other function as Quebec's political minister.

There was a hot and heavy debate about who, Masse or Benoit Bouchard, would become the Quebec lieutenant. Masse had the edge in experience, but he was oft criticized for his frequent absences from Quebec caucus meetings. Bouchard, on the other hand, was close to the caucus. One of Masse's most ardent supporters was Bill Fox, then the PMO Communications Director. Later, after a few unpleasant run-ins with Masse, Fox said dejectedly, "And to think I was the guy who pushed hardest to have him named the Quebec political minister."

The PMO — to say nothing of the Prime Minister — would be particularly incensed months later, when in November, the Minister of Energy went absent without official leave for at least two days after a run-in with Bernard Roy.

The story began when Roy prevented Masse from using a jet belonging to Petro-Canada, the Crown oil firm, for a trip he had planned to Mexico and Venezuela to meet with his counterparts. Masse, knowing that his predecessor, Pat Carney, had used the Petro-Can plane before, was in such a fury that he left town without telling anyone where he was going. Not the Prime Minister, not his closest staff members, apparently not even his wife, with the result that when Mulroney went looking for him, he couldn't find him. He would say after a desperate search for Masse, that it was discouraging to try to run a country when you couldn't find your Minister of Energy when you wanted him. Masse eventually emerged from his hiding place — outside the country, apparently — and, with the help of his friend Paul Curley from the Big Blue Machine, attempted to settle his differences with the PMO. Although I fully agreed that the Prime Minister had to be able at all times to reach any of his ministers wherever they were in the world, I was one of the few in the PMO that was sympathetic to Masse. Since he had become political minister for Quebec, the frustrations had been accumulating. In fact, though Mulroney had put great importance on our strategy in that province, our organization there was a real circus. On top of appointing Masse to his political responsibilities, Mul-

179

roney had also parachuted in one of his own staffers, veteran organizer Pierre-Claude Nolin, to sort out the mess in Quebec, with the inevitable result that Masse and Nolin were fighting over who was really in charge. The minister also complained bitterly to me once that he couldn't do his job if he couldn't meet with the Prime Minister or his Principal Secretary once in a while. He was of course exaggerating for dramatic effect, but I'm sure he had a point — and I actually believed it enough to bring it to the attention of Bernard Roy. I didn't know what the future held for Marcel Masse when I left the PMO, but he didn't have too many friends left there when I packed it in. This was still in the far future on the day of the "Maz" shuffle.

It was the third principle of the shuffle that was the most important. Its name was "Maz." There was an almost super-human myth around Donald Mazankowski, the Member for Vegreville in Alberta. The Prime Minister's boundless admiration for him was summed up when he declared one day, "He never has problems in the House, never!"

Compared to some of the other bunglers on our team, that made him a rare gem. Maz also had the advantage of being generally well liked by people on both sides of the House, and he was, into the bargain, well respected by the media. The way people were talking about him, after he replaced Nielsen as Deputy Prime Minister, I was afraid the expectations being built up around him might prove crushing. Every time something came up, we handed the ball off to Mazankowski.

At the beginning I don't think anyone really knew what his role was supposed to be. We didn't in the PMO, and I don't think they did in Mazankowski's office, either. The Prime Minister finally explained to us, after the media requests for clarification and our own silence on the subject had become clamorous, that he remained Chairman of the Board, but that Mazankowski would function as his Chief Executive Officer. It didn't quite make it clear to everybody, but at least we had a line for the press. I came to understand, with time, that what Mulroney had done was simply to dump most of the unpleasant tasks on Mazan-kowski, particularly those that kept him in Ottawa. The object of the exercise was to free the Prime Minister once again to exploit his greatest strength, his talent as a campaigner.

Maz and his crew moved into the second floor of the Langevin Block, signalling that the post of Deputy Prime Minister had taken on considerably more importance and clout under Brian Mulroney. In Pierre Trudeau's administration, the post had been largely honorary. Where Nielsen had been Mulroney's handy-man, Mazankowski truly became his right arm.

For some time Mulroney had also been preparing a major shuffle of the senior bureaucracy. We at the PMO were also consulted on that one. My general indifference toward the bureaucracy was such that I didn't really consider myself qual-ified to pass judgement on people's whose capacities I didn't really know. But certain of my colleagues were clearly out to square some accounts, and spoke of a virtual purge to root out Liberal partisans who had burrowed into the upper echelons of the public service.

In fact, the Prime Minister's Office went so far as enlisting the help of a career civil servant who traced the political lineage of many senior bureaucrats, noting their patrons, Liberal or otherwise. The civil servant in question knew all the networks operating in Ottawa, and talked at one point of a "gay network," apart from identifying the hard-core Liberals. I don't think all he said was taken seriously by those to whom he reported, notably Bernard Roy, Fred Doucet and Ian Anderson. After a while some people started to think that he was seeing Liberals under the beds. After all, we couldn't allow ourselves an all-out, screaming witch-hunt.

But then, nobody at the PMO cried for Robert Rabinovitch, the Undersecretary of State when the mandarin shuffle was an-nounced in August. Rabinovitch, who had been closely identi-fied with the Trudeau regime, was dispatched to the guillotine.

The big winner in this shuffle was newcomer Norman Spector, who took over as head of the Federal–Provincial Relations Office from Gerard Veilleux. There was a long and heated debate about how the job should be filled; Mulroney regarded it as crucial to his national reconciliation strategy. Trilingual — he spoke English, French and Hebrew — Spector came to Ottawa from British Columbia and fit in as if he had belonged all along, greatly improving relations between the Prime Minister's Office and the Privy Council Office. For me this was proof that the hatchet could be buried between the political personnel and the career civil servants, to allow us all to work to the same end. But these first signs of harmony came late in our mandate, and it's prob-able that our confrontations with the bureaucracy during the early days of the administration won't likely be forgotten.

A few days later, the Prime Minister would make another key appointment, that of Dalton Camp, a legendary party strategist whose myth was based on the key role he played in the overthrow of John Diefenbaker as Conservative leader twenty years earlier. Camp was named Senior Policy Adviser to the Cabinet, a post Mulroney created within the Privy Council Office.

Camp, who had been at the centre of controversy for most of his political life, as president of the Conservative party, a candidate, and a leading strategist for the Big Blue Machine, came under fire once more. This time the charge was that Mulroney was politicizing the civil service. I never could understand the great fascination the media had with this nomination, as though they believed one man could, by himself, refloat the floundering ship of state. I still don't understand the obsessive preoccupation with what he was doing, who was paying him or what he was like.

He was in fact, a pretty ordinary guy blessed with an extraordinary writing talent and a sharp mind. His greatest contribution was his unflappable calm. He'd often tell us in the PMO to relax. Unlike most of us, Camp never raised his voice at meetings. He'd participate in the discussions, but he'd also report directly to the Prime Minister, who had enormous respect for his opinions.

His great advantage was the sheer weight of his experience. His advice was that of a man who had lived a full and instructive life. I remember one occasion just before I left. Camp was disturbed about a leak concerning prospective cabinet appointments that could only have come from the Prime Minister's Office, where the matter had been discussed a few days earlier. We were in a meeting, and when someone asked Camp his opinion on something, he replied, "Since it's impossible to speak privately around this table, I'll give my advice directly to the Prime Minister."

One of Camp's pieces of advice touched on the Prime Minister's performance at press conferences. Camp suggested a more relaxed approach. "He's fighting the questions," he said. Mulroney was told, but by the time I left, Camp was still not happy with the result. The Prime Minister, for his part, told us that Camp was one of the PMO's biggest promoters, that he praised our work to his vast network of contacts.

"He thinks you're very talented and hard working," Mulroney told us at a staff meeting on January 16, 1986.

During the summer of '86 the PMO staff was once again a target. In mid-June, quoting documents obtained under the Access to Information Act, Southam News revealed that the Prime Minister and his personnel had spent $811,000, that had been gouged out of the taxpayers, on three foreign trips: to Paris in February, to Washington in March, and to New York in October, 1985. Of that, $520,024.17 went for the Paris trip alone. The details of the Paris trip, including the rates at the luxurious Plaza-Athenée, where we stayed, were particularly damaging. The Prime Minister's suite alone cost $3,400 a night.

Once again, this one was lost from the start. We could go on about how the French government had given us a choice of three hotels, and that these hotels had been chosen for security reasons. We could have said that we chose the one we did because it was the one closest to our embassy, and that it wasn't even the most expensive of the three. But it was easier for the media to go on about how much the PM's suite cost, or Fred Doucet's or Bill Fox's; I was glad that I'd stayed at the media hotel, the Meridien.

A month later a furious Prime Minister learned that the French government, had in fact, picked up the tab for his hotel expenses to the tune of $28,525 and that the celebrated suite, about which there had been so much tut-tutting in the media, had cost the Canadian taxpayers not one sou. The letter from External Affairs that confirmed this fact, too late, was then leaked to the CBC. Once again the damage had been done.

"When you think of what my wife and I went through. . ." asked Mulroney afterward.

There was also the story of our in-house "camera crew" travelling aboard the government Hercules aircraft. The crew in question was under the direction of the Press Office, hence mine. From the very beginning of our mandate, production personnel hired by the Privy Council Office had travelled aboard military Hercules or the smaller Buffalo transport planes. Fox and I had decided to use the military planes because it was cheaper and more efficient. Our technicians would lose valuable time flying commercial, and often the delicate equipment they travelled with was damaged en-route on commerical carriers. We also knew that the plane would be routinely used for training flights. They'd fly whether we were using them or not. But the media and the opposition wanted to turn this into a national scandal by insinuating that we were squandering thousands on the Prime Minister's "home movies." It was one of the worst distortions of reality that I saw during three years with Mulroney.

There never was a camera crew. Yes, we had a technical crew that travelled with us everywhere, just as preceding Prime Ministers had had one. They were responsible for setting up the equipment we had to bring along for each stop, and they were sound engineers who made sure that the Prime Minister could be heard and recorded at each event. The greatest irony of the whole affair was that reporters would often, when they had missed something through negligence or otherwise, come to us with a request for a tape of this or that statement that they didn't have.

Part of the crew's equipment was a video camera. There was nothing unusual about that; the Press Office had authorized its purchase. It was a standard piece of equipment in this high-tech age. Had we not had one we could legitimately have been taken to task. And yes, the crew, once they had set up the sound equipment, would sometimes videotape the PM's speech. But anyone who imagined that these tapes would wind up being used for electoral purposes should have seen the dismal quality of the tapes.

Mulroney, as far as I was aware, knew nothing about any of this, because we never felt that the Prime Minister should be troubled with such picayune details. When the media tried to make something of it, he was caught completely by surprise. His first reaction was to ban the Hercules flights for the technicians and the use of the video-cam. I thought he was making a mistake. This was an admission of guilt, yet we'd done nothing remotely reprehensible. One of the technicians told me later, "It doesn't bother me. The cognac is free and the seats are a lot better on Air Canada." Anyone who has ever flown aboard a Hercules, sitting in nets that are basically baggage racks, would understand.

But that was nothing compared to the shabby number they pulled on Bill Fox at the beginning of September. We were in Montreal at the Ritz-Carlton when we got wind of the affair. The Cabinet was in a special session on the second anniversary of the glorious Fourth of September. My office told me that Bob Fife and Tim Naumetz, two Canadian Press reporters, wanted to talk to Fox about something personal. I thought it best to call them first to find out what it was about. Fife, who remains a top notch reporter and one of my good friends, didn't want to tell me anything, insisting it was a personal matter and that only Fox could respond. This didn't augur well, but I told Fox, who was with us in Montreal. He went off to phone the CP reporters straight away, and when he got back he looked like someone who'd just been told his dog had died and he was next.

184

The reporters had combed through the expense account he had submitted after the 1985 Nassau trip for the Commonwealth conference. His "entertainment" costs, which tend to be drinks that we in the Press Office buy for our media charges during the normal course of trips abroad, amounted to $569 for a ten-day trip. The reporters had checked with others mentioned on Fox's expense sheet as recipients of his hospitality, and a number of them said they'd never had so much as a soda water with Fox during the trip in question. My own entertainment bill for the trip had been $421.

Fox made a mistake trying to explain himself. He should have said flat-out that he had nothing to apologize for. But he wavered, and said that perhaps his accounts "may not have been as exact as possible," and that like anybody else on a business trip, he was trying to lose as little money as possible on his expenses.

The flagrant hypocrisy of the affair was that everybody knew it was standard practice among Press Gallery reporters to put our names on their expense sheets when in fact they've been out with someone else. I'm sure that if I'd eaten all the meals and consumed all the liquor attributed to me on media expense accounts, I'd weigh two tons and see nothing but pink elephants. The CP reporters seemed to find the whole thing quite funny that night, but when it was there in sober black and white the next day, it wasn't funny at all.

"I've got kids who are going to read that," said Fox sadly. "They're basically saying I'm a thief."

I was beside myself. I came close to blowing my cool when I ran into Tim Naumetz in the Press Club that week. If Margot Sinclair, one of the radio reporters, hadn't got between us I would have started a brawl right there. The next day, to show how stories amplify as they spread, I got a call from Jeff Sallot of the *Globe and Mail*, who asked if it was true that Naumetz and I had come close to getting into a fight the night before. I told him that nothing had happened, that I've had words with a lot of people in my life. I never saw anything written about it, but I nevertheless warned the Prime Minister, who said I should cool it because I still had to work with these people every day. In other words, he was telling me to get a grip on myself. Bernard Roy told me later that this was precisely his worry, that his career would end abruptly one day when he was sufficiently provoked to slug a reporter.

This was the backdrop for what was to have been our rebirth in September, 1986. After a summer of racing around the country, along with a few days in London for discussions on South Africa, the Prime Minister was ready for a new beginning. We'd been battered, but we still had great expectations.

PART FIVE
Tailspin

"Politics in its more primitive and vigorous manifestations is not a game or a sport, but a form of civil war, with only lethal weapons barred."

John W. Dafoe, *Clifford Sifton*, 1931

CHAPTER TWENTY-ONE

The Peekaboo PM

We had developed a strategy to minimize the damage to The Boss, by keeping him on the road, out of the country, out in the regions — anywhere but Ottawa. Things were going wrong, and the Prime Minister had made it clear that he wanted an approach to communications that would distance him from the disasters, so that was what we did. The difficulty was that we had fallen into the trap devised by Mulroney's obsession with the media; instead of trying to run the country, he was trying to persuade Canadians that he was doing a good job or, at least, that someone else was responsible for all the screwups. Thus, we had Don Mazankowski on hand to be the Tough Cop in Question Period, while The Boss was out in the boonies doing walkabouts and being the Soft Cop.

Fine, as long as nothing went wrong, but when it did, voters were bound to ask: who's in charge, here? If it's Mulroney, he has to take the rap; if it isn't, why isn't it? When things went well, we were unable to cash in on that, either. The fact is that the Mulroney administration had racked up the finest economic record of any government in recent history. Unemployment was down, and the dollar was up; we were making inroads on the deficit; inflation had been brought under control, interest rates were down, and investment soared. Canada's export trade was booming, and the central part of the country was booming in response. While there were difficulties in other regions, we were doing more to rectify them than any predecessor government. Why couldn't we get credit for this?

My own theory is that we were the victims of our own oh-so-clever manipulations. We spent our time reacting to the media, instead of governing.

Did Mulroney have any overall plan in mind? I never knew, and I don't know of anyone else who knew, either. At base, he appeared to be in power to be in power. He meant well, no one could deny that, but what did he mean? No one could explain that. His grand agenda, if there was one, seemed to shift in response to the day's headlines, so that we had major policies which had never been presaged in the election campaign — such as the free trade initiative — and sudden switches that seemed to come from nothing more than a reading of the previous day's headlines, such as the announcement that "Air Canada is not for sale" (when it clearly is), or a sudden change in our South African policy.

The Boss wanted everyone to like him, which is a fine quality, but not a prime ministerial one. He wanted the media to say nice things about him — which, ditto. He forgot, and we forgot to remind him, that what counts in the savage game of politics is not fondness, but respect. If we knew what we were doing, we could survive scandals — Trudeau had come back to power on the heels of some of the most malodorous scandals in the nation's history — but if we didn't know what we were doing, our successes would be put down to luck and our mistakes to malice.

Indeed, that is what happened to us. Those of us in the Prime Minister's Office, especially those of us in the press operation, were partly to blame. However, in the end, the responsibility has to lie with that decent, flawed man, Brian Mulroney. He helped us to forge a new approach to administration — the media is the government — because we became so preoccupied with the unrolling scandals that we lost control of our agenda, if we had one.

Essentially, Mulroney became a manager, in charge of damage control, instead of a leader. In private industry, where you determine your own personnel, management is easier; if someone screws up, you fire him and get someone better. Politics doesn't work that way; you're stuck with the help the public chooses to send you, and if you can't make them work, why did you apply for the job? For all his personal skills, Mulroney never seemed to understand that pretty pictures of himself and his wife in the

Canadian boondocks were not a substitute for a coherent political philosophy. (I write this with the earnestness of one who
has no political philosophy, but then, I don't want to be Prime
Minister.)

So, while we were right to guess that we could survive the
scandals by showing The Boss in a good light, we, and he, were
wrong to suppose that that meant getting good coverage on TV
and avoiding the cameras when trouble loomed. The public hates
the media, by and large; in Britain, in the United States, in Canada during the Trudeau years, we saw leaders consistently re-
elected in the teeth of hostile and even vicious coverage. Yet,
we spent much of our time whining after the journalists, and
raging when they wouldn't make nice.

"So, what are the Boys saying?" started as a routine inquiry,
but ended as an epitaph. Just once, I should have responded,
"It doesn't matter Sweet Fanny Adams what the Boys are saying.
Get on with the job."

The strategy, in the end, wasn't so different from what we'd
tried the year before: to show Brian Mulroney at his best in
controlled situations. We felt we had to cut down on the Prime
Minister's public appearances, because, seeing him on TV every
night, the voters would identify him with everything that bothered them about the government. However, with a televised daily
Question Period in the Commons, it wasn't easy to duck the
cameras. And with a temperament like Brian Mulroney's, it wasn't
easy getting him past a huddle of reporters without having him
give in to the temptation to take a few cracks.

From the fall of 1985, on the recommendation of Bill Fox,
recently named Director of Communications, we suggested the
virtual elimination of scrums, those impromptu crap-shoot press
conferences where the Prime Minister usually wound up looking like a cornered animal. Mulroney thoroughly agreed with
the recommendation, but he still found it hard to resist the lure
of the cameras and microphones. He couldn't block out the
questions they shouted at him, and when he picked up what he
thought was "a good question," he'd give in and answer. But
once he stopped, he was trapped, and then other questions,
mostly not so good, would come fast and furious.

I can't remember all the times he embarrassed Fox or me
when, after having told us that he had no intention of stopping,
he'd do exactly the opposite. This made us look especially bad
in the eyes of our media charges, whom we would have told
before that "No, there wouldn't be a scrum today." After a while

I learned to say that he wasn't inclined to scrum, but you can never tell what might happen.

By the fall of 1986, he was much more inclined to go along with the strategy. As for the House, the previous year he had been nicknamed the "Peekaboo PM" because he'd decided not to be there every day, since Question Period is essentially the opposition's forum. Many of our trips were deliberately scheduled so that we would be gone before the 2:00 p.m. Commons Question Period Monday to Thursday, and 11:00 a.m. on Fridays.

We still planned to spend a lot of time on the road, but this time, when he was away, he could count on a new Deputy Prime Minister, who wasn't thoroughly detested by the opposition, to carry the ball back in Ottawa. It was all very well to tell him to keep quiet, but when his ministers were letting the government be lambasted what was he to do? Still, observers who remarked on the PM's low profile in the Commons in the fall of 1986, were right on the money. The strategy was deliberate, even though by the next January, Mulroney started getting antsy about getting back into the fray. While he had agreed with the low-bridge strategy in the fall, he now felt it was time to be more visible.

To give us time to position ourselves better, the new Parliamentary session was put off until the last day of September, when Jeanne Sauvé read our new Speech from the Throne. But the real main event at this session opening was the election, for the first time ever, of a Speaker by the members of the House, an innovation that was part of the Mulroney government's Parliamentary reform package. I don't know exactly how it was engineered, and there seemed to be only a few people around the Prime Minister who knew what was going on, but I'd been there long enough to know that John Bosley's resignation was no mere happenstance. It was the wish of "those higher up." As for John Fraser, he was, despite rumours and reports to the contrary, our man from the outset. One journalist went so far as to write the next day that Fraser's election had been a slap in Mulroney's face. But then it was hard to convince people after the fact that we'd won this round, though it would have been even worse for Fraser's chances had we shown our hand before the vote. Fraser has since gone on to become a first-rate Speaker.

Our troubles had started in mid-September with a Vancouver speech that should have been a dress rehearsal for the Throne Speech, according to our communications strategy. Speaking to the Canadian Chamber of Commerce, the Prime Minister briefly turned to the drug problem in Canada. He said, "Child abuse is tragically on the increase and drug abuse has become an epidemic which undermines our economic as well as our social fabric. Before this Parliament has run its course, we will have enacted important legislation dealing with these problems."

He said nothing more in a speech that went on for twenty minutes. No one in our organization thought that the same Sunday, September 14, President Reagan would come out with a virulent anti-drug speech. But it didn't escape the attention of the media, for whom the rest of the speech was merely a rehash of platitudes and cliches. John Ferguson of Southam News was the first to come up to me after the speech.

"This drug thing, is it new?" he asked me.

I didn't know what he was talking about. I'd scanned the speech only briefly before it was delivered, and in any case, I'd been assured that the essential message dealt with free trade. Nobody had mentioned new anti-drug programs, and I hadn't noticed the reference in the text. I shrugged and told him I'd find out. Less than two minutes later, David Halton of the CBC came to me about the same thing. I could sense the ditch we were heading for: another spate of stories about how Mulroney acts as Reagan's puppet.

I made my way to where the Prime Minister was sitting, to warn him that he could expect more of this on his way out, with frantic reporters demanding details. It didn't seem to bother him when I told him that for some of the most influential reporters this was the most important part of the speech. To my surprise, Mulroney stopped to answer questions on his way out, saying that he'd heard a CBC radio special that very morning on the drug epidemic in Montreal. He said the government would introduce criminal measures as well as education programs to combat the epidemic.

The next day Liberal Leader John Turner accused him of aping Ronald Reagan. The Prime Minister, meanwhile, held a session with fourteen members of the *Vancouver Sun's* editorial staff, where the drug issue featured prominently. He was asked if he favoured mandatory drug testing by employers and replied, "I am not offended by the notion personally. I am not offended by the notion of a test. Other people are, and we are examining the Charter implications of that."

He was then asked if he was for imposing drug tests should the law allow it, and to that the *Sun* took his answer to be, "Uh huh."

On that basis, the newspaper ran a major story which had Mulroney favouring the notion. The next day, during a stop in Brandon, Manitoba, he was beset with the question once more. Impatiently, he said that he'd never said he was for mandatory tests.

Back in Ottawa, I listened intently to the tape of the session at the *Sun*, which I'd attended. There was no "uh huh" on the tape. I'd been there for the interview, and I remember him nodding his head and murmuring something, but I knew him well enough to know that he didn't give a categorical reply. I couldn't believe that the *Sun* would base such a major story on such feeble evidence. The session was to have been exclusive to the *Sun*, but this time I played the tape to the other reporters, convinced that it would prove our point.

But no matter; even though we were probably on the right side of the great majority of public opinion on this one, we'd let ourselves become absorbed for four full days with something that wasn't even on our agenda. The anti-drug offensive had been approved by the Cabinet at the meeting in Saskatoon back in July, but we weren't ready to mount a communications campaign on it by any means. Like complete amateurs, we'd blundered onto a slippery slope of our own making, and Mulroney, rather than applying the brakes by saying, as he should have, that he couldn't comment before the Throne Speech, plunged blindly ahead. We were doing what we swore we wouldn't do: letting others dictate our moves.

There was too much of this, like the little favour we did for Grant Devine when we delayed the announcement that the notorious CF-18 maintenance contract, worth $1.4 billion, would go to Canadair in Quebec, and not Bristol Aerospace in Manitoba. For months there was no doubt in my mind that the contract would go to Quebec, even though Bristol had submitted a lower bid. But there was still the damn Saskatchewan election where Conservative Premier Grant Devine was one of Mulroney's most loyal allies. The contract would affect only Manitoba, but the bad reaction there was bound to overflow into neighbouring Saskatchewan. Devine, as the results showed, was in a close race, and any negative gesture by Ottawa at this point could be devastating. Devine won his election on October 20. The CF-18 contract announcement came on the 31st, and, as expected, Manitoba's NDP Premier Howard Pawley hit the roof. I always thought that the NDP in Manitoba, Ottawa and elsewhere were mostly upset about having lost an election they thought they should have won against the Tories in Saskatchewan. Mulroney had snookered them politically, trailing the doubt about the contract until the election was won. But while that may have been fine and dandy for Devine, it cost the federal party dearly in the west. And, paradoxically, it didn't bring many dividends in Quebec.

Mulroney urged us to get reporters to ask NDP leader Ed Broadbent if the contract shouldn't have gone to Quebec, but both Broadbent and Turner kept their heads down on this one, saying only that the bidding process had been short circuited. I agreed that the reporters should have forced Broadbent to stand up and contradict Pawley, but they wouldn't play our game, preferring to devote their space to Pawley's complaints.

The Prime Minister agreed to meet Pawley in Ottawa on November 3, but it was mostly to tell the Manitoba Premier to his face that he didn't appreciate his public comments and the personal attacks Pawley had added to his litany of complaints against the federal government. After the meeting Mulroney told us that henceforth all federal business in Manitoba would be done over Pawley's head, that he should share none of the credit when the federal government had something favourable to announce, and that he was to be kept in the dark as much as possible. It took months before peace was restored.

Later Mulroney got his revenge on a public platform when he cut Pawley off at the ankles at the first ministers' conference in Vancouver on November 20 and 21. He reminded Pawley, who had, as expected, attacked the federal government's "sense of fairness" in the CF-18 affair, that the Manitoba Premier hadn't questioned his sense of fairness back when he went to Manitoba to defend Pawley's bilingualism policy before the local Conservatives. Mulroney had been waiting patiently for this opportunity to ambush Pawley. And it was obvious that he had succeeded. It was pure Mulroney. There was nothing better than being underestimated by your adversary was one of his favourite maxims.

The softwood lumber tariff problem had been building for months now. A US lobby group, the Coalition for Fair Lumber Imports, had already asked its government to slap a thirty-two per cent countervailing duty on Canadian softwood lumber which they contended was unfairly over-subsidized in Canada. In 1983, Canada had been faced with similar accusations and won its case in the US courts, thereby avoiding the tariff. But the Mulroney government was persuaded this time that with the rise of a powerful protectionist surge in America, and on the eve of the US midterm elections, the battle was lost before the first shot could be fired. On October 16, the US Commerce Department announced the imposition of a fifteen per cent tariff on Canadian softwood imports which, according to the previous year's figures, would amount to $2.9 million. It would be levied on imports from British Columbia, Quebec, Alberta and Ontario. I was on tour with The Boss in the Maritimes when the tariff decision came down. The Prime Minister's first reaction was that fifteen per cent was at least not the thirty-two per cent demanded by the American producers. It wasn't a victory, but it wasn't a total defeat either. Nevertheless, Trade Minister Pat Carney was dispatched to find a better solution.

I understood the political implications of the issue, but the technical details puzzled and bored me. The first time I took a real interest in it was when Pat Carney arrived at the Prime Minister's temporary office at the Hotel Vancouver, where the annual economic conference with the premiers was taking place. Carney, accompanied by senior officials from her department, appeared to be in an advanced state of excitation as she told of the "miracle" that would allow a more amiable settlement of the lumber dispute. The nub of it was that American Commerce Secretary Malcolm Baldridge, who later died in a freak rodeo accident, had agreed to replace the US tariff, that would have gone into American coffers, by a fifteen per cent Canadian export tax, that would leave the money in this country. According to the minister, Baldridge had agreed to withdraw the US producers' petition, even though it was beyond his power to do so.

From that point on, the items on the conference agenda, such as women's rights, the constitutional debate and regional development were all but forgotten. The news angle for the media, as well as the preoccupation of the premiers, lay with the softwood lumber question. Mulroney was trying to get a common front of premiers behind him in seeking a negotiated agreement with the Americans, rather than pursuing a court fight we stood to lose. We knew that David Peterson would turn out to be the biggest problem, even though the great bulk of our lumber exports are from B.C., Quebec and Alberta. During one of the supper breaks, Robert Bourassa, a fellow Liberal, tried to talk Peterson into changing his mind. I can still see them now, standing there together in the corridor, surrounded by their advisers, with the Quebec Premier defending the federal position. How times had changed! In an effort to achieve consensus, Mulroney had scheduled a special evening meeting with the premiers to deal with the lumber question that had landed on the conference agenda like a fly in the soup.

Before it began I was told that it wouldn't last long, maybe fifteen minutes at the outside, because apparently we had an agreement. The Quebec delegation had phoned the Prime Minister shortly before to say that Peterson had been brought onside. That made me happy for two reasons: there was good news and I could knock off early. I was afraid the meeting would drag on all night. They all crowded into a little meeting room at the far end of the grand ballroom away from where the TV cameras were set up. After a few minutes the door flew open and the Prime Minister emerged with a thunderous look on his face, practically running, with his senior adviser, Fred Doucet, trotting at his heels. It was obvious something had gone wrong. Having seen The Boss's expression I didn't dare go into the office, but I found out a few minutes later that Ontario had welched on its original agreement to go along with us. Why? Had we misunderstood the message from Quebec? The answer could only come from David Peterson, because when I went to see my Quebec counterpart, Ronald Poupart, he was equally perplexed. The common front never came to be.

As usual it all culminated in a catastrophe, this time during the holidays between Christmas and the New Year. Pat Carney was in Hawaii. There were suggestions from Vancouver that she wasn't in the best of health, but every time I wanted to talk to anyone about it, it was as though I was asking for the key to the mystery of Easter Island. Fred Doucet and Bill Fox, neither of whom took many vacations, took over the dossier at that point. Their Christmas holiday was largely spent on the phone or in conference. In the end, the fifteen per cent solution was imposed by Ottawa and all we reaped from it was criticism.

The notorious Port Cartier prison, "my poor prison" as the MP for Manicouagan, who had the additional misfortune of being Prime Minister, used to call it, was also prominent in the news that fall. First, because a government source leaked the allegation — almost certainly true — that the Prime Minister had intervened personally to have the prison built in Port Cartier, in his home riding, instead of Drummondville as originally planned, and also because Auditor General Kenneth Dye maintained in his annual report that shifting the prison would waste millions of dollars. Never mind our arguments about the need to help hard-hit areas; never mind the fact that the original site had been a patronage plum for ex-Liberal minister Yvon Pinard; this is another one that was lost from the outset.

Well, at least some things are predictable. When the delegates to the Liberal convention confirmed John Turner at the end of November, it was as Brian Mulroney had predicted all along. We would have liked him to get a little less than the seventy-six per cent support he got from the delegates. If he'd been in Joe Clark's grey area, between sixty-five and seventy per cent, the infighting in the party would have continued with even greater vengeance, with Jean Chrétien's guerrillas hacking away steadily at Turner's authority. We could only hope that his subsequent surge in the polls, also predicted by Mulroney, would be temporary.

As autumn drew to a close in 1986, the Liberals had climbed from thirty-six to forty-five per cent in public opinion, while we slid from thirty-five to thirty per cent and the NDP hovered between twenty-nine and twenty-five per cent. But the numbers didn't discourage us because on December 5, the Prime Minister gave his best press conference since taking office. To the great satisfaction of his partisans, not to mention a few members of the Press Gallery, he clothes-lined Claire Hoy of the *Toronto Sun*, who had been hard on Mulroney from the day he arrived in Ottawa.

Hoy asked a potentially explosive question, wanting to know if Mulroney felt he could regain the trust of the electorate, and if it bothered him that some people were calling him "Lyin' Brian."

Mulroney responded calmly, without a moment's hesitation. "The Liberals and the New Democrats," he said, "will have to decide if there is any great market in character assassination and sleazy personal attacks. You'll have to decide whether people believe that. I think that you are going to find that in the long run, people who read bitter personal attacks and carping personal criticism on a daily basis usually find the author more offensive than the target."

The Boss was back in shape. We thought we were getting back on the right road, and even some of the commentators seemed to think so, saying that perhaps we'd finally gained control of the agenda. It was a phrase that gave me shivers, like the sound of thunder on the morning of a parade.

CHAPTER TWENTY-TWO

The Ladies and the Tramp

When it became common knowledge among my former colleagues that I was writing a book about my time in the Prime Minister's Office, a number of people coyly asked if it was going to be a "kiss and tell" book. It didn't take me long to develop a stock response, "It's the other way around with me," I'd say. "I kiss, they tell."

It's something I can laugh about now, but the reference is to the bitterest, most excruciating episode during my stay in Brian Mulroney's press office.

It was the first week of November, 1986. That Monday, the media mob was squeezed into the entrance hall of the Langevin Block where we would occasionally hold semi-official press conferences, which tended to be more like semi-organized scrums. That day's special event was a visit by Manitoba Premier Howard Pawley, who had come to complain to the Prime Minister about the hotly contested CF-18 fighter maintenance contract.

Among the group camped at the doorstep of the Press Office was Derik Hodgson, sometime journalist, sometime gossip columnist for the *Toronto Sun*, and now head flack for the Canadian Labour Congress. Hodgson, with whom I used to joke regularly, had adopted Fox and myself as two of his choicest targets some time ago. At one point he cited an unnamed Conservative source to the effect that the Tory caucus had nicknamed us "Null and Void." I didn't find this too pleasant, but I readily accepted it as part of the game. And that's precisely what

I told him that morning about one of his recent little items about me.

"It's okay, I don't take what you write seriously," I said.

Maybe he misunderstood; I'll never know. But what he wrote about me during the next few days was nothing to be laughed off. I was about to get a lesson in what "serious" means.

The next day, November 4, began badly. Somehow it had escaped my mind that I'd arranged an early morning meeting with the executive of the Parliamentary Press Gallery, who were as important to me in my function as voting taxpayers are for an MP. I took my time, doing a few things around home that I'd put off too long, and it came as a great surprise when the office phoned to tell me that Fox was wondering where the hell I was while he and my assistant, Vera Holiad, were confronted by the ten members of the Gallery executive. Since I was the Press Secretary, shouldn't I be there?

I dropped everything and rushed off to the Langevin Block, and arrived out of breath at Fox's office just as the meeting was drawing to a close. I couldn't have been there for five minutes before they were all gone.

Fox was still in a state of semi-shock when he came into my office afterward. "You're really something else," he said. "You set up a meeting, and then you make a cameo appearance!"

He laughed heartily, while I felt like a complete idiot. Maybe what happened next had absolutely nothing to do with any of this, but maybe it was also a signal that my planets were in poor alignment, that my karma was scrambled that day. About three o'clock in the afternoon, I was lingering over the remains of lunch at the Press Club, listening to what some of the Boys were saying. There was an announcement on the loudspeaker that there was a phone call for me, but then this wasn't unusual; it happened about every fifteen minutes whenever I strayed into this den of iniquity.

It was Hodgson of the *Toronto Sun*. He started off telling me that he found it very difficult to say what he had to say to me, stuttering at one point that he wasn't really talking about sexual harrassment, quote, unquote. These two buzzwords never fail to provoke a searing reaction in Ottawa's bureaucratic atmosphere; their very mention close to home makes strong men turn to jelly. Hodgson went on about two women members of the Press Gallery who apparently claimed that I had asked them out socially. He named Judy Morrison, a CBC radio reporter, to whom I had apparently made such advances while she was asking me for an interview with the Prime Minister, and mentioned another reporter, not named, with whom I'd supposedly behaved in the same manner while she was seeking a similar interview.

Were they suggesting that I had tried to exchange interviews for sexual favours? No, apparently that's not what they were saying.

It was then that I made my big mistake, flying off the handle and threatening to run a platoon of hobnailed lawyers up his back if he dared to run anything in his scummy rag that so much as alluded to any such thing. He told me not to threaten him, saying that he was trying to be fair. He also told me that other people were working on the story. In other words, I'd better get ready for a few more calls like this.

I'd known Judy Morrison pretty well for at least five years. She was the Vice-President of the Press Gallery when I was President, and she succeeded me as President when I joined Mulroney's office. I also knew her husband, Phil Kinsman, a former reporter for the *Ottawa Citizen* and the *Ottawa Journal*, whom I'd always admired as a fine writer. And maybe it was true, though for the life of me I can't remember the specific instance, that I joked with Judy about going out on a date. But surely, after all these years, she couldn't have taken me seriously? That's what I told Hodgson in the end. My first reaction, once his hideous conversation was over, was to phone Judy Morrison.

At her office they said she wasn't available, but one of her colleagues, Brian Kelleher, took the call and said he had a few questions to ask me. Basically, they were the same questions that Hodgson had asked a few minutes before. I told Kelleher that I was always kidding around like that, and that no doubt I'd asked him out a few times, too. He laughed, and never did anything else with the story.

But not Derik Hodgson. The next day his story ran on page three of the *Sun*, right next to the paper's daily teeth and cleavage photo subject, whose name that day, oh, irony of ironies, just happened to be Judy. The lead paragraph read, "Two female reporters say they were asked out on dates by the Prime Minister's Press Secretary, Michel Gratton, when they attempted to arrange interviews with the Prime Minister."

The next paragraph quoted one of the female journalists as having said, "I did not feel sexually harassed. I just felt insulted."

Hodgson wrote that the two reporters said they did not believe I was trying to trade favours for an interview. "But both thought it was tacky and hurtful."

I was totally floored. Why was he writing this? I hadn't been accused of sexual harrassment, and I hadn't tried to trade favours. What could possibly be the point of this story? That I was heterosexual? I tuned into the Commons Question Period with considerable apprehension that day. If this business was going to blow up, this is where it would happen.

The Liberals didn't touch it. One of John Turner's assistants told me later that they deliberately stayed away from it because they didn't think it was serious enough to merit being raised in the House. And I'm still grateful to them for their restraint, knowing well that their usual tactic was to go for the jugular.

Ed Broadbent, to my everlasting disappointment, didn't have the same rein on his troops. NDP Member Margaret Mitchell rose to advise the Prime Minister that he should caution his staff against asking women reporters for dates, even if it was all simply in jest. This was it, Hodgson's "news" item now had a life of its own.

I got a tip from one of my old friends in the Gallery just before the next bombshell went off in my face. All he said were two words: "Kathryn Young."

It took me less than a whole second to figure out what he was talking about. Two years earlier, after a long evening at the Press Club, spent mostly with a group of Canadian Press reporters, I offered one of their reporters, Kathryn Young, a lift back to her place. It must have been about two in the morning. I'd had a fair amount to drink, maybe a fair amount too much, and on the way to her place in the cab I made a pass at her, perhaps inelegant, but unmistakable. I'd spent a good part of the evening talking to her, and I can't bring myself to apologize for finding her physically attractive.

When we got to her place, even after my advances in the cab, she invited me up to her apartment. It was a highrise, and contrary to some rumours, I did not scale the exterior wall. I rode up in the elevator, like any normal maniac. She, in turn, opened the door with her key and ushered me in, like any normal victim.

Once we were inside she offered me something to drink, a coffee or something like that. But I still had momentum from the party at the club, so I asked if maybe she had something a little stronger.

"I've got some rum," she said.

"I hate rum," I said, gallantly.

"It's all I have."

"What have you got to mix it with?" I asked.

"All I have," she replied, "is pink lemonade."

And that's how I came to have a rum and pink lemonade at Kathryn Young's place at about 2:00 a.m.

It was the first and last time I've ever had a rum and pink lemonade. But I have to admit, I drank it all that night. Maybe I even had more than one. And yes, I must admit I made it clear that I would have liked to share the fair Kathryn's bed. Had she wanted to, I would have shared her floor. But whether she changed her mind or whether she never intended to in the first place, she finally said No. And maybe, under the influence of the pink lemonade, I was more insistent than usual, but her No was obviously final. So, with my pride deflated, I left her place at about 4:00 a.m., telling myself that there's always a next time. The fact was that I liked her a lot and was sincerely hoping to see her again. As for rum and pink lemonade, never again.

This was strongly reinforced the next morning by the hammers ringing inside my skull. But even that didn't prepare me for the nasty start I got when Glen Sommerville, one of the CP reporters and a good friend, phoned me at the office later in the day. Sommerville, a gentle, even-tempered soul, who nevertheless liked a good party now and then, had been part of the group at the Press Club the night before. What he told me made my hair stand on end — as if my head wasn't hurting enough already.

Kathryn Young had apparently called him in the middle of the night in a highly excited state, saying that I'd attacked her in her apartment. I was speechless. How could she have felt attacked? Did she really think I was just interested in a cup of tea when she invited me up? I tried to explain my side of the story to Sommerville, who reminded me that I was in a special position, that I had an important job, and that I had power. Maybe it was naive on my part, but I'd never made the connection before, and as Deputy Press Secretary to the Prime Minister I sure didn't feel as if I had a lot of power. I immediately phoned Kathryn and apologized, saying that if I had hurt her, I deeply regretted it, that I liked her and that I hoped, above all, that our professional relationship wouldn't be affected. Needless to say, I immediately abandoned all thoughts of trying to see her again in intimate circumstances. As far as I was concerned, the affair was over. In fact, I couldn't see any affair there to begin with. Two years later, the ghost of that night's misadventure rose to haunt me.

The headline over Derik Hodgson's story in the next day's *Sun* was: "Reporter alleges PMO sex advances." The first paragraph read, "A female reporter says the Prime Minister's press secretary made sexual advances to her both in a taxi cab and in her apartment."

Hodgson also wrote that Leslie Shepherd, the newly elected President of the Press Gallery, said that Young was "about" the fifth female journalist to complain about Brian Mulroney's official spokesman, Michel Gratton. After the article appeared, Shepherd demanded a meeting with Bernard Roy, the Prime Minister's Principal Secretary. Neither the article nor the President of the Gallery mentioned the names of any more women involved. Meanwhile, Kathryn Young claimed, again according to Hodgson, that she didn't file a complaint at the time of the incident because she didn't want to make waves.

"I made no official complaint," he had her saying. "I was a junior reporter at the time . . . I wanted the whole thing to go away."

Hodgson's story went on: "Young said she kept her silence about the alleged incident until Wednesday when she heard Conservative MPs and fellow reporters laugh at NDP Margaret Mitchell's questions about the matter."

Like Judy Morrison, she did not allege that I tried to exchange any favours for access to anyone. But she insisted, "When you are a representative of the Prime Minister, the highest office in the land, you do not go around doing that to anybody."

This was incredible! How could they drag out a two-year-old episode like this, something that was settled way back then? By then, I'd had enough of this nonsense and I went to see John Nelligan, the lawyer I'd engaged after the first story appeared. But he wasn't terribly encouraging. He told me that there was nothing libellous about calling someone tacky.

"They must have had this checked by their lawyers before it went through the desk," he said, examining the latest piece in the *Toronto Sun.*

Bernard Roy, one of my most solid supporters throughout the affair, called me into his office and asked, "Are there any others?"

Any others? Does McDonald's sell burgers? I didn't want to start counting right there, but a number of names and faces flashed through my mind, and for the first time I started to fear for some of the people I've loved. If they'd dug up Kathryn Young, where would they stop?

And it's not as though it was all one way. I got furious thinking of the female reporters who had called me during the past two years with invitations to socialize. And what about the "gentlemen" of the Parliamentary Press Gallery, who were forever chasing the skirts of female personnel in my office? I believe it's called hypocrisy! Glen Sommerville had told me I had "power." Some power! I'd never felt so vulnerable in my life. Worst of all was the thought that the man with the responsibility for running the country, Brian Mulroney, would have to occupy himself with his Press Secretary's sexual problems.

The Prime Minister, I was told, was 100 per cent behind me. He phoned me at one point and advised me, among other things, not to drink too much, fearing perhaps that I'd stumble into a situation that would aggravate the whole affair. But he did not rise in the Commons to defend me when Margaret Mitchell went after me again after the second *Toronto Sun* article recounting the Kathryn Young episode, just as he had remained silent when she asked her first question two days before. I was deeply hurt — so hurt that I sent a message to Mulroney via Bernard Roy, wondering how he could defend everybody else in his entourage that came under attack, but leave me twisting in the wind. Bill Fox tried to explain to me that it had been the consensus of the PMO strategy group — whose meetings I hadn't been attending that week.

"If we'd let the Prime Minister answer the questions, the whole affair would have been inflated even more," he said. It was cold comfort at the time, but looking back on it now, I understand.

On November 7, Judy Morrison and Kathryn Young, accompanied by the Vice-President of the Press Gallery, Patrick Crampont, of Agence France Presse, met with Bernard Roy and Fred Doucet as Gallery President Leslie Shepherd had requested. Crampont was there as an observer. Not having attended the meeting myself, I had to rely initially on an account that was broadcast on CBC radio's World Report on November 10. "The meeting lasted more than an hour," the report said. "The women agreed to a request to make no public comment afterwards. But CBC Radio News has learned the meeting was an unpleasant one from the very beginning. The women were put on the defensive, cross-examined and felt chastised. When the meeting ended, both women were very upset."

The report also quoted Derik Hodgson of the *Sun*, who, it should be pointed out, was a member of the Gallery executive, as was Kathryn Young, who was the Secretary. The CBC report continued:

"The next day (Friday) Mr. Gratton arrived at a meeting of the press gallery executive. He was uninvited and was accompanied by his lawyer, John Nelligan, one of Ottawa's toughest trial lawyers. *Toronto Sun* reporter Derik Hodgson says it was a blatant act of intimidation. Both Judy Morrison and Kathryn Young were there. Mr. Hodgson says Kathryn Young was escorted from the building through a back door so she could get legal help."

This was taking on soap opera proportions. The report continued with a clip of Hodgson saying: "I'm not suggesting that the lawyer or Mr. Gratton were threatening her in any physical form or with legal papers, but the fact that they showed up unannounced is pretty rough stuff. This is the Prime Minister's Office playing hardball and they're playing it against people who don't deserve it."

I couldn't believe this was being broadcast on the national radio network. What had actually happened is that I had gone to the meeting with my lawyer to try to clear up the situation with the Gallery executive. He advised me that the important thing at this point was to establish whether the "five women journalists" Leslie Shepherd was talking about really existed. After all, no matter how we proceeded, with an apology or by going to the courts, we had to know what we were up against.

I was in John Nelligan's office when I phoned Patrick Crampont, the Gallery Vice-President, who was then meeting with the rest of the executive. I asked Crampont if we could meet with them shortly. He consulted them briefly, called me back at the lawyer's office and said the rest of the executive would rather avoid meeting with us just then.

"Are they meeting now?" asked Nelligan, whose manner and appearance always reminded me of film star Jimmy Stewart.

"Yes . . . on the Hill," I answered.

"Let's go," he said, the way Jimmy Stewart would have said it.

We walked the short distance from Nelligan's office to the Centre Block on Parliament Hill and went directly up to the second floor to the Press Gallery lounge, where the Gallery executive generally holds its meetings. We went to one of the Gallery clerks and asked him to take a message in to the executive in the lounge next door to the effect that we wanted to talk to them. But they remained adamant, despite Nelligan's pleas that all we wanted was to know who my accusers were. Later that day Nelligan issued a statement saying that I was anxious to meet with the Gallery executive to settle the problem.

The next day, I learned that a letter signed by Michael Enright, Managing Editor of CBC Radio News, had been sent to Bernard Roy, asking me to submit a formal apology.

After a week of hurtling along on an emotional roller coaster, I still found it hard to believe that something so intimate as my sex life could become the subject of public debate. On Saturday night I talked to a few Gallery members whom I still counted as friends. They all tried to convince me to apologize if I'd offended anyone. But I still didn't think there was anything for which to apologize.

After a night of tossing and turning, I found myself at Bernard Roy's place. Bill Fox was also there. We tried to figure out what our next move should be, and what they could say on my behalf. For the first time Bernard seriously raised the possibility of a public apology.

"Apologize for what?" I asked, exasperated.

For me, an apology would have been an admission of guilt. But at that point I was more confused than anything else. Maybe I had done something wrong. I didn't know any more. The next day, after dragging myself out of bed, I decided to apologize, just to get it over with. By this time, I was persuaded that it was the only way; if I was going to continue as Press Secretary, having to deal with the Gallery on a daily basis, things couldn't go on like this. For more than a week now, I had been not only useless to the Prime Minister, but a serious liability. My lawyer prepared a two-page statement, accompanied by personal letters of apology to Judy Morrison and Kathryn Young.

The letter to Young said, among other things: "On November 7, 1986, the *Toronto Sun* carried a story reporting on an incident following a social occasion some two years ago. My recollection is that on being informed the next day that you deemed my conduct unbecoming, I apologized to you on the telephone and expressed the hope that the incident would not interfere with our professional relationship. I believe that professional relationship has been maintained on a firm basis since. However, as the incident has now been made public, I wish to repeat publicly my apology of two years ago."

To Judy Morrison I wrote: "I have known both you and your husband professionally for many years, having worked with you both prior to my appointment to my present position. At no time did I intend to embarrass you or to hurt your feelings in any way. If you have taken offense, I apologize most sincerely and assure you this will not happen again."

That pretty well put an end to it, and everybody breathed a sigh of relief. Still to come was a vitriolic column by Claire Hoy in the *Sun*, demanding my dismissal, and a couple of nasty cartoons in the *Citizen* and *Le Droit*, which my brothers and sisters delighted in framing and presenting me with that Christmas. And if that wasn't enough, the country's two biggest papers, the *Toronto Star* and the *Globe and Mail* ran the story of my apology along with a picture of another Michel Gratton, Minister of Revenue in the Quebec Cabinet. This provoked another round of stories on Gratton (the minister) protesting half seriously, half tongue-in-cheek about the case of mistaken identity.

What followed was the remaking of Michel Gratton (the Press Secretary) or at least a tidying up of his act. Bernard Roy called me into his office and said, with all the sincerity I had come to know in him, "Michel, you know me . . . you know how I think and you know that what I'm going to have to ask you is very difficult for me . . ."

I knew what was coming. I was going to effect a substantial improvement in my appearance, because people were starting to ask questions about who I was and what I was doing near the Prime Minister, said Bernard. I had to get a haircut and a few new suits. No more cowboy boots and blue jeans. I could only agree, and even if I hadn't agreed, I didn't have an ounce of strength left to fight him. This whole business had left me completely drained. He didn't tell me, but I understood that the orders had come from the top. The next day, Bonnie Brownlee popped into my office.

"Have you decided where you're going to shop for your new clothes?" she asked. "Do you want me to make an appointment for you with Rinaldo?" Rinaldo was the Prime Minister's barber.

I couldn't have found a better consultant. Hadn't Bonnie been learning at the knee of Mila Mulroney, the quintessence of chic? I asked her who put her up to this, but she said she was only trying to be helpful. I didn't doubt her sincerity, but I was also pretty sure about where the initial suggestion had come from. Anyway, Bonnie and I had a good laugh when we set off to transform my image, starting at a haberdasher's on Bank Street.

"Tell me, are you working today?" asked the owner, looking down his nose at my boots and jeans.

"Sure," I said.

"I see," he said. "You certainly are, uh, casual, aren't you?"

"Will this tie do?" interrupted Bonnie, indicating my favourite, which I happened to be wearing that day, by way of trying to make a start on the new image.

"It's awful," he said, and that was it for the favourite tie.

I felt like Eliza Doolittle to Bonnie's Professor Higgins. My new wardrobe cost more than $1,000. Bernard Roy found our adventures most hilarious. The next day it was Rinaldo's turn to work his magic on my locks. He asked me if the Prime Minister had ever objected to my longish hair. I said No, he's not the type to be intolerant about things like that.

I remember telling my assistant Ann Charron back at the office that a few months from now on we'll be laughing about all of this, and sure enough that's the way it worked out. A few months after I'd resigned from the PMO I was invited to be one of the speakers at a farewell dinner for Derik Hodgson, who was leaving the *Sun* to join the CLC. I was introduced by none other than Judy Morrison, and everyone sat there slack-jawed as I walked to the head table with a baseball bat over my shoulder.

But any tension dissolved immediately with my opening line: "I always carry this weapon," I said, "but I usually keep it concealed."

It brought the house down.

CHAPTER TWENTY-THREE

The Oerlikon Affair

W e were all gathered in the second-floor boardroom of the Langevin Block. It was Friday January 16, 1987. The players were roughly the same as they had been one year before, almost to the day. The Prime Minister was assembled with his senior staff to issue his instructions for the months ahead. I knew how important the meeting was to him when I saw Mila Mulroney walk in shortly after it had started — only she could afford to be late — with Bonnie Brownlee. Her presence there was highly unusual and revealing as to the state of frustration they had both arrived at as the events of the two previous years had unfolded.

The Prime Minister then delivered his "morality" speech.

"We will get an agreement with the United States on free trade; we will get an agreement with Quebec on the Constitution; we will get tax reform through," he said. "But that's not enough. It doesn't catch the people's imagination . . .

"You know, they talk about patronage . . . It is true that we have made a lot of non-partisan appointments, more than any Liberal government, but let's face it, we've appointed a lot more Tories than we've appointed anyone else. We must de-politicize the appointments . . . We need a morality package. It should include appointments, conflict-of-interest rules for elected officials and party financing."

The next day, Saturday January 17, the Oerlikon affair blew up.

I had an inkling that something was coming from a remark Bernard Roy made on Thursday — the day before the "morality" speech. We were at the usual morning staff meeting and the talk turned to a certain minister who might find himself in trouble before very long.

"Yes, and there might be another one, too," said Roy, tersely. He didn't say another word, but I could read in his troubled eyes that something big was tearing him up inside. Still, no one at the table could imagine the dimensions of the firestorm that was about to hit us.

The next afternoon, just after the "morality" speech, Roy briefed me on an article that was likely to run in that Saturday's Montreal *Gazette*, implicating André Bissonnette, the junior transport minister. This is the first I heard of what would shortly become the notorious "Oerlikon affair." Bernard asked me to remain available in case the hammer came down on the weekend.

The timing couldn't have been worse. I had my three young daughters — whom I wasn't seeing nearly enough of already — all set to spend the weekend with me. But I knew that if Bernard's fears were well-founded, I'd have no choice but to climb into my press secretary's harness when the call came.

And sure enough, there it was in Saturday's *Gazette*, a front page story by Claude Arpin, that I hadn't even had time to read all the way through when the phone rang. And sure enough, it was Roy, asking me to come to the office right away. Not having a baby-sitter handy, I trooped off to the office with Valérie, then eight, Marie-France, six, and Brigitte, five, in tow. When we arrived at the Langevin Block, one of the Press Office secretaries, Marie Terrien, took over and transformed a corner of the office into a temporary daycare facility.

It was in Bernard Roy's office on the second floor that I finally got to read the *Gazette* article all the way through. It involved the sale of a piece of land in St. Jean, Quebec, whose price-tag had soared from $800,000 to $2.9 million in the space of eleven days. The land was to be the site for a plant that would build components for Canada's new radar defence system, which had been contracted out to Oerlikon (properly, Oerlikon-Buhrle-Konzern), the giant Swiss military equipment manufacturer. Ian Anderson was also at the meeting, and Bill Fox joined us a little later. Once I'd finished reading, I shrugged. For the life of me I couldn't see what was damaging to Bissonnette in the article. Roy agreed with me, on the basis of what the article included, but I could read in his expression that there was a worm under the rock.

He then showed us an organizational chart that in effect laid out the basics of the *Gazette* story, how the 100-acre property had changed hands a number of times and increased dramatically in value with each flip. In other words, he drew us a picture. It still wasn't clear why we should be taking this so seriously.

"But," he said finally, "the smoking gun is here . . ."

He held up his diagram and pointed to a square a little apart from the rest that indicated the existence of a private, unregistered agreement between the property's last vendor and a certain Normand Ouellette who happened to be the president of the Conservative riding association in St. Jean-d'Iberville and a close personal friend of André Bissonnette's. Worse yet, he was an administrator of the blind trust into which Bissonnette had placed his assets when he joined the Cabinet, in conformity with the Prime Minister's conflict-of-interest guidelines.

I collapsed into my chair. Once again we had a problem that threatened to overshadow everything else. It was already taken for granted then that Ouellette would have to resign as riding association president, but there remained the bigger question as to what would become of Bissonnette.

Fox and I were convinced that appearances were so damaging that the minister would have to resign, at least until the matter was officially cleared up. Bissonnette, according to Roy, was vehemently protesting his innocence and claiming that he didn't see anything so terrible in all of this. That's what he had told the Prime Minister and his Principal Secretary.

Roy hesitated. He liked Bissonnette, and I think he still does, and he was one of Bissonnette's most ardent defenders seven months earlier when Mulroney wanted to dump him from the Cabinet. He also didn't want to be sucked into the media's sensationalist game, or to serve up Bissonnette's head on a platter for the opposition without incontrovertible good cause.

We left things on that indecisive note for that day.

But that Saturday, one thing was irrefutable, and this was my greatest preoccupation at that point: we were on the run. We couldn't claim ignorance later if all the details of the transaction were revealed. Fox and I were convinced it was only a matter of time before someone went to the *Gazette* with the connection to the heart of our organization, now that the real estate transaction had been the subject of a major story. As Fox said, "In a town the size of St. Jean, I bet everybody knows." I could already see the Prime Minister trying to weather the opposition assault in the Commons in a scene borrowed from Watergate. "What did you know and when did you know it?" Above all we had to avoid the mistakes of the tuna affair.

Roy went off to try to root out more information. As for me, I went off to put the children to bed. They had spent a joyful afternoon running merrily through the corridors of the Langevin Block. I deeply envied their carefree exuberance.

The next day, we had just finished watching the latest rerun of Sesame Street when I was called back to the office. I feared the worst, and I was right. With the air of a judge about to pronounce a death sentence, Roy told us that fresh information he had gotten as late as that morning indicated that Bissonnette should be made to resign from the Cabinet. I felt a curious mixture of disappointment and relief, and I'm sure everyone around the table felt the same way. We'd moved quickly to amputate the infected limb, but we also knew that we'd have an enormous price to pay in terms of public opinion, which was already hostile toward us. It was terribly unfair, I thought. Particularly for Brian Mulroney, who had put his confidence and credibility on the line for this guy.

I was assigned to help Fox, who was always the man of the hour on such occasions, to prepare the statement that the Prime Minister would make to the press that afternoon, announcing Bissonnette's resignation.

It was particularly important that we leave nothing out as far as the events that had led to the decision.

Bernard Roy had been contacted by Roger Nantel and Jean Bazin on Tuesday, January 13; he had told the Prime Minister of his worries while he was on holidays the next day; the Prime Minister had then ordered his Principal Secretary to make further inquiries, and, what was of capital importance, was that only the information received that morning finally justified the request for the minister's resignation.

The final draft of the statement read as follows:

"On Tuesday January 13, 1987, my Principal Secretary, Bernard Roy, met with Senator Jean Bazin and Mr. Roger Nantel at their request.

"He was informed of certain facts related to property transactions in the St-Jean-sur-Richelieu area linked to the Oerlikon plant.

"On Wednesday January 14, 1987, Mr. Roy informed me of those facts. I immediately entrusted him to make further inquiries into the matter and to consult with appropriate government officials. Pursuant to this, and in light of information obtained this morning, I requested and received the resignation of the Honourable André Bissonnette from Cabinet.

"I have also asked the Royal Canadian Mounted Police to conduct a complete investigation into the matter. All information assembled has been turned over the the RCMP."

Once the draft was completed in the press office, where my assistant, Ann Charron, was playing baby-sitter that day, we crossed Wellington Street to Parliament Hill where Brian Mulroney was meeting with his Cabinet, sans André Bissonnette, and he had just informed them of the forthcoming resignation over lunch. He then moved on to a meeting of the national Conservative caucus where, according to people who were present, he gave one of his most moving speeches ever.

I felt a constriction in my throat when I went to face him that day. The full weight of his office seemed to be leaning on him, and his drawn features bespoke an immense sadness. There were moments, in the intimacy of his office, where he let his rage boil over to relieve the intense pressure of the situation. He felt betrayed, and he cursed his misfortune in strident tones. "The irony of it," he told me then, "is that I was going to drop him from the Cabinet last June."

He said that at the time he thought Bissonnette "just wasn't working out." But he was persuaded to let him stay. I could imagine the turmoil he must be in at this moment. The last Gallup poll, taken from January 7 to 10, had cast us into third place for the first time with twenty-eight per cent, compared to thirty per cent from the NDP and forty-one per cent for the Liberals. During the ensuing press conference, Mulroney didn't shy away from the evidence staring everyone in the face. When Doug Small, Global TV's Ottawa bureau chief, asked point-blank what effect this most recent affair was going to have on his party's fortunes, The Boss responded, "I will tell you without hesitation that I don't think it will help us."

It didn't take long for the prophecy to fulfill itself. In the February Gallup the bottom fell out on us. We plunged to twenty-two per cent, the lowest reading for a government since Gallup began taking polls during the thirties.

Facing the media in the National Press Theatre, consternation was evident on all our faces. One of the Press Gallery veterans, hardened and cynical, who had seen Brian Mulroney drag him-

214

self over difficult spots in the past, told me in all sincerity afterward: "He really is unlucky."

It was the first time I'd ever felt any real sympathy from journalists toward Brian Mulroney. It reminded me of an earlier episode when Pierre Trudeau went through a difficult period while separating from his wife Margaret. I thought Mulroney was superb that day. I'd rarely seen him so natural, so convincing. He seemed resigned to accept that what had been done had been done, and that nothing could change things now.

Now we had to get ready for the storm that was waiting for us in the House of Commons. Mulroney went in and took the full frontal blast from a furious opposition head on. The Liberals, who seemed to have their own sources of information on this affair, were particularly voracious. The media had a fresh screaming headline every day as details of the affair came out in dribs and drabs.

The opposition, the Liberals in particular, behaved more irresponsibly during this period than at any time during the two-and-a-half years following the election. Not content with only André Bissonnette's head, our political opponents wanted to maintain the climate of scandal, and, above all, to get at the Prime Minister himself.

It was a strategy they had used often in the past: lash out at the Prime Minister by going after his friends. In the Oerlikon affair the link with the Prime Minister was none other than his good friend Jean Bazin, a prominent Montreal lawyer and former law school chum, who was to be sworn in as a Senator in the weeks to come. And he made an ideal target, as had been foreseen by that veteran of this sort of trench warfare, Don Mazankowski, when he was shown the story in the *Gazette*. Mazankowski was right. Bazin had been marginally involved in the land transaction, acting as a lawyer for Oerlikon in the matter only after the suspect transactions had taken place. But he was a long-time close friend of Brian Mulroney's, so the opposition trained its guns on him.

With every passing day, tension mounted in the Prime Minister's Office. We were scheduled to leave for an extended trip to Africa that Friday, and suddenly we were facing a replay of the Asia trip, where our success on the international stage was almost totally eclipsed by the Sinclair Stevens affair back home.

As it turned out, we were a little luckier this time, as the affair showed signs of petering out with our departure. But they were waiting for us when we got back. The Liberals, whose attack had been led by Sudbury MP Doug Frith, played the Bazin card to the hilt by demanding, among other things, that the Prime Minister delay Bazin's swearing-in as Senator, scheduled for February 3.

I was of the opinion that the best thing would be for Jean Bazin to give a press conference to explain his involvement in the affair fully and to show that he wasn't afraid to stand up in public and face the cameras. Up to now, he had insisted on responding to various accusations with official communiques, a tactic rendered largely obsolete in the TV age. I begged Bernard to talk to his friend Bazin, but it was a lost cause. Having failed to convince him, Bernard suggested I call Bazin myself to give it a try.

Bazin was someone I'd come to like, and we'd shared more than a few laughs. But this particular phone call was one of the toughest I've ever had to make in my life because after a few seconds it degenerated into an argument so furious that I was convinced we'd never be able to have a civil conversation again. I must have called him every name in the book, and vice-versa, as I tried to remind him that he was letting down the Prime Minister, his friend, who was, among other things, responsible for that fact that he, Jean Bazin, would soon accede to the life-long security of the Senate.

"If that's what it's going to be like, I don't want to be in the Senate. I don't need it!" he shouted.

"You know damn well you can't do that," I told him.

I could understand that he was upset by the glare of the bad publicity to which he'd been exposed. I'd gone through my baptism of fire in that respect just a few months before, so I knew exactly what he was going through.

Bazin never did give a news conference before he was sworn in as a Senator. I was told later that aides had put him through a test grilling, asking him the kind of questions that would be put to him at a press conference, and it was concluded that such exposure could be catastrophic at a time like this when he wasn't in full possession of all the facts.

He was sworn in as scheduled on February 3, after saying a few words to the reporters on the way in, but without really answering their questions directly. The opposition attacks miraculously abated, which only reinforced our original conclusion as to their intent. Also the same day — a day too late, in fact — I learned that the brother-in-law of Liberal Doug Frith, the same Doug Frith who had been leading the charge against us, was not only a lawyer employed by Bazin's firm, but had done the title search for Oerlikon's purchase of the St. Jean property. Frith had been unbearably sanctimonious in reproaching Jean Bazin for not having warned the Prime Minister of the affair earlier than he did. So why did his brother-in-law not say anything to him before then either? If I'd had that ammunition a week before, maybe the story would have been different.

Bernard Roy couldn't get over the fact that it had become a liability in this country to be or to have been at one time, a friend of Brian Mulroney's. It was a total absurdity as far as he was concerned, and I could only agree.

"It wasn't like that for Trudeau," he told me at the time.

"No," I agreed. "But then Trudeau didn't have any friends."

CHAPTER TWENTY-
FOUR

Graceland

After having carried the government on his shoulders throughout the Oerlikon affair, Brian Mulroney didn't really deserve what happened to him on this Friday, January 23, 1987. Nothing, not even the prime ministership for which he strove most of his life, is as important to him as his family. Some people find that hard to believe, but I often saw the proof, no more so than on this unfortunate day. We were to leave for Africa the next day, but the Prime Minister had already promised long before to speak at an Italian community event that night in Toronto. The plan was that he would fly up on the Challenger and come back to Ottawa after the speech.

Brian and Mila Mulroney never made it to Toronto. During the flight, an urgent message was relayed to the Challenger. The family's eldest son, Benedict, had been involved in an accident at school and been taken to hospital. No one knew how serious his injuries were, but the word hospital is enough to make any parent frantic. The Challenger turned around halfway to Toronto and headed back toward Ottawa as the Mulroneys desperately tried to get more information, but the phone on the Challenger kept being cut off.

Finally, back at the Billy Bishop Lounge at the Armed Forces hangar in Ottawa, they found out that their son had hurt his back, but that the injury was not serious. Tears flowed down Brian Mulroney's cheeks.

But the wheels of our wagon kept turning. We were awaited on the other side of the globe. In Rome first, where we would meet Pope John Paul II and Prime Minister Benito Craxi. Then it was on to Harare in Zimbabwe, and finally to Dakar in Senegal. It was a trip to test our sanity. In all we would spend more than thirty-eight hours aloft in the Armed Forces Boeing 707: eight hours between Ottawa and Rome, eleven hours from Rome to Harare, a two-hour return flight to Victoria Falls, nine hours to Dakar, a two-hour return flight to Sahel and, finally, an eight and one-half hour flight back to Ottawa. And all this in the space of ten days with a skeleton staff.

The media criticism of the Paris and Asia trips, denouncing the excessive entourage, had had an effect. The Prime Minister ordered his adviser for foreign trips to reduce the delegation to a strict minimum. But if ever there was a trip where we needed all the hands aboard we could get it was this one, with its complex itinerary, long distances, and difficult climatic conditions, in which we never knew who would take sick the next day. Even Bill Fox, who had advanced the visit and was one of the few who had seen all the sites, wasn't on the trip. We decided to leave him back in Ottawa to handle the continuing fallout from the Oerlikon affair. The official version was that he was "needed at home."

Therefore we were a relative handful of PMO staffers on the Africa trip: Fred Doucet, the delegation head; myself and Marc Lortie from the Press Office; Gerard Godbout, the translator; and two executive assistants, Rick Morgan with the Prime Minister and Bonnie Brownlee with Mila Mulroney. Our normal complement of technical and support staff was also sharply reduced.

As well, we were carrying a media pack that was watching our every move, poised for the slightest slip after the week we had been through back in Ottawa. Usually on these trips they watch each other very closely because there's nothing more embarrassing than to have to tell your editor that you've missed a story that somebody else has. Editors back home, who tend to regard these trips as pleasure jaunts, find it hard to understand how someone on the same plane can miss a story. So the situation, paticularly between the radio reporters, is generally tense. But this time it was even more so because of the government's current discomfort and our own paranoia about the media.

It had all started badly a few days before when Tim Naumetz of Canadian Press, as a result of a gaffe on my part, wrote a story saying we'd bring a blood bank along with us because of the prevalance of AIDS in Africa. The story wasn't true, but we had created the confusion ourselves when the possibility of such a blood bank was raised by the organizers of the trip.

It never went much farther than that because it was practically impossible to transport the blood we would need without refrigerating it. When Naumetz asked me about the blood bank, I said I'd heard some talk about it because they'd asked me for my blood type, but that I hadn't heard anything more about it. Then he told me that he hadn't been asked his type, and, eternally suspicious, believed that the blood in question would only be for the Mulroneys and the PMO staff, and not the poor scribes at the back of the plane. I never pursued his ridiculous story; it was typical of the kind of thing we could have done without, but which kept cropping up.

Naumetz was back at it in Rome, asking me about a certain satellite dish that had supposedly been set up to allow the Prime Minister to catch newscasts from home. This time there wasn't a shred of truth to the story. We never had a satellite dish anywhere in the world, because the costs were so exhorbitant. We did, on occasion, as in Paris where we stayed for several days, have cassettes of taped newscasts flown in by commercial carrier, but the space-age stuff was strictly in the reporters' imaginations. The print reporters don't know much about "the little details" of intercontinental communications in the satellite age. They thought it was as simple as plugging in a toaster.

When we arrived in Rome, we had a little time to play tourist, and I took full advantage, knowing it was the last break I'd have for the rest of the trip. That night, the Prime Minister surprised us by inviting all the staff to dinner at a restaurant in the heart of Rome — and sure enough, I had to tell some reporters the next day that we'd all paid our bills separately. It was a wonderfully relaxed evening, one of those rare occasions when we could all get together in these difficult times, for the purpose of having fun. The Prime Minister was always handy with a special gesture when someone left, or on people's birthdays, but never had he extended so intimate an invitation.

The centrepiece of the next day's activities was the visit to the Vatican. This wasn't like another factory visit, and even for someone who'd been around, it was most impressive to meet our host here, who has become a legend in his own time. Since there wasn't a photo session at Buckingham Palace, I was in no position to make comparisons, but I was hard pressed to imagine a place in the world more impressive than the papal apartments at the Vatican. Room after room after huge room, adorned in luxury as close to celestial as can be found on this earth. You could see your reflection in the polished marble floors, and lose your breath looking at the frescoes splashed across the walls and ceilings — frescoes by people of the calibre of Michelangelo. The popes of antiquity knew how to encourage the local talent. We were escorted by gentlemen in black habits who are, for the most part, ordinary Romans who perform these honorary functions on special occasions. We were told to wait in one of the rooms and Fred Doucet tugged my sleeve and indicated one of the windows.

"You know when the Pope talks to the people in St. Peter's Square from a window?" he asked.

I looked to where he gestured.

"Well, that's the window!" he said excitedly.

If only I'd finished seminary, I thought. To my great surprise we were then informed that we would join the Pope and the Prime Minister in the room where their meeting took place. But I still wasn't prepared for the scene when the door was opened to the next room where, escorted by our guides in black suits, we were not only ushered into the Pope's presence, but introduced, each in turn, by the Prime Minister. His Holiness gave each of us a souvenir medallion embossed with the effigy of Christ. There were three kinds: gold, silver and bronze. I got a bronze one; the Pope must have heard about the debauched life I'd led.

You have to be made of stone not to be moved by the sheer presence of the man who leads the Catholic church, particularly this man. His face, like his voice, is a blend of saintly calm, yet absolute firmness. He's built like a linebacker, but he wears his habit with a natural ease that makes it seem as though he was born in it. From all points of view you get the impression of being in the presence of a colossus.

It was right after that that Mario Proulx, one of the Radio Canada reporters, did something about which he'll be able to tell his grandchildren. In effect, he "scrummed" the Pope. It happened when, to their great surprise as well, the Pope went over to talk to the reporters as we exited. As he approached, Proulx dared ask him in French, "Will you come back to Canada, Your Holiness?"

As he said later, with the Pope you have to be polite.

"Oh, I think it's enough for now," he said laughing, indicating that he'd been to Canada already and that other parts of the world still awaited his first visit. But later he added, "But I still have an obligation; it's to the Indians. We'll see what we can do about that because I'm committed, I gave my word." On his 1984 visit to Canada, the Pope was scheduled to visit Fort Simpson, in the Northwest Territories. Bad weather cancelled the trip, but he said he'd be back.

He then withdrew before any of the English reporters could work up the nerve to ask the question in English. Hence the only voice clip from the Pope was in French that day. Some of the English radio and TV reporters were furious, but the French reporters were laughing. They kidded Claire Hoy of the *Toronto Sun* who had said, when asked what he, a unilingual anglo, would do in a French country like Senegal, "If it's important, they'll say it in English."

The French reporters took delight in telling him that it couldn't have been important because the Pope didn't say it in English. And Mario Proulx told me afterward, "There were miracles here today. Everybody bought me a beer."

The Pope, by answering the question, had done us a considerable service. He had given the media a story for that day, and we could breathe easier, knowing they wouldn't be looking for targets the rest of the day. They certainly weren't interested in our meetings with the Italian leaders.

That evening, after nightfall, we took off for Zimbabwe, where we were awaited the next morning. I found out at that point that the Prime Minister was sick as a dog, running a temperature and barely able to stay on his feet. I couldn't see how he could make it through the insane schedule that we'd prepared for him. Few people in the entourage were aware of it and none of the media were to find out, otherwise it would become the day's story.

The welcome in Zimbabwe was impressive after eleven hours in the air. Our hosts chanted and danced, and what drew our attention most were the wild turkey calls they made to demonstrate their joy at having us there. I'm not trying to poke fun at them; for them it's the same thing as singing "Na-na-na-nah, goodbye" at the Forum during a Habs–Nordiques game. But for us, from the other side of the Atlantic and the far side of the equator, it was like arriving on another planet.

Harare, as a city, doesn't much resemble most other third world capitals. Its avenues are broad, the vegetation is lovely and well tended and people don't appear to beg or sleep in the streets at night. It's relatively safe for a stranger. The South African commandos are a lot more dangerous than the local criminals. Our hotel, a Sheraton, was a spanking new golden cube on the city's outskirts. There we didn't get the impression that we were in a country with a war on its doorstep, in Mozambique, and slowly being choked by the apartheid regime in South Africa.

This is why Brian Mulroney was here. In keeping with the strategy devised at the Commonwealth conference in Nassau, he wanted to "tighten the screws" gradually on South Africa. He was the first leader of a western nation to visit Zimbabwe since its independence. The reporters on the tour found it hard to believe when our high commissioner in Harare, Roger Bull, told them that the local authorities feared for Mulroney's safety, being so close to South Africa. In fact, a month after our visit, the South African Air Force, under the pretext of flushing out an encampment of rebels, bombed the Livingstone Road, the road the Prime Minister took to Zambia. Moreover, Bull later gave a sparkling briefing, basically a press conference not for direct attribution, that fascinated everyone present including myself. A few people said afterward that they should all be like that, and I felt good. The wind was shifting slightly in our favour and the paranoia of the early phase of the trip was abating.

All day long Mulroney fought down his flu; through the arrival ceremonies and meetings with Prime Minister Robert Mugabe and President Rev. Canaan Banana, he never flinched. I remember him saying at the debriefing that night that he wasn't at the top of his form, but I never heard him complain, and that night he had to give a speech at a dinner that the Prime Minister of Zimbabwe was giving in his honour. As if that wasn't enough, there was trouble on the home front, where the controversy over the Canadian—France treaty on east coast fishing rights was about to erupt.

Meanwhile, we were trying to cope with the intricacies of Zimbabwean protocol. Our hosts were nice people, don't get me wrong, but they could change their minds about things from one minute to the next with disconcerting frequency. Maybe this isn't a compliment, but our logistical and technical support machine for the Prime Minister was just that — a machine. There's nothing that worries us more than to be uncertain about details of an event in which the Prime Minister will take part. The Zimbabwe people, on the other hand, were much more laid back. With the result, for example, that on the evening of January 27, minutes before the state dinner, I wasn't able to tell our reporters, particularly those who wanted to tape the event, whether the Prime Ministers would speak before dinner or after, before the soup or after the soup, before dessert or after dessert.

It was chaos as far as we were concerned. Finally, we got a decision from the protocol chief that the speeches would come after the soup. We were lobbying to have them before the meal, as is our custom in Canada, but the compromise was more than acceptable.

I took that to mean that our reporters should stay outside the banquet hall until after the soup was served, then slip in when the speeches were announced.

So there we were, relaxing behind the closed doors, making conversation, when suddenly the doors were flung open and there was Robert Mugabe, at the lectern, already well into his speech. The protocol chief had taken it on himself to announce to his Prime Minister that he would speak before the soup. We bolted into the room like bulls into a china shop. After that, the next time a Canadian reporter asked in Zimbabwe, "What's happening now?" I had only one answer, "Haven't a clue."

The next day we went about an hour by road into the bush to a place called Kutama where there was a mission founded by Marist Fathers, most of them from Quebec, and where Robert Mugabe had gone to grade school. His mother, who still lived in a nearby village, accorded the Canadian Prime Minister the rare honour of coming to meet him, something that is just about never done according to Zimbabwe's cultural traditions.

The welcome we got from the local population was unbelievable. We'd expected a few hundred, but they were there by the thousands, to see the Prime Minister from the land of snow step down from the helicopter with their local hero, Robert Mugabe. The air was thick with the wild turkey cries that we first noticed at the airport, and there was a deliriously joyful confusion as the security men steered away the most enthusiastic revellers. We'd never seen anything like this in our lives. I told Fred Doucet, "Before we leave, get the name of their organizer so we can sign him up for the next election."

The highlight of the Zimbabwe visit was the side trip to Victoria Falls, one of the highest in the world, where Mulroney was to meet with Mugabe and the leaders of three other "front line" states, so called because they were directly affected by reprisals from their white-dominated neighbour, South Africa. Coming in from the air was a breath-taking experience, as we overflew the Zambezi River, cutting through its towering banks of sheer rock that looked as if they were gouged out of the jungle by a giant bulldozer with an impeccable sense of symmetry. As for the falls themselves, try to imagine Niagara twice as high. It makes you feel very small.

Mulroney was scheduled to meet the four African leaders on Zimbabwe soil, then cross the border for an official visit to Livingstone in Zambia, accompanied by the country's impressive president, Kenneth Kaunda. The meeting was preceded as usual by a photo session. Another little photo op, I told myself, relaxing on the terrace along with a few crocodiles and some of the reporters. Everything seemed to be going perfectly when, by force of habit, I went down to the press room to see what was happening. There I found out that the photo op was still in progress twenty minutes after it had started. I immediately started to worry because these things were supposed to take five minutes at best.

"How can it still be going on?" I asked, panic mounting.

Without waiting for an answer, I rushed off to the meeting room. There, to my horror, I saw that all of the leaders were giving little improvised speeches before the TV cameras. What was going on? I noticed Marc Lortie and threw him a desperate look. All he could do was shrug his shoulders; this wasn't his doing, either. I found out later that once the pictures had been taken, and at the point that the media pool is usually ushered out, Mugabe invited them all to stay and hear the opening statements of the meeting in which the leaders, among other things, justified the use of violence against South Africa. Mulroney spoke last. No one in our organization was aware of the arrangement. Mugabe had proposed it at the last minute, and Mulroney had graciously accepted — only he'd forgotten to tell us.

But Mulroney was no dupe. He knew very well that this was a chance for these African leaders to get their message across to public opinion in the West by way of the TV cameras we'd brought along. Our media later suggested that Mulroney had walked into a trap beside Victoria Falls that day, but as far as I was concerned, he knew exactly what he was doing and what his gesture meant to the fight against apartheid.

Once the meeting was over, we all crossed the border to Zambia, where the Press Office's main concern was getting a picture of the Prime Minister with the falls. It was like the Citadel in Quebec and the Great Wall of China — a natural for the front pages. But at the last minute, saying he was dead tired, Mulroney changed his mind and decided not to go. I couldn't believe my ears. The plan was being changed after we'd come all this way. But the Boss was adamant. He went as far as the bridge over the Zambezi with the President, where they could see the falls from afar.

The next day the Prime Minister was scheduled to hold a press conference. We were worried about the way Mugabe and the other African leaders had advocated violence against South Africa in his presence, and we expected the initial thrust of the questioning to be along that line. It was. The Canadian media wanted a clearer answer from the Prime Minister as to whether he agreed with the speech put forward by the front-line states. Mulroney handled the questions deftly, saying he couldn't really put himself in the place of a Robert Mugabe, who was living a totally different reality and who had even been imprisoned for a number of years.

We all thought that he not only handled himself well, but that he was excellent. As always, he was at his best when speaking from conviction, but I also felt that the role of Prime Minister suited him more and more, and far from enfeebling him, the difficulties he'd been through had given him a kind of serenity.

From there, it was on to Senegal where another reality awaited us. The extravagant welcome, fit for a conquering emperor, was matched only by the human misery that reigned on the streets of Dakar, a city which is, in essence, an open sewer except, of course, for the oasis of affluence where foreigners stay, and where the capital's wealthy minority lives. There were perhaps a million Senegalese massed along the route from the airport to the capital, cheering frenziedly as though we had just liberated the city. They chanted: "Abdou, Abdou . . ." in honour of their President, Abdou Diouf. I was at the head of the motorcade, in the army trucks carrying the photographers and cameramen filming this incredible scene. Except for a short distance, the President and the Prime Minister stood in their convertible limousine, waving to the delirious crowds along the road. A motorcycle escort brought us to the centre of the city where they gave way to scarlet-coated cavalry reminiscent of Napoleon's lancers. I couldn't help but think that they should see this back in Canada, where people were going on about our presidential airs. Our little podium was chickenfeed compared to this.

But the pomp and ceremony laid on by our hosts obscured another world that lay in the over-populated capital, where famine was a daily fact of life, where children, often blind or deformed, begged in the streets, where you took your life in your hands going for a walk after sunset. The third world is full of contradictions. The reality is something most of us prefer to know from afar, and to forget most of the time, without having to confront it close up.

Fortunately, there are people more charitable than I, like the French doctor who ministers to lepers in a colony outside the city that Mila Mulroney went to visit. What struck her, she said later, was the dauntless joy she saw on the faces of the lepers and the children of lepers who live isolated from the world, hoping for cures which are fortunately becoming more frequent. Perhaps there was joy on the faces of the children, but I couldn't help but think how I'd react if someday I was told I had leprosy, or worse, that my child was stricken. We were a long way away from tuna and Oerlikon. Everyone, including the reporters I convinced to come along, were shaken by the experience.

However, politics would soon bring us back to our artificial little world. Along with several meetings with leaders of neighbouring states, Mulroney was scheduled to deliver another speech. As far as I was concerned, it was to be another routine speech; certainly no one told me otherwise. Moreover, the speech was in French, so it would have to include something stupendous to interest our anglo press contingent.

But I was wrong. In his speech Mulroney said that Canada had imposed sanctions on South Africa, and that more would follow. The words didn't mean that much in themselves, but they roused the reporters, sensitive to the diplomatic implications of Mulroney's statement. It was CBC radio veteran Brian Kelleher, one of the best reporters in the Press Gallery, who asked me if this signalled a change in our policy toward South Africa. Up to then the Prime Minister had spoken about applying more sanctions, but always qualified it by saying that this would be done if South Africa made no more progress toward desegregation. But there was no "if" in the Dakar speech. Kelleher had spotted it right away.

I didn't know what to say. I dodged and darted a bit, but I was basically cornered. I had to agree that the Prime Minister's statement was more categoric than any he'd made before. I did so fully knowing that he hated having us interpret his speeches, but I didn't have much choice. Back at the hotel, I phoned Fred Doucet in a panic, telling him, "I got snookered. Nobody told me what was in the speech."

Doucet started out by saying that there was no change in the policy, or any difference between the speech and our position up to now. I couldn't believe that he didn't see it. He finally admitted that maybe I was half right, but later, after a conversation with the Prime Minister, he reverted to his original stance. Cy Taylor, the Under Secretary for External Affairs, repeated the same thing to the media at a briefing that followed, and there was general confusion. Fortunately, it was Saturday; most of the papers weren't publishing the next day, and the TV networks weren't as exercised about it as the print reporters. For a while I thought I'd ruined the whole trip, and I had some choice words for the guy who was supposed to edit the speech.

Still to come was the trip to the South Sahara with the great sand dunes that we've all seen in our geography texts. The reporters and cameramen wouldn't stop kidding me because I was wearing a shirt and tie. Everybody, including the Prime Minister, wondered if I'd gone off my nut: here he was having so much trouble getting me to dress right in Ottawa. All along the media hounds found it hilarious to see me changing my outfit four times a day. Inevitably whenever we would arrive at the hotel I thought I'd be able to relax a bit like everybody else, but there was always a call from the presidential palace. The Prime Minister wanted to know what the Boys were saying.

The desert air was almost impossible to breathe. There was sand everywhere. From the air there seemed to be a veil of dust cloaking the immense stretch of dunes as far as the eye could see. With every breath it seemed as if your nostrils were clogging with dust. The sun, in the cloudless sky, beat down mercilessly, and the wind carried more sand that stung the skin and burned the eyes. And yet, people had been living here for thousands of years.

Modern science has been taking these traditions into account and working miracles, in part with the help of Canadian aid. We saw immense vegetable gardens in the middle of the desert, where nothing had ever grown before, thanks to modern irrigation and new techniques to hold back the inexorable march of the dunes. Once more, even though we made reference to Canadian foreign aid programs, we felt far removed from mundane political concerns.

I climbed back aboard the Canadian Forces 707 on Monday February 2nd with the feeling that I'd just been on the most amazing voyage of my life. That's what I told the Prime Minister when he called me up front for our usual chat. I'd rarely seen him looking so serene, like someone who had done what he saw as his duty, no matter what anyone thought. The conversation on the way back from Africa, in which Mila Mulroney joined, was one of the most pleasant we ever had.

When I got back to my seat I felt as if I'd capped this whole adventure just perfectly. Already, in the back of my mind, my power trip was over. I didn't want to be around much longer. I also felt, after the improbable success of this long and exotic voyage, that I'd done my bit. It was time to say goodbye, not only to Africa, but to the PMO.

Epilogue

The fun had gone out of it.

Not that it was ever much fun. As the song goes, the good times were too few and too far between. But, at least, in the beginning, there was a belief in doing something worthwhile, a belief in ourselves, a desire to make Brian Mulroney the best Prime Minister Canada had ever had, a commitment to the man himself.

The love and admiration for him and for her were still there. But the passion had left me. And you can't do a job that owns your life, as it should in such a high office, without passion . . . a great deal of passion. I felt empty. It wasn't worth fighting any more; I was going nowhere . . . fast. It wasn't the polls. It was just a feeling of being wasted, of not having what it took to perform any more. It was hard to accept. I had always told myself that if I got on the roller coaster, I'd stay for the whole ride through the next election campaign, win or lose.

I'd never really liked politics from the inside. Too many things, the infighting among friends, the hypocrisy, the scheming, were against my nature. My imagination, dormant for almost three years, was craving the creativeness that you can't find in a world of half-truths and back-stabbing. I wanted out.

Upon our return from Africa, morale was low in the Prime Minister's Office. The Oerlikon affair had taken its toll, and minister Roch LaSalle was about to resign over the fact that members of his staff had not undergone the proper security checks. One of them had been associated in the past with a nude dancer club in Joliette and had a criminal record.

The media guys were talking privately about "our thugs in Quebec," hinting at kickback schemes that had been going on for the last two years. I advocated what I called the "shotgun theory." The Prime Minister could not afford more scandals. We had to clean the stable once and for all. We had to shoot every-

231

thing that moved — no pity for ministers or anybody else. Bernard Roy said that, in the course of that reflection, we should perhaps also look at our own individual situations. I agreed totally. We had to give the Prime Minister the option of releasing us. We had to make it easy for him.

When I walked out of that morning meeting, I wrote my letter of resignation. I went to see Bernard, walking casually into his office as I usually did. He read it and said simply, "I think everybody here should do the same thing before the Prime Minister leaves for his holidays."

I don't know if anybody else actually wrote a letter. I think most resignations were offered verbally. I sent my letter to the Prime Minister of Canada. The feeling at that moment was one of letting him down. I explained that I thought that basically I was no longer useful to him; that in the course of rebuilding his image, he had to make a change at the helm of the Press Office.

I had already told Bernard Roy I thought that our profile was too high and that the only solution was to turn down the heat by appointing bureaucrats to the key positions. People with government method and discipline. People who would do their jobs systematically and quietly and not become media stars themselves. With that in mind I recommended that Marc Lortie, a career External Affairs diplomat, be appointed to my position. He was well liked and respected by the media and would most probably not get into the kind of trouble I was constantly flirting with.

The Prime Minister did not acknowledge my letter for almost three weeks. We even made a trip together on the Challenger, and he never mentioned it. The feeling on that last journey together was strange, almost unreal.

I remember Mila Mulroney telling Bonnie Brownlee and I that a speech she had given at a roast that week was a success because her husband had written it all. Bonnie and I were dumbfounded. We had written that speech! That Mila would say that to other people who had listened to it is fine; that's our job. Nobody should expect her to announce that the author is Michel Gratton or her Executive Assistant. But why, in the privacy of the plane was she telling us that? It was out of character. I felt something was wrong. Later in the day, on the way back, she would correct herself and thank me for my co-operation on the same speech. But something must have been troubling her and I wondered if it wasn't me.

The Prime Minister came back from holidays without announcing the expected changes in his personal staff. The capital was buzzing with rumours of an imminent shake-up, although many commentators believed that Mulroney's legendary loyalty to his friends and allies would not let him make any major moves.

In the PMO, a number of us, led by Fox and myself, started pleading for something to be done, whatever it might turn out to be. For the sanity of everybody involved it had to happen. The rumours had slowed the operations of the PMO to a crawl.

David Halton had had a report on the CBC the week before listing the upcoming casualties in Mulroney's entourage; he quoted from an apparent hit list that Senator Norm Atkins, godfather of the Big Blue Machine, had given the Prime Minister. Halton had phoned me in my hotel room in Quebec City where I was discussing matters concerning the Francophone Summit, to ask me if I'd heard about this hit list. I hadn't, but I said I wasn't surprised. There were six names on it: Bernard Roy, Fred Doucet, Bill Fox, Ian Anderson, Charley McMillan and me.

On March 9, the acceptance of my resignation by the Prime Minister would mark the beginning of a watershed in the history of Brian Mulroney's stay in power. The end of an era. Of the people who were close to him on "Manicouagan I" or in the Ottawa campaign headquarters, of those who stayed on after the September 4th triumph, those who brought him there and stuck with him after, almost none were left.

Fred Doucet was sidetracked and named "ambassador" to the summits Canada was to hold over the next year (Francophone, Commonwealth and Economic). He moved out of the Langevin Block for another government building in nearby Vanier, along the Rideau river.

Ian Anderson resigned to go into business for himself.

Bill Fox stayed on for a couple of months in a position that eventually became redundant with the appointment of Derek Burney as the new chief of staff (who had a different management style). Fox also went into business for himself and returned partly to his first love, journalism, writing a weekly column in the Toronto *Sunday Star*.

Charley McMillan resigned after the Venice Economic Summit in June and was alive and well living in Toronto and pondering his return to teaching at York University.

Bill Pristanski was appointed chief of staff to James Kelleher, the then Solicitor General.

Patrick MacAdam was awaiting a controversial diplomatic nomination in England.

Bernard Roy and Geoff Norquay were to stay in the PMO but both would see their responsibilities reduced with Burney's arrival. The only two major players left were Bonnie Brownlee, perhaps the toughest of the bunch, who would remain where she always was, at Mrs. Mulroney's side, and Keith Morgan the Boss's riding liaison man, who would sadly witness the departure of "my buddies" knowing he had no choice but to stay on in a job nobody else could handle, as the PM's representative and unelected MP for Manicouagan.

All this happened over a period of about three months in the spring of 1987.

Peter White, Peter Ohrt, Lee Richardson and Hubert Pichet had all left before.

We had paid the price of power. As for me, I did a little writing and went back to the love that had never really left me, as a columnist at large for *Le Droit.*

The circle is complete.

On March 9, 1987, Brian Mulroney gave me back my life.

Some Key Dates

1983

June 11	Brian Mulroney wins PC leadership

1984

June 16	John Turner wins Liberal leadership
June 30	John Turner sworn in as PM
July 9	Federal election called for September 4
July 16	"Old whores" story breaks
July 18	Apology press conference in Sault Ste Marie
July 24	French debate on TV
July 25	English debate on TV
August 1	The "Chatham Massacre"
August 15	Women's issues debate on TV
August 3	CTV poll puts Conservatives in front for first time
September 4	Federal election: Conservatives win 211 of 282 seats
September 9–20	Papal Visit to Canada
September 24–October 7	Royal Visit to Canada
November 6	"Nanny" story breaks
November 23	"Gag rule" for bureaucrats announced

1985

February 12	Defence Minister Robert Coates resigns
February 14	First ministers' conference in Regina
March 17–18	The Shamrock Summit in Quebec City
April 30–May 2	London visit
May 3–5	Bonn Summit

May 23	First Wilson Budget
June 26	David Peterson becomes Ontario Liberal Premier
June 27	De-indexation of pensions withdrawn
September 17	Tuna scandal breaks
September 23	John Fraser resigns as Fisheries Minister
September 25	Marcel Masse resigns as Communications Minister
October 3	Blais-Grenier uproar breaks
October 15–22	Nassau Summit
November 1	Don Getty becomes Conservative Premier in Alberta
December 2	De Havilland sale announced
December 12	Robert Bourassa Liberals win in Quebec

1986

January 9	Gallup poll shows Liberals ahead for first time since July, 1984
January 30	Erik Nielsen admits eavesdropping on Liberals
February 17–19	First Francophone Summit, Paris
February 26	Second Wilson budget
March 6	Andrée Champagne scandal breaks
March 10	Senator Jacques Hébert begins hunger strike
March 17	Washington Summit opens
March 18	Howard Pawley's NDP re-elected in Manitoba
March 19	Sondra Gotlieb slaps her secretary
April 29	Sinclair Stevens affair breaks
May 4–6	Toyko Summit
May 12	Sinclair Stevens resigns
May	Michel Gravel scandal breaks
June 30	Major Cabinet shuffle
September 5	John Bosley resigns as Speaker
September 14	Mulroney's "Drug Epidemic" statement
October 16	United States imposes softwood lumber tariff
October 20	Grant Devine's Conservatives re-elected in Saskatchewan
October 21	CF-18 contract awarded to Quebec

1987

January 17	The Oerlikon affair breaks

January 19	Gallup poll shows Conservatives in third place
January 24–February 2	Trip to Rome and Africa
March 9	I resign